ROMANISM AT HOME.

LETTERS

TO THE

HON. ROGER B. TANEY,

CHIEF JUSTICE OF THE UNITED STATES,

BY

KIRWAN.

NEW YORK:
HARPER & BROTHERS, PUBLISHERS,
329 & 331 PEARL STREET,
FRANKLIN SQUARE.
1852.

TO ALL MEN,

WHETHER PAPISTS OR PROTESTANTS,

WHO CAN

READ, REFLECT, AND REASON,

WHO DESIRE THE EXTENSION OF

CIVIL AND RELIGIOUS LIBERTY,

These Letters are Dedicated,

BY THEIR FRIEND,

THE AUTHOR.

PREFACE.

The history of the following pages is very soon told. A few years ago I addressed some letters to Bishop Hughes, stating my objections to Popery, confining myself mainly to its unscriptural and absurd doctrines. A controversy ensued, upon which the country has pronounced its opinion. My objections are yet unanswered, and are likely to remain so. I know of nothing that promises relief to the good bishop save a "winking Madonna," which the alms of the faithful, if liberally contributed, can readily secure. Any thing in that line is supplied to order at Rome.

Fatal to Popery as are the objections drawn from its doctrines, yet more fatal are those drawn from its "external arrangements," its government, its despotism, its spirit, its legends, its relics, and its influence on the moral, social, and political interests of the world. I have been often solicited to present this aspect of the subject to the public; but to do this as I desired, I must needs see Romanism at home—I must visit "the Lady of the Seven Hills" in her own house, where she is permitted to exercise her maternal authority just as she wills. With this object in view, I made a flying visit to Europe within the last year, in company with a friend, who has attained a distinguished rank in the medical profession, and who witnessed with me nearly all the scenes on the Continent described in these letters, and who will testify that they are not overdrawn. The present volume is the first fruit of that tour.

I design these letters to be an appeal from the priests to the people of the Romish faith; hence I address them to a layman of that faith. Upon the face of the earth there is no people so robbed, deluded, and degraded by a priesthood, or upon whom so many motives and interests are pressing to assert their mental and spiritual independence.

I design these letters to reach and to influence, if possible, the men of education and influence of this land, whether Papists or Protestants. Hence I address them to a man distinguished for his mental training, and by his high social and judicial position. No greater curse threatens this nation than the spread of Romanism in it. Almost any other evil would be a blessing in comparison with this. And the man who courts the priest to get the votes of his dupes—who flatters the spies of the despots of Rome for the purpose of securing their assistance to vote him into power, should be regarded as selling his country for a mess of pottage.

I speak in these pages as I feel about the priests, and as all must feel who study them at home, and who witness the outrages they commit, and the lives which they lead. If any complain of a want of reverence, I plead guilty, and offer as my excuse an unconquerable besetting sin to reverence only the sincere and the true.

No new thing will have happened unto me if these letters bring upon me the curses of the priest. I will consider it a sufficient compensation for all that, if they only bring upon me the blessings of one poor soul saved by grace from their wiles, and made to rejoice in the glorious liberty of the children of God.

March, 1852.

CONTENTS.

LETTER I.

Introductory.—Object of these Letters.—Reasons for addressing them to Chief Justice Taney .... Page 13

LETTER II.

The Beginning to be understood.—A Church of God.—The Jewish Church became Corrupt—had Reformers and Reformations.—Mainly corrupted by Priests.—The Christian Church became Corrupt—through what Causes.—The setting up of Mohammedanism and Romanism.—Romanism not the Church Paul found in Rome ... 20

LETTER III.

The Basilica of Saint Peter's a Temple of Art, not a Church.—A Type of the Romish Church.—Romanism a System of Policy to retain Power.—The Power it claims—its means of supporting them.. 27

LETTER IV.

Romanism not the Religion of the New Testament.—A Combination of various political Elements.—A political Compound.—Great Delusions always put forth monstrous Claims.—Priestly Pretensions to be spurned 35

LETTER V.

Romanism as a religious System.—Naples.—St. Paul Major a Type of the Paganism of Romanism.—Holy Water—how made.—Its Uses and Ends.—St. Anthony's Day.—The Origin of Holy Water 42

LETTER VI.

The Sistine Chapel.—Angelo's Painting.—The Artist's Reply.—Incense.—Its Pagan Origin.—Candles: their Use, End, and Origin.—Candlemass in Rome.—The Light of Candles can not supply the Light of Truth 50

LETTER VII.

St. Patrick never in America.—Our Poverty in Holy Wells and Places. —The Holy Wells at Ballahadireen.—Ballina.—Downpatrick Head. —Their Origin.—The Cell of St. Mary in Via Lata.—The Atrocity of opening fabulous Wells, and suppressing the Fountains of Truth..Page 58

LETTER VIII.

The Market-place at Naples.—A ludicrous Disaster at its Gate.—Images every where revered.—Church of St. Augustin.—Scene witnessed there.—The Image of Peter at St. Peter's.—Worshiped by Pope and Cardinals.—The Pantheon: Scene there.—Rome, Pagan in Fact, Christian only in Name 65

LETTER IX.

Cumulative Evidence of the Paganism of Romanism.—Landing at Naples.—Appearance of the Ecclesiastics.—Convent house.—Church of Capuchins at Rome.—Preserved Monk.—Horrid Burying-place.—Nuns—how manufactured.—Whence Monks and Nuns, and for what. —Tools of the Priests and Corrupters of the People 74

LETTER X.

Letter from Rome dated A.D. 90.—The Paganism of Rome then, the exact Picture of Papal Rome now...... 82

LETTER XI.

Sham Miracles.—Altar in the Catacombs.—St. Januarius—the Liquefaction of his Blood.—A terrible Incident for the Priests.—Ara Cœli. —Bambino.—A Scene.—History of Bambino.—Its wonderful Powers 91

LETTER XII.

Sham Miracles.—Holy House of Loretto—its History—Flight—Dimensions.—Miracles.—Litany of our Lady of Loretto.—Perpetrators of such Frauds, Impostors 99

LETTER XIII.

Sham Miracles.—St. Anthony of Padua.—The Virgin of Modena.—Blood of Thomas à Becket.—Miracles of St. Patrick.—Miracles at Downpatrick.—St. Dagland's Grave.—The Boy exorcised.—Xavier's Miracles.—The wonderful Crab.—Priests not to be trusted ... 108

LETTER XIV.

Relics.—Scala Sancta.—Sancta Sanctorum.—Relics of Santa Croce—of St. Praxede—of St. Peter's—in Milan—in Cologne.—Sanctioned by the Church.—Made to Order.—That they should be true, not essential.—Their Effects upon the People.—These Forgers of Relics unfitted to be our moral Teachers .... Page 117

LETTER XV.

Legends.—Sabbath evening in S. Carlo.—Gorgeous Scene there.—Legends from Butler—from Lives of English Saints.—Dr. Duff's Testimony.—Foolish Legends of the Dark Ages revived.—The Religion of Legends not fitted for America 128

LETTER XVI.

The Mass not the Worship of God.—A theatrical Exhibition.—Waldensian Church in Turin.—High Ceremonies of Rome all theatrical.—Feast of the Nativity.—Visit of the Wise Men.—Procession of Palms.—Judgment-hall of Pilate.—Procession at Bonville.—Sabbath evening Service in Edinburgh.—Popish Plays and Play-actors not suited to America 139

LETTER XVII.

Romanism tested by its Fruits in Rome.—No personal Liberty there—two Cases in Proof.—No security of Property—two flagrant Illustrations.—No Religion there—no Sabbath—no Bible—no Preaching—no worshiping Congregations—no serious Devotion there.—Is Popery the best form of Religion for our Country? 150

LETTER XVIII.

Fruits of Romanism.—Idolatry in Rome.—A Prodigy.—Pictures of Mary—her Names and Worship.—Immorality of Rome.—Scene at Naples—Key to priestly Profligacy.—Experience of Luther.—Mass for the Soul of Gregory XVI.—Vespers in the Sistine.—Cardinals—their Character.—Feelings of the Romans toward the Priests.—A Chat at Civita Vecchia.—Romanism detested at Rome 160

LETTER XIX.

Avignon.—Hotel de l'Europe—mine Host.—Captain Packenham.—Elasticity of Romanism—the Pope—Priests.—Despotism of Romanism.—Friends of the Pope.—Neapolitan Catechism.—Priests the Watchmen of Despotism—their horrid Use of the Confessional—it should be the Abhorrence of all Flesh 171

LETTER XX.

Character of Priests.—A Walk in Turin.—Bishops in England and America Spies of Rome.—Ecclesiastical Preferments the Rewards of Spies.—When Priests and Despots are in League, no Hope for the People.—Examples of priestly Despotism.—Curse from the Altar.—Case of the Antrim Miller.—Priests the Curse of Ireland.—Can they be a blessing to America? .... Page 182

LETTER XXI.

Ballenglen.—An Incident.—Persecution of Converts.—Thrilling Fanaticism at a Funeral.—The Way the Priests get Money.—An Incident.—Cursing from the Altar.—Hard Case of Donovan.—Doing Penance in Sheets.—Priests' Power giving Way.—Anecdote of a Girl.—The Milkman.—Taking the Bull by the Horns.—The Curse of Ireland 192

LETTER XXII.

Deceivings of Priests.—Nunneries.—Taking the Vail.—Stories about Luther and Calvin.—Case of poor Bruley.—The Vaudois Monsters.—Bridge of Purgatory broken.—Father O'Flanagan.—Why these deceivings?—Priests deserve Purgatory 205

LETTER XXIII.

Rome Intolerant.—Persecutions sanctioned.—Bishops sworn to persecute—Deposed if they do not.—Wiseman's reply.—Proofs of Intolerance—Waldenses—Castelnau—Bezières—Morland's Address—St. Bartholomew—Edict of Nantes revoked—Irish Massacre of 1641—other Evidences.—Two Skins 217

LETTER XXIV.

Bad influence of Popery on the Nations.—Results from its Principles.—No exceptions.—Naples.—Rome.—Sardinia.—Female Degradation.—Ireland.—Protestant and Papal States compared.—Spain.—Colonies of Papal States.—Is Popery the best Religion for our Country?—Protestantism has made the United States what they are.—What will they become if surrendered to the Jesuit and the Priest? .. 230

LETTER XXV.

Emigration—must increase—mostly Popish.—What to be done for them—Liberty—Conscience—American Spirit.—Tide stayed until now.—Right of all Men to the Bible—Wickedness of withholding it.—

Differences between Protestantism and Popery.—Edinburgh Irish Missions.—Rev. Mr. King.—Character of Priests.—Pilgrim of Struel. —Treatment Priests deserve........................Page 243

LETTER XXVI.

Strictures on Popery ended.--Popery to be extirpated—its End hastening.--Friends of Freedom Enemies of Popery.--Suspended Wrath.—Religion essential to national Greatness.—What true Religion is.—Nature of the Church of God—its Object and End.—Tendency to vicarious Religion.—Great Curse of Christendom 260

KIRWAN'S LETTERS

TO

CHIEF JUSTICE TANEY.

LETTER I.

Introductory.—Object of these Letters.—Reasons for addressing them to Chief Justice Taney.

MY DEAR SIR,—It will probably strike you and others with some degree of surprise that I address to you the following series of letters. And you have a right to ask, and I confess myself under obligations to give, the reasons why I select you from all the distinguished and honorable men of these United States for this purpose. Permit me to state these reasons in the briefest manner.

It may have come to your knowledge that, within a few years, I addressed a series of letters to the Right Reverend John Hughes, the Roman Catholic Bishop of New York. In those letters I stated my objections to the doctrines and teachings of the Roman Catholic Church, with the view of bringing them before the bishop and the country for a new consideration. I obtained my object in part. The bishop read my letters —twice attempted a reply—and feeling the objections to be less vulnerable than their author, fled the controversy, and sought to cover his retreat by a few letters, famed for their weakness, low personalities, and want of manliness. But, although every where denounced by papal priests and their press, my objections have received some consideration from the country, and with what results a future day must fully reveal. I return again to the discussion, with the desire to appeal from the bishop and the priest to the people; and who, Sir, from the ranks of those holding a nominal connection with the Romish Church in this land, could I have selected to whom to address these letters in preference to yourself? The motives which led me to select Bishop Hughes from the prelates of this Church have led me to select you from its people. And in saying this, I protest against the inference of wishing to reduce you to the level of the bishop.

Again; ours is a great and growing country. Within your remembrance—yes, within the years through which your name has been known in our public affairs, it has vastly extended in territory, population, and power. And in all the elements of greatness it is constantly augmenting. Already do we, as a people, stand out before the world as one of its great powers; and, if second, as only second to Britain, in maintaining free institutions, and in recommending them to universal adoption. It is of unspeakable importance that the moral power of our country should grow with its growth. And you, Sir, as the chief and honored judicial officer of our republic, are in the very position to appreciate this truth, and to see it in all the magnitude of its application. And how much to do with the moral power of a nation, and with the right exercise of its physical, has the form of religion which obtains among the people! Believing in my heart as I do, and as I shall attempt in subsequent letters fully to place before you, that the prevalence of Romanism in our land will have only the tendency to reduce our country and people to the low level of Italy and the Italians, I wish to forewarn, and thus to forearm the American people. And this I shall aim to do, not by appeals to passion or prejudice, but by a careful and honest statement of facts, and examination of principles, and reference to history, and to the state of things now actually existing. And in order to attract toward my statements the attention of our entire country, I address myself to you. The higher our glorious flag is hung, the more eyes will behold its stars and its stripes.

Again; I address these letters, Sir, to you, because I desire to appeal from the priests to the people; and especially to the people yet under the influence of the teachings of Romanism. With the people is the remedy for all our civil wrongs. This is a principle to which you have given your individual, political, and official sanction. Government is for the benefit of the people; and when rulers pervert the government to their own purposes, and trample upon its written Constitution, and oppress the people, then the remedy is with the people—peaceably if they can, by revolution if necessary. A government perverted by cunning from its great ends is no longer binding upon its subjects; it is their duty to restore it to its original foundations—peaceably if they can, by rebellion if they must. No American—scarcely any monarchist—will question these positions as to civil affairs. And are they not of equal application to our religious? If an institution was ever set up in our world for the good of mankind, it is the Church of God. Good will to men—to bind all men in love to God, and in love to one another—is its great mission. And I hope to prove to your entire satisfaction, that as far as the Romish Church is concerned, its priesthood have perverted it, as to its constitution, doctrines, and institution, so as to debase and grind the people—and for their own ends; that they assume the position in the Church which absolute monarchs do in the state; that the Church exists by them and for them. Now, Sir, when men by craft obtain the possession of high powers, whose exercise brings them great gain, they are slow to relinquish them; they are proof against all the weapons of reason and logic. And this is especially true of high ecclesiastics, who have ever manifested an amiable tendency to the belief of a divine warrant for as much oppression as may be needful to support their claims and their pomp. Where and when did they ever freely surrender unlawful power? Not among the Jews—nor among the heathen—nor under the shadow of the crescent—nor within the dominions of Romanism. Priestly power, always intrenching itself behind divine sanctions, has never yielded save before the power of the people; and not even then without thundering its anathemas against those who had overthrown it. Need I stop, Sir, to give illustrations of all this? They stand, thick as the trees of our unbroken forests, along the history of our race. The power of the Romish priesthood is terrific; and it claims even more than it can exercise. It has sought to crush every thing that opposes it. Where it is the controlling power, it has put out the light of the Bible and of general literature; it has put its shackles upon the press and upon human liberty. Nor will the Pope or the priest relinquish the power they wield so disastrously to all the interests of man, and for their own benefit, but at the bidding of the people. I desire to enlist the people in one great and united effort for the overthrow of this power; and hence, with the hope of thus better reaching them, I address these letters to you. I hope the time has forever passed when the voice of the people was forbidden to mingle with that of ecclesiastics in controversy upon religious systems and topics. Look at Scotland, and England, and Italy, and then ask, have the people no interest as to the form of religion which shall obtain among them? If they have, I wish them to show it; if they show it not, then let them bare their necks for the priestly yoke.

Again; you are yourself, if not really, at least nominally, in connection with the Romish Church. Descended, as I learn, from an honorable family of the Roman faith, you have received from them that faith as an heir-loom, which, although treated by you with indifference, is not yet cast away as a gross imposture. Indeed, presuming on your fidelity to that system of hoary error, a Romish prelate has recently dedicated to you a work on Theology, which embodies in it a vindication of the ferocious and infernal Inquisition! The priests and people of that faith seek to make out of your name and position all that they fairly can for its support. If not a reasonable, this is, at least, a common way of argumentation. Perhaps we all seek an argument for our systems from the honorable and worshipful names that have embraced them. Now, Sir, I have a desire that the facts and statements which I have to make should pass in review before your well-trained, logical, and judicial mind. Brought up to a profession which proverbially sharpens the intellect for just discrimination, and having risen to the very highest honors of that profession, you are as capable of separating the false from the true, the fiction from fact, the seeming from the real, as any other American citizen. Hoping and believing that you have not surrendered to a gossamer theory the right of private judgment, I venture to address my letters to you, with the expectation that if they receive the attention which their subject-matter deserves, you will openly renounce the entire delusion, and withdraw from its support your honored name and official station. May I not hope for more than this? If, on review, you find the system false, and blighting in all its direct influences, may not the expectation be indulged, that a mind signalized as is yours by so many triumphs at the bar and on the bench, stimulated by philanthropy and a love of country, will rise above the trammels of early education, and the fear of denunciation by foreign prelates and priests, and devote its energies to the saving of our land and its institutions from all the influences and machinations of Romanism? If I have no line by which to measure the insolence of a priest that would dedicate a work, containing a vindication of the Inquisition, to the Chief Justice of the United States of America, neither have I any line to measure the good that you might effect by throwing yourself into a hearty opposition to a system whose only fit name is "Mystery of Iniquity."

Such, Sir, in brief, are my reasons for addressing these letters to you. I have no desire to draw you into religious controversy of any kind, nor to withdraw your attention from the high duties which your country has devolved upon you. As I address you anonymously, no law of controversy or courtesy requires you to reply. Although unknown to me, save as you are known to the whole country, by character, for that character I have the very highest respect. And should your many and important public duties permit you to give sufficient time duly to weigh the statements which I shall present for your consideration and that of the public, it will give me unfeigned pleasure in any way to hear from you. I have no fear that, like our friend in New York, you will commence answering my letters before you read them; and, should you reply, I have no fear that you will write a line unworthy of your name and station. The characteristics which entitle a man to wear the ermine as Chief Justice of this great republic, are very different from those which secure for a cunning priest a foolish fillet made from the wool of holy sheep.

With great respect, yours.

LETTER II.

The Beginning to be understood.—A Church of God.—The Jewish Church became Corrupt—had Reformers and Reformations.—Mainly corrupted by Priests.—The Christian Church became Corrupt—through what Causes.—The setting up of Mohammedanism and Romanism.—Romanism not the Church Paul found in Rome.

My dear Sir,—In all discussions which involve great principles and interests, it is always well to begin with the beginning. When the beginning is well understood, we may carry a stream of light with us to the end. And we may so simplify the most abstruse and erudite subjects as to place them within the comprehension of the great masses of men. Permit me, then, in the present letter, to ask your attention to some statements as to the Church of God, and the rise of the Church of Rome. As I have never heard to the contrary, I will take it for granted that you are a believer in the Bible. May I not hope that, as the chief expounder of the laws of a great and Christian people, you make it the man of your counsel and the guide of your life?

Admitting the truth of the Bible, it is beyond all question that God has erected a Church in our world. Until the coming of Christ, that Church was confined to the Jews, and its rites were administered under the Mosaic economy. Although existing under types and ceremonies, the shadows of good things to come, it was truly the Church of God. Yet how sadly was it corrupted! How deeply, at times, did it sink into the most gross idolatry! How often were its true members reduced to a few who bowed not the knee to Baal; and while false priests were offering their incense upon a thousand altars, and the people were clamorous in the praises of false prophets, who daily fared sumptuously at king's tables, how often were the true priests, and prophets, and people, compelled to seek refuge "in deserts and in mountains, and in dens and caves of the earth." In its day and dispensation, the Jewish was the true Church of God in our world, and yet it fell into an idolatry as gross as any that existed among the surrounding heathen, and its priests and people became to every good work reprobate. And the great object of heaven in raising up the prophets who successively appear in the progress of its history, was to recall the minds of the people from their idols to the consideration of first principles and of God's revealed will; and by reforming their sentiments, to reform their lives. And Elijah, and Elisha, and Isaiah, and Jeremiah, were only the Luthers and the Calvins, the Melancthons, the Whitefields, and the Wesleys of the dispensation which has vanished away, each blowing a reformation trumpet in Israel, calling upon priests and people to return from their idolatry and wickedness unto Israel's God. Every thing, Sir, with which man has to do, is liable to corruption and perversion, because, in his best state, man is an imperfect being. And I make this statement for the purpose of impressing this one truth, that while God was the God of the Jewish, as he is the God of the Christian Church, he permitted that

Church to fall into a state of backsliding so awful as to render successive reformations absolutely necessary. And the Bible reveals the pregnant and warning truth, that the priests, high and low, and the pretending prophets, were the main corrupters of the faith and worship of the people. But where, you will ask, was the true Church in these days of backsliding, idolatry, and corruption? In the dens and caves of the earth, with those who clung to the truth of God, and who bowed not the knee to Baal.

In the fullness of time the Savior came into the world, and the Jewish was changed for the Christian dispensation. The Church was continued, but under a new, and better, and brighter economy. The rites and ceremonies of Judaism were laid aside for the things which they signified. The thoughts, the manner of life, the doctrines of the Savior were perfectly simple, and equally simple was the dispensation which he introduced. The power of his religion lay in its truthfulness and simplicity, and in its adaptation to the moral wants of the world. He laid down his life for sinners, that through the efficacy of his atoning sacrifice, all of every nation, tongue, and people, who should believe on him, might be saved. The only qualification required for admission to his Church was belief in him—the belief of the heart, which manifests itself in a holy life. And he set apart a class of men, the models of a perpetual ministry, in his Church, to proclaim to the ends of the earth that God was reconciling the world unto himself through his Son. The object of the ministry was to preach salvation through a Savior; the duty of all who heard them was to believe in the Savior preached; and the privilege of all who believed was to connect themselves with the company of believers, called the Church, and there to unite their energy and influence with those of others in extending the news of the common salvation to the ends of the earth. Such was the Church of Christ as it came from the hands of its divine founder.

But it was committed of necessity to imperfect men; and although the promise was given that the gates of hell should not prevail against it, yet that promise did not protect it against assault from without, nor against corruption within. A true ministry and true believers never have, and never will, cease from the earth until the great ends are obtained for which the Church was established; yet we see in the Church of Christ the very things recurring which in previous ages had befallen the Jewish Church. Converts from Judaism were multiplied to the new faith, who brought with them Jewish prejudices and notions, which they sought to ingraft on the Church, and not without success. Converts from the heathen were multiplied, who brought with them their prejudices and notions, and which, with like success, they sought to ingraft on the Church. New systems of philosophy arose, which sought to incorporate themselves with the teachings of Christ, and thus to render those teachings subservient to their ends. As the martyr age passed away, the Church became secular, its ministry unconverted, and its entire spirit changed. It sought to gain the world by relaxing its severe morals, and sinking its great truths, and by conformity to existing customs and habits. In the worst sense of the passage, it became "all things to all men."

The ambition of priests soon led them to model the Church after the fashion of the state; and thus, by gradual stages, the work of corruption and of external conformity progressed, until in a few centuries the Church of Rome was fully developed, which, although it contains more truth, bears a no more striking likeness to the Church established by Christ than does Mohammedanism. While the systems of Rome and of Mecca agree in some things, they differ much in their setting up. That of Mecca was framed by a bold impostor, was most artfully adapted to human nature, and was established at once by violence, while that of Rome was the gradual growth of centuries. One corruption prepared for another—one step toward supreme power and ghostly dominion prepared for another—what was begun in one age was perfected in the next; and thus, by slow but sure stages, "the mystery of iniquity" grew and became compacted, until the Church of Christ was divested of its simplicity and beauty, and its light was extinguished in all its high places. The system of Mecca might be compared to a large tree planted at once, and that of Rome to a tree which grew up from the seed, striking its roots deeper from year to year, and spreading wider and wider its branches. Or, to use a Scripture parable, the enemy sowed tares among the good seed, and the corrupt clergy, finding it would be most to their advantage to cultivate them, fostered and cherished them, and nursed them to a vigorous growth, until they choked the good seed, and flourished almost alone in the garden of the Lord. Romanism is not Christianity; on the most liberal allowance, it is but little more than a caricature of it.

That you, Sir, and all men may see this, just run over the list of things which, when combined, form the Romish system, not a pretext for which can be found in the Christian Scriptures, nor in the life and labors of Christ and his Apostles. They are such as these: a pope, cardinals, the mass, auricular confession, penances, an infallible earthly head, robed priests, purgatory, praying to the saints, feasts and fasts, monks, friars, nuns, celibacy, holy water, mitres, crosiers, palliums made from the wool of holy sheep! These, cemented and jointed by other inventions of men, and some scriptural truths, make up the system of Romanism, which differs as much from the religion of Christ as does the harlequin dressed up to play the buffoon from a plain, sensible, and well-bred gentleman.

You, Sir, will esteem it no answer to all this to say that if this statement is true, the promise of Christ to his Church has failed. This is begging the question. God's Church existed when the priests and people of Judea were idolatrous, and when Obadiah thought that he was left alone. The Church of Christ is with those who believe and practice the truth. Nor especially is it any answer that the Romish is the oldest, and, therefore, the true Church. Age never converts the lie into a truth—the forged into the real. If so, the Jew or the Pagan have the argument against the Christian; and the "old wives' fables," of which Paul speaks to Timothy, may supplant the teachings of the Apostles. The Church, as established by Christ, we find in the New Testament—the Romish Church we find in the decrees of Councils, in the writings of the Fathers, and in the rèveries of enthusiasts. That of Christ is the oldest;

and to it all belong who receive the New Testament, and live as it teaches.

To you, Sir, or to any thinking man, it is no new truth that the best and most safely-guarded institutions are liable to corruption and perversion. The more pure they are, the more are they opposed to our natural selfishness, and the greater will be the effort to pervert them. Have not governments been corrupted? Have not despotic supplanted free institutions? Have not unlawful acts grown into precedents, and precedents become laws? Have not the grants of weakness or of favor been made the foundations of claims of right? Have not privileges enjoyed because of the ignorance, indolence, or weakness of others, been claimed as divine rights? The setting up, in the way that we have stated, of the Romish Church in our world, is no new thing under the sun. And I here aver that the present awfully despotic government of Rome differs no more widely from the old Roman Commonwealth, than does the present Church of Rome from that which was found there by Paul the Apostle, and which was greatly confirmed and enlarged by his labors. Of this, more in the sequel.

With great respect, yours.

LETTER III.

The Basilica of Saint Peter's a Temple of Art, not a Church.—A Type of the Romish Church. — Romanism a System of Policy to retain Power.—The Power it claims--its means of supporting them.

My dear Sir,—On entering the splendid and sumptuous Basilica in Rome, dedicated to Saint Peter, I found it exceedingly difficult to conceive of it as a church devoted to the service and worship of God. And the difficulty increased with every visit made, until every idea of its being a church at all vanished from my mind. I have stood under its great cupola, and have gazed with rapture on the wonders and proportions of architecture above and around me. I have walked around its massive pillars, its magnificent walls, its gorgeous chapels, until wearied with the sensations of pleasure and delight excited by its statuary and paintings. I have explored its subterranean vaults by torch-lights; and from the ball, high in the air, which surmounts its dome, I have looked down upon the old historic city which seemed to lie at my feet. As, on the eighth day of June, 1851, I passed down the "piazza" on which it fronts, I turned round to take of it a full and last view, and, believing that I never should behold it again, a feeling of sadness came over me. I took off my hat, and bowed to it, most profoundly, a final farewell.

But Saint Peter's is not a church dedicated to the worship of God. There is no Bible there on all its altars. There is no preaching of the Gospel there. Masses are constantly mumbled there by crowds of priests, but there are no congregations. In the same chapel I have seen some priests creating God at the altar, while others, with a guide-book in their hand, were criticising the pictures and statuary around them, talking and smiling as if in a museum. And all this on the Sabbath day. You will find young ragged Romans playing "hide and go seek" amid its pillars, and squalid beggars imploring your charity even at the base of the magnificent "baldacchino" which surmounts the altar at which the pope alone can say mass; but the Gospel is not preached there, nor is God there worshiped. It is not, then, a church; it is simply and only a Temple of the Arts, where may be seen, in wonderful combination, the highest efforts of architecture, and the most splendid creations of the chisel and the pencil. And regarded simply as such a temple, it is, beyond comparison, the most magnificent in the world.

Now, Sir, in many things, this Basilica of Saint Peter's is a true type of the entire Romish Church. That Church is far more a system of policy than a religious system; and is framed more with a view to sustain and to extend its power, than to extend the knowledge of salvation through Jesus Christ. And I see but little more reason for calling that system and people, of which the Pope is the head, *a* Church, or *the* Church, than I do for calling the Russian or the English government a Church, as in Russia the emperor, and in England the queen, is the head of the Church. And the Church of Rome, like the governments of England and Russia, is simply a system of policy to perpetuate the power by which it has lorded it over people and nations, and bowed their minds and souls to its will. Permit me to present to you, Sir, a few considerations bearing on this important point.

The Pope of Rome claims to be the successor of Peter, and, as such, to be the vicar and vicegerent of Christ upon earth. In this character he assumes spiritual supremacy over the entire Church, regarding those who admit his claim as his faithful, and those who reject it, as do all Protestants, as his rebellious subjects, but not less amenable to his jurisdiction. In virtue of this spiritual supremacy, he claims a supreme sovereignty over things temporal as well as spiritual—over all the kings and nations of the earth. So that, in the words which have been often applied to him by his votaries, in their literal sense, he bears "in his hand a two-edged sword, to execute vengeance upon the heathen, and punishment upon the people, to bind their kings with chains, and their nobles with fetters of iron." And while the first claim is unfounded, and the second monstrous, yet the whole machinery of Romanism, from beginning to end, from the Arctic to the Antarctic circle, has for its grand aim the support of these unfounded and monstrous claims. The claims are prodigious, and I may admire or despise the gigantic ambition or fanaticism that makes them—the means devised for their support display amazing craft and cunning, and a wonderful adaptation to their end; but what title have the asserters of such claims, or the devisers of the means to sustain them, or those that admit them, to the name of a Church, or The Church? It is an old trick to compensate by arrogant claims for the want of title; and the main elements of the Romish Church are monstrous claims—monstrous means to sustain them—and the monstrous faith of its people. It is no more a Church of God, than is Saint Peter's a temple for his true worship. It is a system of policy to retain power, to strengthen which every thing in the way of doctrine or Scripture is made to bow.

Unlawful possession, whether of property or power, always leads to unworthy means to secure it. With a good title, we are always at rest; when conscious that our title will not bear investigation, we feel always in jeopardy; and to cover one fraud we will commit ten others. A thousand illustrations of this principle will present themselves to your mind; but I ask, Sir, your attention to some of those frauds by which the Romish Church seeks to fortify itself in the possession of the power which it claims, and which it wields with such disastrous effects on all the higher interests of humanity. This is a comprehensive topic, including almost every peculiarity of Romanism, and must not be dismissed with the few barren statements I shall now place before you.

To prop up the power which by fraud and falsehood it has been accumulating for ages, it claims a monstrous authority for its priests. The Pope is the vicegerent of Christ and the centre of unity. Bishops are his agents, and receive authority from him; priests are the agents of the bishops, and receive authority from them. To resist the priest is to resist the bishop, and the Pope, and Jesus Christ himself. To rebel against the authority of the priest, is to rebel against Heaven! The sacrament of "holy orders" means, with them, something more than the giving of canonical authority to men to dispense the rites of the Church; it invests every man, however senseless or immoral, with the power of shutting and opening heaven and hell, and of sending his fellow-men to the one or the other, as they fear him or frown upon him. Is not the attempt to make men believe that "holy orders" or "ordination" confers any such power, the perpetrating of a gross fraud upon the world? You, Sir, are our chief justice, by law appointed—the decisions of your court are binding until reversed. But there are other justices in the world, and administering law under governments very different, in form, from ours. Are they not lawful justices also? And, as the powers that be are ordained of God, have not they divine authority for the due exercise of their functions as well as you? And to make "orders" or "ordination," whether conferred by Pope, bishop, or presbytery, any thing else than the simple authorizing of a man, according to established rules, to preach the Gospel and to administer ordinances, is to perpetrate a priestly fraud, and for the maintenance of priestly power. The liberty of the Church and of the world is bound up in the question of "orders" and "ordination;" and you, Sir, and every other educated layman, should see to it that the pedantic priests and bishops who go through our land flouting their authority and their lawn in our face, and separating us from the gracious care of our Father who is in heaven, because our faith is not large enough to admit their claims, should not have it all their own way. They are all, so far forth, engaged, whether they hail from Rome or from Oxford, in palming an imposition on their race, and are not the less culpable because some of them may be honest.

While the Romish Church thus claims enormous authority for its priests, it virtually forbids the Word of God to its people. I say virtually, because I do not wish to enter into the question as to the teachings of the Church on this subject, which are wisely of such an elastic character as will enable a bishop to assert in New York, and to deny in Rome. Yet a real prohibition of the Scriptures to the masses is not a position very difficult to establish. But what is the actual state of things where Popery is in power? The Bible, as a rule, is unknown in Italy. I have conversed with a noble Christian man who was exiled from Rome for introducing into that city some copies of the Latin Bible. After having in vain sought for a Bible in many shops in Naples, I said to my valet, a sensible man of fifty, "John, have you ever read a Bible?" "No, sir," was the reply. "Have you ever seen a Bible?" Again he replied, "No, sir." "As God has given the Bible to man, why is it not to be found in Naples?" "The bishop and priests forbid its circulation, sir, and forbid us to read it." "And why, John, do they forbid your reading of it?" "O," said he, with that shrug of the shoulders so peculiar to the Italian, "they think that if we should read the Bible, we would become Protestants, and they would not like that." Here is the revelation of the whole secret. And, as the world knows, you can be no stranger to events which have within a few weeks transpired in Florence, where individuals have been exiled, imprisoned, and condemned to the galleys for meeting to read the Bible in private houses. And why, Sir, this fear of the Bible? Because it is the divine charter of the Church of God and of our religious rights. If any man questions your authority, you have no fear of his reading the Constitution of the United States. The Prime Minister of England never thinks of forbidding the people to read its Constitution and laws. If a question should come before your court for decision in reference to a close corporation, which sought to eject a large number of citizens from their lands and tenements; and if, on examination, you found that the said corporation had secreted all papers pertaining to their own claims, and to the title of the citizens, and had forbidden the citizens to make any investigations as to their rights, would you not be liable to infer that there was a dead fly in the pot of ointment; that the corporation wished to perpetrate a glaring fraud? Now, Sir, the Romish priesthood is a close corporation; that corporation puts forth claims in the name of God, deeply affecting your individual interests and mine, as well as those of all men and of all nations. Those claims, if right, must be founded on the Bible; if not there authorized, they are not to be allowed for a moment, and their claimants should be held up to universal execration. That they are not authorized by the Bible, Pope, bishops, and priests well know; and hence their dire, their sleepless opposition to its circulation, and to its perusal by the people. And by withholding the Bible from those to whom God has given it, they are perpetrating a great fraud upon the people, and simply and only for the purpose of perpetuating their ghostly power. Sir, there is just as much to support Romanism in the

Bible, as there is in the Constitution of the United States, and no more. And if Pius IX., or his spy in New York, deny this, I am willing to meet either of them before you, and, after a full hearing on both sides, to leave the decision of the question with you. And surely they will not question your sympathies, seeing they have had confidence enough in their Lateran leanings to dedicate a work to you containing a vindication of the bloody Inquisition.

Romanism, then, is a system of policy framed to sustain and extend its power, and by means such as we now state to you. Can it be a, or the, Church of God? As a system of policy, it is, like Saint Peter's, a gorgeous structure: it contains within it many things which strike the beholder with wonder; but, Sir, can it be a Church of God?

With great respect, yours.

LETTER IV.

Romanism not the Religion of the New Testament.—A Combination of various political Elements.—A political Compound.—Great Delusions always put forth monstrous Claims.—Priestly Pretensions to be spurned.

My dear Sir,—In my last letter I presented for your consideration the statement that Romanism is more a system of policy to retain and extend its power than a religious system. Although a layman, and, from the nature of your profession, not deeply read in religious controversies, yet it must be quite apparent to you that Romanism, as a system, is greatly dissimilar to the system of religion taught in the New Testament. Have you ever seen the Pope in Saint Peter's, or in the Sistine Chapel, at the mass? If not, you have yet to see a farce, and the more laughable because of its mock solemnity. If you have, then let me ask you, do you think Christ was ever so dressed, or that he ever so acted? Can you conceive of any thing at a farther remove from the simplicity of his character as portrayed by the Evangelists? Have you seen the cardinals, with their scarlet carriages, scarlet robes, and scarlet skull-caps, going through their maneuvers in the Sistine? Can you conceive that ever the Apostles condescended to act a part in such a scene of gorgeous buffoonery? You perhaps occasionally visit the cathedral of the city of your residence;

have you the least conception that God was so worshiped by apostles, or ministers, or congregations, in the first age or ages of Christianity? Where, in those days, could they light up their wax candles, or pack away their crooks and their crosiers, or carry their vestments, or burn their incense? A careful comparison, in this way, of Romanism and Christianity, must convince a mind disciplined as is yours that there is scarcely a semblance of relationship between them. Whence, then, is Romanism, as a system of policy? Regarded as a religious system, it is a mixture of Paganism, Judaism, and Christianity; as a system to sustain, and perpetuate, and extend its power, it is a mixture of the various political elements which have risen in the world for governing and grinding the people and nations.

As a system of policy, it has in it a strong element of despotism. This is common to it with all false systems. The external arrangement called "the body of the Church" is simply this: Christ appointed apostles—over these he placed Peter as Pope—to these and their successors he committed the government of the Church in all ages and countries, and the power of the keys to bind or to loose, as they deemed proper. And in virtue of his being the vicar of Jesus Christ, the Pope claims supreme authority over things temporal as well as spiritual. Here is despotism, not as a doctrine of expediency, not as established by the sword, but as set up by the sanction of Heaven itself, and as clothed with divine authority. You, Sir, need not be informed how fully, in past ages, the Pope has acted the despot; nor how fully he acts it now, where he can, nor how fully he would act it over us all, if he could!

Again; as a system of policy, in its external arrangement it is modeled after the old Roman state. The emperors were elective, so is the Pope. Until the transfer of the seat of empire by Constantine to Byzantium, the emperor reigned in Rome; there reigns the Pope. When elected, the emperor was the fountain of all authority; so is the Pope. In all the countries which lay under the shadow of his sceptre, the emperor had his subordinates, and these again theirs, down to the lowest office in the state; so has the Pope. Cardinals, archbishops, bishops, priests, deacons, canons, monks, friars, are but the higher and lower constabulary of the Pope, through which he seeks to collect into his own hands the reins of universal government, and to hold in allegiance the nations to Papal, as the Cæsars held them to Pagan Rome. There can not be a doubt but that the Roman state was the model after which, in its main features, wily ecclesiastics modeled the Roman Church. When Cæsar retired to the Bosphorus, the Pope wisely preferred to remain on the Tiber; and as, by the progress of the consumption which led to the dissolution of the Roman empire, the reins, one after the other, fell from the hands of the weak successors of Constantine, the Pope was very careful to collect them into his own; and thus, by slow but sure stages, he grew up to the possession of an authority more extended and powerful than emperor ever wielded, and in the exercise of which he converted emperors into his waiters and grooms. Need I, Sir, run the parallel farther? The likeness is as striking as is that of the pictures of the Popes in the Vatican to one another. There is not only a family likeness among them, but it would seem as if they were all sons of the same parents, born in the same age, and of the same size, and as if all of them were equally healthy and burly. As they look down upon you from the walls of "S. Paolo extra muros," each looks as if he were a twin-brother to the other; nor do any of them look as if upon their shoulders was laid the weight of all the churches. Any of them might be mistaken for a likeness of the man who was clothed in purple and fine linen, and who fared sumptuously every day.

Again; it possesses a very strong dash of the old feudal system. As a frame-work of policy, Romanism is not the work of an age or a century. From age to age, it has sought to incorporate with itself the strong elements of other systems, that by twining and twisting them together, it might increase its power. Now, Sir, that you may see how much of the feudal it has appropriated, permit me to ask you to read again, as I have no doubt you have read them once, the chapters of Hallam on the Feudal System of the Middle Ages, or the remarks of Robertson on it, in his Introduction to the History of Charles V. As self-defense was the chief care of kings and conquerors, they parceled out countries among their chief followers on the condition that they should appear in arms when required. Persons receiving land were to contribute men and means in the proportion of their grants. These chief men made grants, on similar conditions, to others; and these, again, to others, down to the lowest subdivision. And thus, by grants and conditions, the different classes of society were bound to the next highest, and, through the chief nobles, were bound to the king or conqueror. And in the proportion of their possessions, each were bound to contribute for the mutual defense to the power above them. Each was bound to gird on his sword at the command of his superior. It was at this time, also, that the custom sprang up of nobles dropping their own name and taking that of their estates, which is yet in existence. This system had its strong and its weak points. The weakest point was the absence of a central power to balance and regulate the monarchical and the aristocratic parts; and for the want of which the whole system fell into confusion. From this system, Romanism selected and appropriated its strong features, and supplied the great central, regulating power which it wanted, as any intelligent mind can see in a moment. The Pope is a king; by feudal tenures he parcels out the Papal world among his archbishops and bishops; and these, again, among their subordinates. Cardinals, archbishops, and bishops swear to him allegiance, and their subordinates to them. And when the head of this system is in a strait, he has only to apply to his chief vassals, and they pass the word to the next below, and these, again, to their inferiors; and soon the Papal world is in motion to supply the requisite assistance. Thus it was in the Papal wars—thus it was recently in the collection of the Peter-pence, to sustain a weak and profligate set of priests when scheming and chambering in Gaeta. And see the way and manner in which priests, when made bishops, drop the names which their fathers gave them, as if ashamed of them, and assume the name of the territory over which their king has given them jurisdiction, as a farther evidence of this feudalism. England has its "Nicholas of Westminster"—we have our "John of New York"—and you, ere this, have your Patrick of Baltimore; while in old, dilapidated Rome, a clever and good-looking old gentleman, who is far more a prisoner than a king, and much more of a puppet in the hands of his cardinals than an independent ruler, is acting the universal bishop under the sobriquet of Pio Nono.

All this, Sir, is to suggest a true analysis of "the external arrangement," as our friend of New York would say, which is known as the Romish Church. Take away from it all its despotism, all that it borrowed from the Roman state when governed by emperors, and all that it appropriated from the feudal system, which so widely obtained in Europe from the seventh to the eleventh centuries, and what is there left? Not enough to command the respect of an Alpine cretin, save what it holds in common with Protestants.

And yet, Sir, this compound of various political elements, cemented together by the priestcraft and cunning of ages, is "the external arrangement" which Papal priests would palm on the world as the Church of God, founded on the apostles and prophets, and fortified by divine sanctions, and out of which there is no salvation! Can you conceive of a more monstrous fabrication?

Permit me, Sir, also to remind you of the fact that this thing of dealing out damnation to the nonrecipients of theories is always an accompaniment of grand delusions. The claim of divine authority for priestly nonsense and fabrications is no new thing under the sun. It is put forth as boldly by Pagan as by Papal priests, and is asserted as impudently in Stamboul as in Rome. You know it is death by law, and without benefit of clergy, for a Mohammedan to become a Christian while residing under the shadow of the crescent, and that Paganism thunders its excommunications against all who abandon its superstitious rites. The foundation of all this lies in the inherent weakness of the theories put forward, and of the claims asserted; and the object is to quell scrutiny, and to induce faith by authority and by fear. God is the Father of us all; and Jesus Christ is the Savior of all who believe upon him; and how preposterous for Pagan, Papal, Protestant, or Mohammedan priest to cut us off from the grace and love of our heavenly Father because we deny their claims, discard their rites, and refuse to submit to their manipulations! Sir, the intelligent laymen of this land, and of all lands, should seek fully to comprehend the great interests of humanity involved in these priestly pretensions; and while rejecting them themselves, they should see to it that the most ignorant of the people should not be deluded by our swarming, imported, and ghostly pretenders. For myself, when I meet with a man dressed in ecclesiastical livery, urging upon me or others theories of human device as to the external arrangements of the Church, and seeking to compel my belief in them with the threat of damnation if I reject them, I can scarcely resist the conviction that he is either a knave, or a fanatic, or a fool. And it sometimes requires a little more of the grace of patience than I possess to forbear telling him so.

With great respect, yours.

LETTER V.

Romanism as a religious System.—Naples.—St. Paul Major a Type of the Paganism of Romanism.—Holy Water—how made.—Its Uses and Ends.—St. Anthony's Day.—The Origin of Holy Water.

MY DEAR SIR,—Hitherto I have only asked your attention to the "external arrangements" of Romanism, which is called "the body of the Church." I have stated to you their causes and their ingredients, and that these arrangements form a system of policy to sustain and extend the power and the dominion claimed by the priests. In its external form, Romanism bears no possible likeness to Christianity as it received its simple habit from its glorious and glorified head. I shall now ask you to pass with me to the examination of Romanism as a religious system, premising that, in this respect also, we shall find it at an equal remove from Christianity, as we did its external form.

It was on the morning of the twenty-eighth of May that the steamer Bosphorus came to anchor in the Bay of Naples. As the morning sun was shedding its first bright beams on the surrounding scenery, I opened the window of my state-room, and lo! the summit of the fiery Vesuvius was smoking before me! The desire of many a long year was gratified. Soon we all debarked, and after locating myself in a quiet hotel facing the magnificent bay, and in a room from which I had a view of the harbor, its islands and surrounding mountains, I went forth with my friend and our valet to see sights. It was here that I first touched Italian soil, and that I first mingled with the people of Italy. Every thing struck me as new, strange, and peculiar. Such crowds of soldiers, priests, beggars, and donkeys I had never seen. In beauty of scenery, and in the squalid wretchedness of masses of the people, Naples stands pre-eminent. To the causes of this wretchedness I may allude hereafter. During the morning I made a visit to the Church of Saint Paul Major, which is one of the sights of this beautifully located, but misgoverned, priest-ridden, and degraded city. This is really the old temple of Castor and Pollux transformed into a church. There stand the old pillars of the heathen temple; there, before the door, is the statue of a heathen god converted into a statue of St. Paul: on either side of the great door, and over it, are left remaining the pictures of the heathen priests offering sacrifices, and all over the interior of the building are the representations of heathen mythology, mixed and mingled up with the representations of the myths and superstitions of Popery. Priests in their robes were mumbling mass at its altars, women and beggars were either kneeling before the altars and gazing around, or were pestering you for alms at every turn. And to a person at all acquainted with heathen mythology, with Roman antiquities, and with the way and manner of the worship of the old Italians, the conception, on entering this church, would be neither violent nor unnatural that he was in a heathen temple, whose altars were surrounded by heathen priests, upon which they were offering their unmeaning sacrifices. Such, Sir, was the strong impression made upon my own mind as I walked around the old temple of Castor and Pollux, now called the Church of Saint Paul at Naples. And unless, Sir, you have already given it your attention, you will be amazed to find how largely Romanism has drawn upon Paganism in the formation of that compound which it calls Catholic Christianity. And to the Paganism of Romanism, as symbolized in that old temple of Castor and Pollux, I would respectfully ask your attention.

On entering a Romish Church, the first thing that strikes you as peculiar is the stone or marble basin of *holy water* placed near the door, in which the more ignorant and devout dip their fingers, and then, with their wet fingers, make upon themselves the sign of the cross. Holy water, you know, is a thing of universal use, and to which is ascribed wonderful potency in the Romish system. Have you, Sir, ever seen the farcical ceremony by which common water is made holy? If not, permit me to describe it to you, as I have recently witnessed it myself. Connected with the Basilica of St. John Lateran at Rome is the baptistry said to have been built by Constantine in which to receive baptism from Pope Silvester. Every thing in Rome, you know, must have a history, or tradition of some kind; and these are easily manufactured, if they do not truly exist. Learning that there was to be a peculiar ceremony there of some kind, I sallied out on the morning of the 7th of June to witness it, in company with some friends. We entered the little gem of a building, and in its centre, beneath a cupola supported by columns, was a large antique urn, almost as large as a bathing tub, filled with water. Save a few ragged boys and beggars, myself and friends were the only persons yet present. Soon the voice of melody was heard in the direction of the church, which came from a bareheaded procession, dressed for the occasion, on its way to the baptistry. A sleepy bishop, that we had seen drowsing on former occasions, when boys were swinging their incense vases before him, brought up the rear, most gaudily dressed, and with an umbrella held over his head. Singing, they entered the chapel, and surrounded the urn. The bishop read a little — then all sang, and chanted. Thrice, at intervals, the bishop, with his hand, made the sign of the cross in the water, making quite a ruffle on its surface as he drew his hand through it; thrice, at intervals, he breathed into the water, commanding it at each time to receive the Holy Ghost. Then, from a vessel like a coffee-pot, he poured oil into it in the form of a cross; and from another similar vessel, at a brief interval, he poured some other liquid into the tub, again in the figure of a cross. At another interval he took both vessels by the handles in his right hand, and bringing their spouts near together, he poured into the tub a little stream in the form of a cross, formed by the liquids from both vessels uniting. A powder, something like fine salt, was also cast into it. Then, after mixing up all together, he washed his hands in the compound, which were most reverently wiped by his attendants. Before putting them in the water, his hands were divested of their gloves and rings, and were most devoutly kissed; as was his crook when taken by his attendants. Thus common was changed into holy water by one of the most silly and blasphemous ceremonies it was ever my lot to witness. After sprinkling the faithful around, they retired to the church with procession and singing as they came, where mass was said, without any but the priests and their waiters to hear it. It was thus I saw holy water made in Rome. The supremely ridiculous and superstitious way in which it is ordinarily made, you may see in the closing chapter of Challoner's Catholic Christian Instructed, a monument to the credulity and folly of its author.

While doctors differ as to the object and meaning of holy water, it is commonly regarded as a symbol of the purity with which we should approach God in worship. Grant this to be a good object, and an excuse for the thing, how can this explain its other applications? It is sprinkled upon candles—upon palms on Palm-Sunday—upon the garments of the living—upon the coffins of the dead—upon dogs, sheep, asses, mules, beds, houses, meat, bells, fortifications, and cannon. "Nothing," says Croly, "can be blessed or hallowed without it; neither candles, nor new fruit, nor new-laid eggs. .... Even the butter-churn is sprinkled with it before churning commences, that the cream may work the better. It purifies the air—heals distempers—cleanses the soul—expels Satan and his imps from haunted houses—and introduces the Holy Ghost as an inmate in their stead." And that you, Sir, may not esteem this an exaggeration, ponder the following statement affixed to the wall over the vessels of holy water in the Church of S. Carlo, in Rome. There it is not under a curtain, like some of the miraculous pictures, but where every eye can see it.

"The Church proposes holy water as a remedy and assistant in many circumstances, both spiritual and corporeal, but especially in these following. Its spiritual uses are:

"1. It drives away devils from places and persons.

"2. It affords assistance against fears and diabolical illusions.

"3. It cancels venial sins.

"4. It imparts strength to resist temptations.

"5. It drives away wicked thoughts.

"6. It preserves safely from the passing snares of the devil.

"7. It obtains the favor and presence of the Holy Ghost.

"Its corporeal uses are:

"1. It is a remedy against barrenness, both in women and beasts.

"2. It is a preservative from sickness.

"3. It heals the infirmities of the mind and body.

"4. It purifies infected air, and drives away plague and contagion."

This is the substance, though not a literal or full translation of the document. Must not, Sir, the common-sense, equally with the religious sentiment of the world, brand all this as a vile and wicked imposition?

But this is not the worst or lowest use of holy water. You have heard, no doubt, of the good Saint Anthony, of blessed memory. He was a rare personage, and his festival is on the 17th of January. Balacius, king of Egypt, when persecuting the Christians, was exhorted by this saint to permit God's people to live in peace. The king tore the letter in pieces, and resolved to make Anthony his next victim. Five days after, when riding out, his remarkably tame horse threw him to the earth, and then turning round, bit and tore his thigh so terribly that he died in three days. From this, or some other legend equally veracious, Anthony is made the patron saint of horses, and they have gotten up in Rome the blessing of horses on Saint Anthony's day, and this is done by sprinkling them with holy water. On that day, the horses, mules, and donkeys of the city of Rome and of the surrounding country, gayly dressed, are paraded before the church of this saint, where a priest takes them under the care of holy Saint Anthony, and then sprinkles them with holy water, *receiving some small remuneration* for each horse, mule, or donkey which he thus purifies. And the poor people of Rome are made to believe that, unless their horses, mules, and donkeys are thus besprinkled with holy water, they will stumble, or fall, or die, or receive some serious injury through the year! These, Sir, are some of the various uses and benefits of holy water! Is it possible to conceive of impositions more barefaced or dishonest! And all this is under the eye of the Pope, who patronizes the iniquity by yearly sending his own horses for a sprinkling!

And the question arises, Whence this custom, so wicked, so foolish? There are no traces of it in the Bible; there is scarcely a pretension to this by Papal doctors. It is purely a heathen custom, transferred by the priests from heathenism into the Church for the purpose of facilitating the passing over of the heathen from Paganism to Popery. What was at first a matter of policy became soon a matter of faith; and now a font of holy water is of far more importance to the complete finish of a Romish church than the Bible

Indeed, while the Bible is supplanted by the Mass-book and the Missal, the font of holy water is never absent. Your own acquaintance, Sir, with classic literature and heathen mythology will supply you with the proofs which establish the Pagan origin of holy water. And if you have not time to look them up, I would refer you, for some of them, to "Dr. Middleton's Letter from Rome."

You, Sir, know how much is made of holy water in the Church with which you hold a nominal connection. Its origin, beyond all question, is Pagan, and is so admitted by some Papal writers. And as I have seen priests in Ireland passing through crowded chapels, followed by boys bearing a tub of water, in which he ever and anon dipped a big brush and scattered it over the people—as, in the Madeleine, in Paris, I saw an old monk standing by the door in the railing which fences out some and fences in others, holding a brush wet with holy water in his hand, that the polite Parisians might touch it with their fingers—as I saw the thing manufactured by tubs-full in Rome, and by the priests of St. John Lateran, the holiest church in the world, "Ecclesia urbis et orbis, mater et caput ecclesiarum," I could not help thinking that, so far forth, these Papal were Pagan priests, practicing a Pagan rite, and for no other motive but the gain which it brought them.

I shall return to the Paganism of Romanism in my next.

With great respect, yours.

C

LETTER VI.

The Sistine Chapel.—Angelo's Painting.—The Artist's Reply.—Incense.—Its Pagan Origin.—Candles: their Use, End, and Origin.—Candlemass in Rome.—The Light of Candles can not supply the Light of Truth.

My dear Sir,—As I promised you at the close of my last epistle, I return again to the examination of the Paganism of Romanism. I have already shown you that *holy water*, both as to its origin, and as to its multifarious and ridiculous uses, is of Pagan origin. Let me now ask your attention to other things, forming at all times and places essential components of the Romish service.

As I entered the Sistine Chapel at Rome, so famed in the annals of art, I was strangely overwhelmed with a feeling of disappointment. It is an oblong and lofty room, about thrice the length of its width, and divided by a low railing into three compartments. In the most distant of these compartments, as you enter, is the altar, and the Pope's chair; and around it are benches for the cardinals. The middle compartment is entirely vacant, with nothing but standing-places for the spectators; the outer one has some plain benches, and is appropriated to the ladies during the hours of worship. As there was no person there save the door-keeper, and a painter who was transferring to his canvas the pictures on the walls, I walked leisurely round, and without any let or hinderance. Angelo's great fresco of the Judgment, sixty by thirty feet, and so long the wonder of art, was before me. I gazed upon it from various points to get a clear view of it, but in vain. I borrowed the magnifying-glass of the painter, and gazed through that, but yet in vain. "What," said I to the painter, "is the matter with these paintings? Is it the fault of the light that I can not see them clearly? or have the colors faded?" "No," said he; "it is the effect of that *ridiculous incense* which they burn here at mass;" and he uttered the sentiment with a tone and manner which showed that he, at least, was incensed by the frivolous, but yet, to the paintings of Angelo, injurious ceremonial. And if the cause assigned was the true one, I felt, at the moment, as if every incense vase in Rome should be cast into the muddy Tiber; nor do I yet feel that, by committing such an act, any man would burden his soul with the sin of sacrilege. I witnessed mass afterward in the Sistine, and saw clouds of incense rise and spread themselves all around, and thick enough to set weak lungs a coughing. The last scene of this kind that I witnessed was in St. Gudule, the cathedral at Brussels. It was on a fine Sabbath morning in June, when the feast of some saint brought a large number of clergy and several bishops together. The latter were more richly decorated than any I had previously seen. When the time for offering incense arrived, a short but exceedingly fat man came to the bishops with his censer. So rotund was he, that it seemed as if he could roll as easily as walk; and his efforts to go from one bishop to another, and then his efforts to get round his enormous belly, so as to give the censer the ceremonial swing, made it as ludicrous and laughable as it is a senseless and superstitious ceremony.

In the matter of incense, Sir, you well know that papal priests are very prodigal. You have to smell it, and breathe it, in all their chapels; and it seems to me that the priests would be adding something, at least, to the comfort of the faithful if they would somehow contrive to make it a little more agreeable to the sense of smell, which it is very pleasant to have occasionally consulted. You enter a Romish church to witness the mass: at a certain point a boy, dressed in white, appears with a vessel—the priest puts something in it, and it immediately commences to smoke. The priest takes it and throws it up to the altar, and to the crucifix; the boy then takes it and throws it up before the priest, and other persons and things. And before the ceremony is ended, the smoke, or, as it is called, the incense, fills the house. This, we are taught, is "an emblem of prayer ascending to God from a heart inflamed with his love." But whence this custom? Not from Christ—not from his apostles—not a command or allusion to it in the New Testament. Not a thing sufficient to sanction it even in the typical economy of the Jews. And if an emblem of prayer, why not offer the prayer and drop the emblem? The whole thing, Sir, is transferred bodily from Paganism, as any person informed about Pagan ceremonies must know. Incense was always offered to the gods from Pagan altars, and, as we may learn from the sculpture and pictures which have come down to our day, very much in the manner in which it is now offered in Romish churches—by a boy in white robes, with a censer in his hand. And had an old worshiper of Castor and Pollux risen from the catacombs and entered with me the Church of St. Paul Major at Naples, he would have felt that, although great revolutions had taken place in other things, his old temple and its worship were yet mainly the same. There, at least, were the holy water and the smoking incense, just as he had left them.

Another prominent peculiarity of the Romish service is the use of *candles*. These are seen burning on all their altars, in greater or less profusion, according to the eclat of the occasion, or of the saint or sinner on whose feast-day mass is offered. I have seen them burning on the chief altar of San Carlo in the Corso, in numbers beyond my computation, standing at about the centre of the gorgeous edifice; and I have seen them reduced to about half a dozen on the altar of the Sistine, when the Pope and his cardinals were bowing before it. I have seen them, Sir, in your cathedral at Baltimore, on Christmas day, as thick and countless as trees in a nursery; and the tomb of Peter, under the great cupola of Saint Peter's Church, is perpetually lighted by one hundred and twelve lamps, disposed round a circular balustrade. These lamps never go out; forcibly recalling to the intelligent mind the lights kept perpetually burning on the Pagan altars in Rome, by the Vestal Virgins. You, Sir, will not forget what you learned in your schoolboy days on that subject; but, should you have done so, you can easily refresh your memory by referring to your "Roman Antiquities."

But what mean, and whence, these lighted candles? Hear what Bishop England—in his day a clever man, and an excellent judge of Irish whiskey—says in reply: "Lights are placed on the altar from the usage of the most ancient times. It is an *Eastern custom* to express joy; for, even in the light of the sun, the torches and candles were lighted to manifest this feeling; and, as *our religion* is received from *the East*, most of our ancient customs *are of Eastern origin*." Here is the whole thing confessed by a Romish bishop, with whom, no doubt, Sir, you were acquainted, and who flourished his crook and his crosier in the city of Charleston. The Pagans of the East expressed their joy by lighted torches and candles; and, as Romanists received their religion from the East, they adopted this among other Eastern customs!

In our own happy America, where we have learned how to express our joy without lighting lamps or candles, we have scarcely any idea of the extent to which they are used in Papal countries. With us they are used whenever mass is said, or extreme unction is administered, or any service is performed at the altar or chapel. In Rome, and the countries of Italy, they are used not merely in these ways, but in all ways. I have seen them burning on an altar in the catacombs of Naples—before images of the Virgin at the corners of the streets, in whiskey-shops, and by the way-side—in the gorgeous processions of carrying the Host to some dying person—at funeral processions. Neither the light of the moon and stars by night, nor of the glorious sun by day, is sufficient to express the joy of a Romanist; their light must be increased by that of a few lamps or candles in order to obtain their object and to give vent to their feelings!

To be sure, the silliness of the whole thing should save it from this sifting; but as the origin of the matter is confessed, and these candles form a part of a system addressed to the senses, let us not yet put them out. You know there is an old feast called C-a-n-d-l-e-m-a-s-s, so called from the number of lighted candles used in the procession of the day, and from the custom of consecrating candles on that day for the rest of the year. Have you, Sir, ever seen that procession, or witnessed that blessing of candles? In Rome it is one of the most gorgeous festivals of the year. Sitting in his chair of state, the Pope is borne on the shoulders of eight men into Saint Peter's, attended by huge fans made of ostrich feathers, with the eyes of the peacock's tail, and by cardinals, bishops, prelates, and priests. When every thing is fixed for the senseless ceremony, candles are brought to him in immense numbers. They are incensed, sprinkled with holy water, and blessed. Then they are distributed. Each cardinal approaches, receives a candle, kisses the Pope's *hand*, and retires. Each bishop approaches, receives a candle, kisses the Pope's *knee*, and retires. Each inferior functionary on the occasion approaches, receives a candle, kisses the Pope's *foot*, and retires. On a sudden an immense number of candles are lighted, in the blaze of which the Pope is carried round the church, and retires, granting an *indulgence of thirty years* to all the faithful present! This, Sir, is Candlemass at Rome! And if you, Sir, or I, or any body else, wish an indulgence to cover all the years of our sojourn here, we need only attend the feast of Candlemass at Saint Peter's thrice; for three times thirty years make ninety; and beyond ninety years we will not probably need indulgence, save from our heirs or our nurses.

As, beyond all possibility, this can not be Christian rite, whence is it? Bishop England says it is of Eastern origin; every body acquainted with mythology must confess that it is Pagan. In heathen temples lamps and candles were ever burning on the altars, and before the statues of their deities. Donations of lamps and candlesticks were often made to temples and deities. The use of candles in Pagan feasts and processions is first traced to the Egyptians, who had their yearly festival of "THE LIGHTING OF CANDLES," somewhat similar to that in Rome, in which the Pope acts so conspicuous a part. And some of the Christian fathers thus ridiculed the heathen; "they light up candles to God as if he lived in the dark; but do they not deserve to be called madmen who offer lamps to the Author and Giver of light?" The whole thing, Sir, is ridiculous, and is transferred bodily and confessedly from Paganism. There is nothing in the Christian Scriptures to countenance it. And should some Pagan Roman come forth from the catacombs, as did Lazarus from the grave, at the bidding of Him who is the resurrection and the life, he would see in the lamps and candles which burn in all its temples an evidence that the religion of his fathers was yet there unchanged. O, Sir, it is the entrance of God's truth into the mind that gives light; without this light we may stand amid the concentrated blaze of all the lamps and candles that ever burned on Papal or Pagan altars, and yet be in

Egyptian darkness. The oil of all the whales that swim, the tallow of the cattle upon a thousand hills, the wax of all the bees that have ever buzzed, if manufactured into candles, and blessed by the Pope, would not shed as much light upon the mind as would this one simple text, "He that believeth in the Son hath life"—or this other text, "Then spoke Jesus unto them, saying, I am the light of the world; he that followeth me shall not walk in darkness, but shall have the light of life." O, why should miserable priests attempt the fraud of supplying the light of the truth which they suppress by the light of candles?

I am not yet through with the Paganism of Romanism. I shall return to it in my next.

With great respect, yours.

LETTER VII.

St. Patrick never in America.—Our Poverty in Holy Wells and Places. —The Holy Wells at Ballahadireen—Ballina—Downpatrick Head. —Their Origin.—The Cell of St. Mary in Via Lata.—The Atrocity of opening fabulous Wells, and suppressing the Fountains of Truth.

MY DEAR SIR,—I am not yet through with the Paganism of Romanism; and I will ask your attention in the present letter to some other evidences in proof of their great similarity. In the mean time, I wish you not to forget what I have said about the uses of holy water, incense, and candles.

As good old Saint Patrick, of blessed memory, never visited these American shores; and as, in the days of monkish miracles and legends, and of holy houses flying through the air, they lay beyond the light of the Dark Ages, we are very sadly deficient in holy wells, at which the wondering saints drank, or in which they washed their feet, and in holy places, where miracles were wrought when none were needed, to gratify their whims or their appetites, or to strike with fear their enemies. And may not this, Sir, be one of the reasons why Romanism flourishes so little here, and why so many educated in that faith, in other lands, on reaching these shores, lay it aside as a compound of old wives' fables? Whatever may be the cause of the effect, whether it be our poverty in holy wells and places, or our open and ennobling institutions, it would really seem, especially as to our emigrants from Ireland, that they carry their Popery in the pockets of their corduroys; for as soon as they lay aside the one, they seem to get rid of the other. But if we are poor in holy wells and places, they abound in those lands where Romanism yet reigns and rules.

In some letters addressed, not long ago, to our magnificent friend of New York, I had occasion to advert to these holy wells. I described one that I had seen in my boyhood. Knowing how to shoot a gun round a corner to the entire satisfaction of many of the faithful, he sought to throw discredit upon the whole statement. He knew and knows that they exist in almost every county of Ireland; but he was ashamed to own them, and afraid to denounce them, lest he should break their charm over the vulgar mind. Now, Sir, as I have recently made a pilgrimage to some of these holy wells, permit me to describe a few of them to you, and of the least celebrated.

Near to a small town called Ballahadireen, in the county Mayo, is a holy well of some female saint, whose name I forget, and whose festival is on the 10th of August. On the 13th of last July I was all around it. It stands in a secluded spot, and is surrounded by a very rough wall of stones, upon some of which are cut Popish hieroglyphics in the most primitive style of the art. I found old rags between the stones in place of mortar; and in lifting up some stones, I found knots of thread under them; and upon the branches of the little shrubbery by which it was surrounded, there were tied pieces of old cloth. These were left behind as mementoes of their visits by the poor devotees, who go there to make their stations; that is, to go round it upon their knees, praying to the saintess of the well for her intercessions. Miss H., the noble and pious sister of the proprietor of the place, told me that she saw one day a woman at this well pull the hair from her head, and tie it to a bush on its side. "Why," said she to the woman, "do you do so?" Her reply was, "If God will overlook me in the judgment, holy Saint Patrick will look on this hair and remember me, and will speak to God for me." If Irish Popery is true, heaven is no place of rest to good Saint Patrick. He has his own troubles there. The feast of this saintess is kept on the 10th, and there is a great carousal on the 11th of August; and within a few years three awful murders have occurred at these carousals. So I was informed on the spot.

Another of these holy wells is near to Ballina, in Connaught, and on the side of the public highway. This is one of the many called after Saint Patrick, whose fame is very great for many wonderful things in "the Island of Saints." It is surrounded with mud, which was so deep on the 15th of July as to prevent me from reaching its brink; and through that mud all the poor devotees wade in making their stations. After making the required prayers around the well, they cross the road, and pass over a stone wall into a field, in which is a rock. They walk round this rock praying, dropping at each circuit a little stone upon it. When the required circuits are all made, they return to the well, and gaze into its shallow waters until they see the *holy trout*, whose appearance is an evidence that their prayers are answered! The well-known Dr. John Edgar, of Belfast, one of Ireland's noblest sons, was with me on this pilgrimage. He stated that he saw once a pilgrim at this well watching for "the holy trout," that he might have an evidence of the acceptance of his prayers. Of a sudden he exclaimed, with astonishing emotion, "I see the holy eel!" But, on examination, it was found that "the holy eel" was only a long, rotten twig, thrown by some wag into the well. And as I passed from this holy well through the town, I saw half a dozen of lazy and carnal-looking priests fishing for salmon in the River Moy, which passes through it. I felt for the moment as if I should like to have seen them at least knee-deep, if no further, in the mud which surrounded the well in which the victim of their cruel superstition saw "the holy eel."

I visited, also, the holy well, and drank of its waters, which springs up in the moor as you approach Downpatrick Head. There were the beaten paths of the pilgrims, along which they perform their stations; and there were the old rags stuffed in between the stones; and I learned by our guides that hundreds flock to it on the day when prayers offered there have a peculiar efficacy. But what need, Sir, of dwelling longer on these wells? If slippery John of New York, whose memory is often very conveniently treacherous, knows nothing about them, there are millions who do. Who has not heard or read of the famous well of Saint Patrick, in the county Down? Who is ignorant of Saint John's well, at Kilmainham, or of the superstitious rites and licentious practices which are exhibited there on the 24th of June? These sacred wells, places, and spots you meet every where in Papal countries. In

Italy they abound. Down in a dark cellar, under the church "St. Maria in Via Lata," I was shown the holy well, by a burly priest, which miraculously sprung up for the baptism of those converted by St. Paul. And there is scarcely a hill, vale, river, spring, road, church, or village that you meet, which has not its sacred history, and to which somebody does not make a pilgrimage in order to obtain the remission of sin.

And whence, Sir, all this reverence for holy wells and holy places? Surely not from the Bible; surely not from the teachings of Christ and his apostles. Whence, then, are these superstitious customs derived? Most certainly and obviously from Paganism. You, Sir, will not need me to tell you how frequent among the heathen were sacred fountains, and rivers, and lakes, and places. You well know to what an extent, at this day, are pilgrimages to holy places and rivers made by the Hindoos, and the votaries of Bhoodism over all the East. This, also, in the language of Bishop England, is "an ancient custom, of Eastern origin," and adopted because "our religion has been received from the East."

As I gazed around that cell, under the Church of Saint Maria in Via Lata in Rome, in which the miraculous well of Saint Paul is kept locked and covered up, and which is only opened once a year to quench the thirst of the faithful, my eye lit upon a pillar extending almost to the ceiling of the cell, around which a chain was entwined. "What chain and pillar are these?" said I to our priestly guide. "O," said he, "that is the pillar to which Paul was bound, and that is the very chain by which he was bound." I smiled but was silent, as I did not care to confess my unbelief down there. I did not go to Rome desirous to obtain a martyr's crown from or by priestly hands. I approached the pillar, and found this sentence deeply chiseled into it, "*Verbum Dei non est alligatum*"—the Word of God is not bound. I was amazed. There, down in that dark, damp cellar, was engraved upon stone the glorious truth that God's Word is not bound, and yet, when you go up into the light, you find the Word of God not only bound, but banished from Rome. "There were other fountains," said a friend to our guide, "which sprung up here; what is become of them?" "What were they?" said he. "The fountains called Paul's Epistle to the Galatians, and Paul's Epistle to the Ephesians, and Paul's Epistle to the Philippians, and Paul's Epistle to the Colossians, and Paul's Epistle to Philemon, and probably Paul's Epistle to the Hebrews," was the reply. "These were great fountains which sprung up here at the time you say this holy well did, and where are they?" He replied, with a shrug of the shoulder, "I don't know." And, although a shorn priest, I suppose he did not know.

Now, Sir, how can we estimate the atrocity of that outrageous system of priestly policy which hides from the people the fountains of truth, and the truth by which we are converted and sanctified, and then sends them to rivers, fountains, or old muddy wells, at which some fabulous saints are said to have drank, or to have washed their clothes or their feet, for that cleansing which faith in the blood of Christ alone can effect? They shut up from the people the fountains of truth, the wells of salvation, and send them in crowds to perform stations around these holy wells, and to pray to the saints to whom they are dedicated. I know not, Sir, how all this may impress you, but I confess that, with me, it places a Papal and Pagan priest on the same level, save that the Pagan is the most excusable. You find, Sir, no priests making their stations around these wells. They never dirty their shoes around that at Ballina; they have never been heard to repeat a paternoster around that at Ballahadireen; they are rare as swallows in winter at those holy places to which they encourage the vulgar to go. Why is this? As among the ancient Egyptians, the priests have a religion for the people and a religion for themselves.

The ancient heathen believed, and all the heathen nations of the East now believe, that some places are peculiarly holy, and that a visit to them is greatly meritorious, tending to purify the soul, and to gain the favor of the gods: Popery adopts from their mythology this very principle, and in its pilgrimages and penances we have an exact counterpart of those of the heathen in ancient and modern times. Are you not beginning to see that Romanism is far more Pagan than Christian; that it bears a nearer resemblance to the teachings of the Shaster than to those of the Scriptures?

Nor have I yet exhausted the Paganism of Romanism. More evidence to this point in my next.

Yours, with great respect.

LETTER VIII.

The Market-place at Naples.—A ludicrous Disaster at its Gate.—Images every where revered.—Church of St. Augustin.—Scene witnessed there.—The Image of Peter at St. Peter's.—Worshiped by Pope and Cardinals.—The Pantheon : Scene there.—Rome, Pagan in Fact, Christian only in Name.

My dear Sir,—I am not yet through with the Paganism of Romanism. So manifold are the points in which they touch and blend, and so numerous are the institutions, rites, and ceremonies transferred bodily from the one to the other, that to exhaust the subject would require volumes; but I am not going to write volumes. Yet that you, and the poor, degraded victims of the system may see, as I see, that in many of its main features it is baptized Paganism, I have a few more things to adduce in order to strengthen my position. In the mean time, let me ask you not to forget what I have said about holy water, incense, candles, and holy wells.

There is in Naples a market held in a square called Marcenello, and so called, if our valet spoke the truth, which is not always to be taken for granted in Italy, from the name of a rebel against the government, who rose up from among the fishermen, and who, in this square, put to death, in a barbarous manner, many of the nobles. You enter this market-place by a gateway, on one side of which I saw an image of the Virgin and Child inclosed in a glass case, with candles burning before it, and to which the peasants, as they passed out and in, always bowed the knee. In this gateway I witnessed a most ludicrous scene, which admirably illustrates the piety of the Neapolitans. On approaching the gate, a donkey, laden with vegetables, as I had never seen a donkey laden before, and driven by a brawny and boisterous master, stumbled, and cabbages, onions, and turnips were scattered around. The donkey recovered, and his enraged driver overtook him in the gateway, where for some minutes I witnessed the farce of his bowing to the Virgin, and whipping the donkey, and swearing at him at the same time. The obvious distraction caused by his reverence for the Virgin and his rage at the ass was most diverting. And these pictures and images you see every where in purely Papal countries, and they are held in great reverence by the people. They superabound in Naples.

And they are to be found in all Popish churches. As you enter these churches, they strike a stranger as one of their great peculiarities. You see people kneeling and praying before them and to them. Never, on any occasion, have I seen a more profound reverence manifested than I have seen toward these pictures and images in the churches of Rome, and in the presence of swarming priests. And to multitudes of these pictures miraculous powers are attributed; and healing from diseases is sought from their touch, and forgiveness of sin from their worship. This statement may be denied in theory by the priest, but it is true to the letter in the practice of the people. And that you,

Sir, may be convinced of this, permit me to make a statement of a scene on which I gazed with my own eyes, and which may be daily witnessed in Rome.

On the lovely Sabbath morning of the 8th of last June, I started in company with others for St. Peter's. We took in our way the Church of St. Augustin, famed for its fresco of Isaiah by Raphael. Near to the right entrance is the statue of the Virgin and Child by Sansovino, which, for reasons that I could not learn, is an object of special veneration. Both the Virgin and Child were most gorgeously robed, and were sparkling with brilliants, the munificent donations of the opulent. The church has three naves, and is supported by gigantic pillars, all of which were covered from top to bottom, and on all sides, with hearts made of different metals. Around the statue was a crowd of poor people, each intensely anxious to kiss the toe of the Virgin, and crowding their way to gain their end. Mothers were there, holding up their infant children in their hands, and pushing them over the heads of others, that they might only touch the venerated image. The successful competitors for the holy kiss, sprinkled themselves with water, and, after abstracting a penny or a paul from their rags, and depositing it in a money-box just by the statue, they retired, with joy and pleasure beaming from their countenances. Priests in flocks were passing in and out, but they sought neither to kiss the Virgin's toe, nor to stay the idolatry of the people. And what meant those hearts which hung in thousands from the pillars and walls of the edifice? They were the votive offerings of those who received benefit or cure from kissing the toe of the image made by Sansovino! I heard, subsequently, Dr. Duff portraying with burning eloquence the idolatry of India, but no picture did he draw so gross or revolting as that which I witnessed, and which you may witness in the Church of St. Augustin, which lies within the hearing of a gunshot to the palace of the Pope! This is the church to which the poor in Rome do mostly resort. It lies in a crowded and dirty part of the city.

We passed on to St. Peter's. Here are pictures and statuary beyond number. I shall now only ask your attention to the image of St. Peter. There it is in the great nave, near to the high altar, and just in the position to attract the eye of every visitor. It is a sitting figure, formed of bronze, and resting on a heavy marble pedestal. His face is such as you might expect from his character as depicted in the Scriptures, impulsive and stern; his right hand is lifted as if in the act of blessing; and in his left he holds two ponderous keys. This statue is a great affair in Rome, and has its history and its worshipers. Some say that, save the head and hands, it is the old Jupiter Tonans, with the thunderbolts exchanged for the keys. I have scarcely a doubt but that it is so. And at stated times the Pope and his cardinals go to it in gorgeous procession, and render to it, as far as the external act is concerned, as profound a worship as ever did the old Romans under the name of Jupiter. I saw myself priests bowing before it, kissing its toe, and rubbing it with their foreheads. Indeed, by constant kissing and rubbing, several feet have been worn down; and, as I can testify, the present one is dying of consumption. While measuring its dimensions with my eye, and rubbing with my hand the wasting toes, and thinking of the priestly wickedness connected with the whole affair, I was told that our friend of New York, on his recent visit, prostrated himself before it. If so, it is another evidence of his great fitness to wear the fillet made by withered nuns from the wool of holy sheep.

We, Sir, away in this land of darkness, and, if a star at all in the ecclesiastical firmament, only a wandering star that will not obey the impulses of the sun, and that will not be attracted to the great centre of Catholic unity, are as poor in holy statues and paintings as we are in holy wells; and very much for the same reason. But other countries are very rich in them. Have you not heard, Sir, of the holy image of the Virgin and Child in Lucca—how the shoulder of the image bled when struck by a furious man—and how the blood is preserved to this day, and is exhibited with great ceremony to the faithful? Are you—can you be ignorant of the image of St. Dominic, in Calabria, which was brought from Heaven by St. Catharine and Mary Magdalene, and which, as cardinals, bishops, and priests testify, has raised the dead, given eyes to the blind, and cured all diseases and infirmities? It is yet visited by swarms of pilgrims yearly. This St. Dominic, you will remember, was the father of that wonderfully human institution, the Inquisition, which your good archbishop so manfully vindicates in that erudite work on theology which he has so kindly dedicated to you. Have you not heard of the picture of Mary, painted by St. Luke, kept in a church near Florence, which is brought out in solemn procession in order to avert any calamity which may be feared as impending over Florence or Tuscany? But, Sir, the time would fail me to tell you of the numbers beyond number scattered over Southern and Northern Italy, Spain, Portugal, France, Germany, and Holland; and which, even in our day, are regarded as possessing wondrous and healing efficacy. Where there is a mixture of Protestants among the people, these things are kept behind the curtain, and are but secretly encouraged; but where the people are unmixed Papists, they are openly patronized, and, in many cases, are of more value than mines of gold to the priests. I met these things every where in Italy—in churches, by the road-side, in market-places, at the corners of the streets, in cigar shops—and, in multitudes of cases, I have seen the people offering to them, at least in appearance, the most profound worship.

If, Sir, you have not seen, you have surely read of the Pantheon, the most perfect and celebrated monument of ancient Rome. Although built before the Christian era, there it yet stands, in all its original proportions, unaffected by the revolutions of two thousand years. Although various are the interpretations given to its name, yet in this temple all the gods of the heathen were worshiped; and, when new countries were conquered, their gods, or duplicates of them, were sent to this temple, that the people from those nations, visiting the then metropolis of the world, might have their accustomed images before which to bow. And for this purpose it was most admirably arranged.

This gem of antiquity, originally built by Agrippa, the son-in-law of Augustus, and dedicated by him to Jupiter Ultor, Mars, Venus, and, as its name imports, to all the gods, was dedicated by Pope Boniface IV. to the Virgin Mary and all the saints. With this single change, it remained as it was. Mary took the place, perhaps, of Venus, and the saints of Jupiter, Mars, and the other heroic gods of the heathen. The old images remained, but with new names, and they were passed off upon the deluded populace as the veracious images of Christian heroes! And as the heathen found there all their gods before which to bow, so now do Papists find there their favorite saints before which to pray. Several times did I stand beneath its beautiful dome, and witness the ceremonies at its several altars; and, as I saw the few that resorted there looking for a few minutes around, and then filing to the right or left as they discerned the picture of their favorite saint, how could I resist the impression that it was yet in substance and form a heathen temple, or suppress the fear that it was so in fact? I assure you, Sir, that I regarded the dirty and clumsy priests I saw there more as the priests of Jupiter than of Jesus, and the persons I saw worship there more as Pagans than Christians.

Now, Sir, the question again arises, and imperatively demands an answer, Whence these images—whether of the chisel or the pencil, the carpenter or mason—which every where crowd Papal churches, and which are multiplied to a surfeit in Papal countries, and which have so much to do with the genuflections, prostrations, prayers, and beads of ignorant Papists; and, as in the case of the statue of St. Peter, even with those of the Pope himself, and his crimsoned cardinals? Whence all this? Not, surely, from the Scriptures of the Old

Testament, because we are taught nothing by them more clearly than that God, in his anger, visited the Jews with war, famine, pestilence, and dispersion, to punish them for the sin of setting up images after the manner of the heathen. Not, surely, in the Scriptures of the New Testament, where we are taught that there is but one mediator between God and man, and that we must worship God in spirit and in truth. Whence, then, is it? Clearly from Paganism. And so undeniable is its paternity, that many Romanists not only will not question it, but will absolutely defend it as a capital stroke of policy to bring over the people from Paganism to Popery without their knowing it; and what was once, on this ground, a stroke of policy, is now retained and defended as essential to impress the senses of the vulgar, with whom spiritual conceptions is a work of great difficulty!

And as it is in the Pantheon, so it is in the other heathen temples that yet remain in Rome; they have pulled down one idol and set up another, or merely changed its name. The sweet little temple of Vesta is now possessed by the Madonna of the Sun; that of Fortuna Virilis by Mary the Egyptian; that of Saturn by St. Adrian; that of Romulus and Remus by Cosmas and Damianus; and so on to the end of the chapter. And with Dr. Middleton I can truly say, that I would rather give divine honors with Pagan Rome to the founders of empires, than with Papal Rome to fictitious saints, whose miracles and holiness have nothing to sustain them but the miserable legends of the monks of the Dark Ages. If I must bow before pictures or images at all, give me Vesta, and Saturn, and Romulus:

and I will give the Madonna of the Sun, and Adrian, and Cosmas to the Pope and his priests.

Are you not now beginning to see that Romanism is far more Pagan than Christian?

With great respect, yours.

D

LETTER IX.

Cumulative Evidence of the Paganism of Romanism.—Landing at Naples.—Appearance of the Ecclesiastics.—Convent house.—Church of Capuchins at Rome.—Preserved Monk.—Horrid Burying-place.—Nuns—how manufactured.—Whence Monks and Nuns, and for what.—Tools of the Priests and Corrupters of the People.

MY DEAR SIR,—I am not yet through with the Paganism of Romanism. The evidences of the paternity of the religion of the Seven Hills grow with investigation. Like the ruins of Pompeii, they lie concealed beneath a slight external covering, which is easily removed.

On landing at Naples, I was struck with the large number of ecclesiastics, in different garbs, that were to be seen in all the streets. They all looked extremely fantastical and self-satisfied. Some wore a three-cocked hat, and some no hat. Some wore shorts, and stockings, and shoes with large buckles, and some wore sandals without stockings; but, whether they wore shorts or not, I could not tell from their flowing dress. Some wore an elegant priestly coat of black cloth, girt with a sash around the waist, lifted up a little on one side in order to facilitate their walking; while others wore a coarse garb, flowing from their shoulders to their feet, with a cord around their loins. I soon learned that the fat, well-fed, and well-dressed persons, with large shovel hats, were priests; and that the persons without hats, wearing sandals and no stockings, and a kind of a shoe with no hind part to it, and which flapped against the sole of the foot as they walked, were monks and friars of various and varying orders. Of these persons I had often read, but now they were before me a living reality. The walk, the look, the whole appearance of the priests seemed to testify that they belonged to the better class of society; and, as I was subsequently informed, they were persons whose parents had purchased for them admission to the priesthood as the cheapest way of securing to them a competent support for life. But the monks and friars that were swarming every where bore the strongest evidence of a mean origin. Their low foreheads—their shaven pates—their unwashed faces and uncombed hair—their coarse and filthy garments, and their unwashed feet, bore evidence against them. Of these monks and friars there are many orders in Naples. Some you see with bags on their backs, and others with baskets in their hands, begging from door to door; while others are confined to their rooms in their houses, the voluntary subjects of rules and customs the most superstitious and degrading. On the side of the hill which rises up in the midst of Naples, and which is surmounted by a strong fortification, is a monkish house. It is a very large establishment, making a hollow square, with the grave-yard in the centre; and each of the posts of the fence by which the grave-yard is inclosed is surmounted by a naked skull. These monks never speak, and never eat at the same table, save on the Sabbath! And these establishments you find every where in Italy. I visited one of their churches in

Rome, where I witnessed the most revolting sight I ever beheld. It is the Church of the Capuchins, where is the magnificent painting of the Archangel by Guido. In a glass case, under one of the side altars, is the body of a monk, laid out in his old robes, in a state of *miraculous* preservation. Whether it was dried flesh or *wax* I could not tell; I suspected the latter. I asked the monk that attended on us why the flesh of this man was preserved, while that of others decayed. His reply was most ludicrous. Putting his hands together, and turning up his eyes, like a duck in a thunder-storm, he answered, "Because he was a good fellow." The burying-place of these monks is a horrible sight. It seems to have been gotten up to outrage all the feelings of humanity. It is partly under the church, and is entered from the yard by a series of arches. The burial spot may be twenty or thirty feet by seven or eight. The clay of this bed, I was told, was brought from Palestine. In this bed the monks are buried, where they lie until the flesh falls from their bones. Then the bones are taken up, and some of them, after being jointed with wires into a perfect skeleton, are dressed up in their old garbs, and hung up around the place, while the skulls, the bones, and the ribs of others are wrought into fantastical arches and candlesticks, which every where cover the walls and meet the eye. Even Rome does not present a more revolting spectacle. And shreds from an old dirty garment of that preserved monk, whose name was Crispini, are said to have wrought miracles, and have been sold at exorbitant prices. And in this revolting den of superstition and indolence are one hundred and fifteen of these dirty

Capuchins, who, judging from their appearance, stand far more in need of a thorough washing than they do of victuals or wine!

These monks, who spend their time between praying, begging, sleeping, and sinning, you meet every where. One of them was regularly stationed in the hall of the Hôtel d'Angleterre every morning to beg alms from the strangers retiring from the breakfast-room. My traveling friend, who liked them about as much as I did, put his hand in his pocket one morning, as if hunting for a franc for the shorn monk. Fingering his pocket, he went up stairs, and the monk after him, his eyes beaming with hope. At the top of the first stairs, he signified that he could not find any thing to give him. He stopped a little, but cast a longing, begging look after him. Again my friend commenced to finger his pockets, and, again flushed with hope, the monk renewed his pursuit. But, while ascending the next flight, the incorrigible Protestant came down upon the lazy rogue with a thundering rebuke, under which he went down stairs at least as fast as he ascended them.

And you, Sir, must well know how large a space in the history of Romanism is filled by the rise and the progress, the conflicts and the crimes, of the various classes and orders of monks and friars.

It has also called into requisition female monks, called nuns, who have contributed not a little to the extending of its plans. The first of these persons I saw abroad was on a funeral occasion, in the Madeleine, in Paris. The deceased was obviously very poor, and the priest in waiting mumbled a service over the coffin, so hurried and so heartless as to fill me with contempt for him. The nun, who, perhaps, was the nurse of the deceased, was there, and a more common or ugly woman no man might wish to see. There were three of them on the steamer from Lyons to Avignon, and, in appearance and manners, they were the very ditto of her I saw in Paris. The great vulgarity of their appearance in Italy put to flight all the images of beauty, and delicacy, and modesty which I had ever associated with them; nor could I account for what I observed until my visit to the Catacombs at Naples. As you approach these subterranean graves, there are two large buildings on either hand; that on the left is devoted to the care of poor old men, and that on the right to poor young girls, who are deserted by their parents, or "who had no parents," as said our valet. This building is capable of containing between one and two thousand girls, and is usually full; *and all of these are compelled to be nuns.* The fact that they are taken from the very lowest walks of life accounts for the commonness of their appearance; and it is the same fact which accounts for the yet more common, and dirty, and sensual appearance of most of the monks and friars that I saw abroad. Here and there a disappointed maiden may flee to a nunnery to hide her blushes or her shame, and become a lady abbess; or a greatly criminal noble may flee to a monastery to hide his crimes, and to play the gentleman fanatic among boors; but, as a rule, monks, friars, and nuns are from the very sweepings of society, and ever have been. Italian nuns, as far as they came under my observation, needed not the walls of a nunnery to protect them from marriage, for I have seen many females far prettier enjoy the benefits of single blessedness without any to disturb or to make them afraid. And such are the monks and friars that are shipped here in cargoes to civilize and to Christianize us!

But the question again arises, Whence these orders of monks and friars? Whence these nuns of various names, and various colored vails? There is nothing like them in the Old Testament—nothing certainly in the New. Celibacy is nowhere enjoined on man or woman, saint or sinner, in the Bible. Seclusion from the world, like that practiced in monasteries, is nowhere enjoined by the sacred books of our religion. When Paul speaks of persons wandering in deserts and in mountains, in dens and caves of the earth, he refers to those banished from their homes and friends by the ferocity of persecutors. Whence, then, these orders? They are all of Pagan origin. You, Sir, need not be told how orders of priests abounded among the Egyptians and the Greeks, nor how they were copied by the Romans. The merest novice in mythology will remember the Pagan confraternities, to which Franciscans, Benedictines, Dominicans, and Jesuits so nearly correspond, and the Vestal Virgins, to which Popish nuns are so exact a counterpart. How exactly Homer and Plato painted the monks of La Trappe in their descriptions of the priests of Dodonean Jove! Anchorites, hermits, recluses, and monks existed in Asia long before the Christian era; and, at the present time, the countries which profess the religion of Brama, Fo, Lama, and Mohammed, are full of fakirs, and santons, toners, talapoins, bonzes, and dervises, whose fanatical and absurd penances are the arts of deception, and not the fruits of piety. And in some of the countries of Asia at this hour you will find priests and monks under the vows of celibacy without keeping them, with shorn heads, with and without turbans, and wearing peculiar robes tied about their loins, as thick as under the shadow of St. Elmo, or as on the banks of the Tiber.

But why these monks, and friars, and nuns? Has the question ever occurred to you? The bishops are generally engaged in the higher affairs of the state or the Church; the priests are saying masses in deserted churches, and faring sumptuously; and the monks, and friars, and nuns, collected from the common people, and sympathizing with them, are abroad among them, as the curates or assistants of the priests and bishops, for the purpose of filling their minds with fables, and keeping them in bondage. They are priestly spies among the people, save those that go into se clusion; and hence you find them begging for the people, sitting with the people in the streets, mingling with them in the market-places, lounging with the lazaroni, and laughing with them, and all for the purpose of doing the dirty work of the priests, and filling their minds with superstitious legends. The object of importing to our shores monks and nuns can not be mistaken; and as soon as public sentiment will allow it, you will see these lazy and wicked wretches sticking their shorn heads into the cottages of the poor, to warn them against all the elevating influences of Christianity, and flouting their coarse robes in our thoroughfares for the same purpose for which the Pharisees of old made broad their phylacteries. These monkish orders were, and are, the curse of Pagan nations; they wofully corrupted the Christian Church; they were mainly the authors of the lying legends of the Dark Ages, which Papal priests are endorsing even in America; they are now a grievous curse to the Papal nations of the world. O, Sir, will you not join me in the prayer that they may never curse, either by their presence or their arts, our own happy, thrice happy country?

With great respect, yours.

LETTER X.

Letter from Rome dated A.D. 90.—The Paganism of Rome then, the exact Picture of Papal Rome now

My dear Sir,—That you and all men may see at a glance the entire truth of the Paganism of Romanism, which I have already so fully proved and illustrated, will you permit me to go back to the year 90 of the Christian era, and, like my friend "Nicholas, Cardinal Archbishop of Westminster," to address you a letter "out of the Flaminian Gate," describing the religion of Rome, both as to its priests and ceremonies, as then existing?

Rome, A.D. 90.

Sir,—I have just reached this great city after a tedious voyage. I have spent several days in visiting the many temples here erected to the worship of the gods, and in inquiries as to the civil and social state of the people; and I now proceed to detail to you what I have seen and learned.

Domitian has just brought to a close the Dacian war, having secured a peace on very humiliating terms. This, instead of humbling him, has greatly excited his turbulent passions, so that no man is now safe here, unless he would degrade himself to flatter the tyrant and his tools. The philosophers are expelled, Christians are greatly persecuted, and are prohibited from meeting for worship under the severest penalties; and a widespread fear of the emperor is among all the people. Rumors of conspiracies against his life are very frequent, and those who are suspected as enemies are cruelly torn from their families; but what is done with them none even conjecture. The unseen hand of tyranny is every where felt, and every person is in hourly dread of its chains or its daggers.

But very few Christians are to be found here. They are compelled to worship in secret, where the eye of tyranny can not see them. The most frightful immoralities prevail among the people, although the altars and images of the gods are every where to be seen, and although their temples are multiplied and gorgeous, and their worship is maintained with many and imposing ceremonies. And what seems to me surpassing strange is, that the more immoral the people, the more they are attached to their religious rites.

There is here a wonderful array of Pagan priests, filling the temples, and to be met with in all the streets. These are frequently to be seen leading in processions in honor of the gods, which processions are calculated to please the people and render them superstitious. One of these I have just witnessed. The magistrates in their robes were there; the priests in their surplices were there; with wax candles in their hands, and carrying the images of the gods, finely dressed. These were followed by young men in white vestments, singing in honor of the god whose festival was celebrated; and these, again, were followed by crowds of all kinds of people, with candles and flambeaux in their hands. The whole scene was very gorgeous, but very idolatrous. The common people are said to be fond of these things, and they are multiplied by the priests on that account.

The priests here are very numerous, and wield a vast power. I will, therefore, give you some account of them. The chief and head of them all is called *Pontifex Maximus*, or sovereign pontiff. This man is the visible head of their religion, and is the chief of a body of priests, which, in their collective capacity, is called collegium or college. This college is the final judge in all cases relating to religious things; and where there is no written law, they prescribe what they think proper. This college is a body of vast influence, and always sits in secret. When the pontiff dies, it elects a new one, and usually from their own number. The Pontifex is almost worshiped as a god; indeed, he is sometimes called god, although he only claims to be the vicegerent of Jupiter. He claims to exercise among men the authority of Jupiter—he lives in royal state—he levies taxes upon the inferior priests and upon the people, and he claims a respect from the people, which, to me, is just like adoration or worship. Men bow before him as he passes, and none can approach him without kissing his feet. He is the infallible interpreter to whom the people resort; and while he punishes others at discretion, he is not himself amenable to the judgment of the senate or the people. All priests, and almost all things, are subject to him. He regulates the year and the public calendar. He usually wears a gorgeous robe bordered with purple, and a cap in the form of a cone, and holds a rod in his hand wrapped round with wool. But you should come to Rome yourself to understand the power of this man, and the splendor with which he appears in public, and in which he lives in private.

In the train of the Pontifex Maximus there is always a numerous priesthood, divided into several classes. Some of these are called Augurs, some Quindecemviri, some Septemviri; these are the chief. But, besides these, there are fraternities of priests less considerable, though quite influential. These, in the language of this country, are called Fratres Ambervales, Curiones, Feciales, Sodales. Besides these, there are priests of particular gods, as the priests of Jupiter, of Mars, of Pan, of Hercules, and of Cybele, *the mother of the gods.* There are also here women they call Virgines Vestales, or Vestal Virgins, who are consecrated to the worship of Vesta, and who enjoy singular honor and privileges. These all wear peculiar garments, by which they are distinguished from one another and from all the people. Their dress tells who and what they are, wherever you meet them, and you meet them every where. And all these priests have servants, who wait upon them when they are performing rites at the altars of the gods.

The houses erected to the gods are many and beautiful. These are called Templæ, or temples. I have just returned from the Pantheon, where I witnessed a ceremony which I will describe to you. As the morning here is regarded as the most propitious part of the day, their great ceremonies are all ended before noon. The priest entered by a door, dressed in a white robe called *alba,* and ascended by a few steps to the altar. He wore, also, a tunic of various colors. His head was shaven, which struck me as singular, and he had upon his breast a richly-decorated covering called a *pectoral.* He wore, also, a vail. The whole dress struck me as very fanciful, nor could you conjecture, save from his head and face, whether he was a man or a woman. When he had washed his hands, he marched round the altar, and, having made obeisance before it, he stood fronting the people. Lighted tapers covered the altar. The servants and inferior priests burned incense, while the priest made many prostrations. He always spoke in Latin, which I do not sufficiently know fully to comprehend him. When the ceremony was ended, the god in whose honor it was performed was carefully locked in a little box upon the altar, and then the priest dismissed the people with these words: "Missio est." And after being sprinkled by the inferiors with water mingled with salt, which is called "lustralis aqua," or holy water, they left the temple, smiling and talking, and apparently gratified. And, with little variation, this is a picture of what I have witnessed in all the temples I have yet visited. The sacrifices, as I had supposed, did not always consist of slain animals; sometimes nothing is offered but a little round wafer, which is called *mola*, and the offering of which, as they declare, removes the sins of the people. This was instituted by Numa, and is called "*the unbloody sacrifice.*"

Nothing here more sorrowfully impresses a true mind than their great multiplication of gods. They have twelve superior gods, with whose names you are familiar; and they have gods inferior, which they multiply without end. These latter are persons selected for divine honors from the ranks of men, and who, for their virtues or merits, are placed among the gods. When the Collegium, of which I have already spoken, has resolved to deify any person, they proclaim his apotheosis, which proclamation places him among the gods. Immediately the ignorant people begin to pray to him, and to invoke his aid. First they make a god of him, and then they make him pay for the honor conferred! From these small gods it is customary for classes and professions to select a patron. Musicians have selected Apollo; sailors, Neptune; farmers, Ceres; soldiers, Mars; cities, towns, and persons select their guardian gods. Rome has selected Jupiter Capitolinus, and Athens Minerva; and families have their gods in their houses, and individuals carry their patrons in their pockets. And to these gods they give the honor and prayer which are due only to the only true God. I saw a poor sailor, the other day, who had escaped drowning at Ostia, hang up his coat as a votive offering in the temple of Neptune, and prostrate himself before his image as if it were our God!

I find also here a belief of a state somewhere between hell and the Elysian fields, where the souls of the departed go which were not bad enough for hell nor good enough for heaven. I know not whether they borrowed this doctrine from Virgil, who is here in great repute, and who teaches it; or whether it was older than Virgil. Probably he only embodied what was a popular superstition in his fine poem. But the use which the priests make of it has strongly impressed me with their want of honesty. They pretend to the power of abridging the awful sufferings of souls in this intermediate place by prayers and sacrifices, and for which they charge very high prices when the people are able to pay. In this way the Pagan priests here draw enormous revenues from the living for the saving of the souls of the dead. They speculate on the sorrows of the living; and from hearts broken by afflictions and trials they draw some of their chief revenues.

But I may weary you with these details which I make, and which you must read with sorrow. This is a wicked city, and its priests are the most wicked of its people. It is a most superstitious city. But the power of these Pagan priests is gradually giving way, and the influence of superstition over the people is becoming less and less. The true Gospel of Jesus Christ is here as a leaven—may it leaven the mass. It is the only remedy for the sins and follies of this great but wicked people.

Very truly your friend.

Now, Sir, if you will turn to the history of Rome at the date of this letter; if you will turn to any writer on Roman Antiquities; if you will read Adams on the Religion of the Romans, commencing with page 234 of the New York edition of 1826, the one now before me, you will find that I have given you an exact account, as far as such an account can be drawn from history, of the priests and ceremonies of Paganism, as far as I have gone, and at the time selected. Were it necessary to go further into the conduct of the priests, and the manner and character of their ceremonies, I could have brought out other things that would equally astonish you. And now, Sir, I would seriously ask you what is the difference between Pagan Rome in the year 90 of the Christian era, and Papal Rome in the year 1852? I assure you, Sir, I can see but little. The Pontifex Maximus you have in the Pope; the Collegium in the sacred college of cardinals; the priests of various classes you have in the varying classes of the monks and nuns; the multiplication of demigods you have in the canonization of the saints; the ceremonies described in the Pantheon you have there at this very hour, almost unchanged; the wafer called the "mola" you have in the "*unbloody sacrifice of the mass;*" the intermediate state between Hell and Elysium, as sung by Virgil, you have in Purgatory; and the cruelty of Domitian and his tools, and their persecution of the Christians, you have in the infamous, detestable conduct of Pius IX. and his cardinals; and so on to the end of the chapter. Popery, therefore, is little else than Paganism extended. All unbiased minds on earth, capable of forming an opinion on the subject, must admit this, especially if they visit Rome, and examine the subject, as I have done, in what were once Pagan, and now are Papal temples.

And here, Sir, you have one of my chief reasons for addressing these letters to you. A man high in character, station, intelligence, and influence, you are claimed as a Romanist by Papal priests. Whatever may be your private views, you would prefer the name of Christian to Pagan; while a thorough Papist, can you be less than Pagan? And, as the able and tried friend of your country and its institutions, would you not prefer that it and they should be under the molding influence of the religion of Jesus Christ, rather than under that of the old Pontifex Maximus of the Seven

Hills? Is not the Bible a better book for our people than the traditions of the Sybils, doubtfully or dogmatically interpreted from Papal altars? Are not ministers of Christ better teachers of the people than the commissioned spies of the holy college of cardinals—than the lineal successors of the augurs, the curiones, the sodales, the Virgines Vestales of the days of Domitian? Are you doing your duty to your noble country, the hope of the aspirants of true liberty in all the earth, by giving even the approbation of your silence to the efforts of priests from Ireland, Austria, and Italy, to transplant to our shores nominally Popish, but really Pagan institutions, whose very best influences have been always adverse to the highest interests of humanity? Honor yourself and your posterity, and bless your country, by a wise and powerful effort, such as you can put forth, to prevent Papal priests from Paganizing our country.

With great respect, yours.

LETTER XI.

Sham Miracles.—Altar in the Catacombs.—St. Januarius—the Liquefaction of his Blood.—A terrible Incident for the Priests.—Ara Cœli.—Bambino.—A Scene.—History of Bambino.—Its wonderful Powers.

My dear Sir,—Having, as I trust, satisfied you, and all my readers, that Popery, in its forms, ceremonies, and external arrangements, is nothing but the Paganism of the old Roman state, which Christianity found there on its first introduction into our world, permit me to proceed to the consideration of some other topics.

On entering the Catacombs at Naples, the first thing that strikes you, so as to attract attention, is a rude Papal altar, covered with all the insignia of Romanism. You ask, Why is it there buried under a high mountain, and shut out from all save those visiting this wonderful receptacle of the dead of the heroic ages of Italy? The reply is, that "it marks the spot where the bones of the far-famed St. Januarius were found." "How long did they remain here," said I to our guide, "before discovered?" "About three hundred years," he replied. "But how tell, at that distance of time, whose bones they were?" "By miracle," he replied. Of course, I could say no more. In the cathedral church of the city, dedicated to this saint, is a beautiful chapel, where are two vials of his blood; I was shown the case in which they were locked up; but my eyes were unworthy of seeing them. "How," said I to the guide, "could they get this blood, when it was not known where his body was for three hundred years?" "By miracle," was again the reply. "When, and how is it," I asked, "that this blood liquefies?" "In September, May, and December," he replied, "and at other times when the bishops pray. And the blood melts when the saint's head looks at it." "But the head is dead—how can it look?" "By miracle," was the reply. "But how does the look of the head melt the blood?" "By miracle," was the answer. And, egregiously absurd as the whole thing is, it is by these sham miracles that Romish priests, in all lands where belief in them is the vulgar faith, seek to retain their ascendency over a deluded people. And in all this they prove themselves to be the worthy and true successors of the Pagan priests, who sought by prodigies and omens to excite and strengthen the vulgar belief. Let me place some of these miracles before you.

There, in two old vials, is the fabled blood of St. Januarius. On the set time, these vials are brought out by a priest; and the head, which was cut off about the year 306, and which must have been often renewed in nearly sixteen hundred years, is brought out and placed near them. The blood melts at the sight of the head. The Rev. Alban Butler, a most erudite scholar in lying wonders, tells us, "that when the blood is brought within sight of the head, though at a considerable distance, it melts, bubbles up, and, upon the least motion, flows on all sides." Then a boy holds up a lamp behind the vial to make the liquefaction visible. Then the faithful, usually composed of beggars, press toward the altar, when a priest touches their forehead and lips with the wonderful vials. When persons in a clerical dress approach, which is rarely the case, it is touched to their forehead, lips, and bosom; and surely, like the soothsayers of old, they must laugh when they look each other in the face. It would seem to me that the man who left the company of waiters upon the priests, who were saying high mass for the purpose of showing us the wonders of the church, was laughing in his sleeve at our apparent credulity as he was describing to us the miracle-working relics. And that miracle of stupid credulity, Rev. Alban Butler, tells us, with all seriousness, that in 1707, the shrine of St. Januarius, carried in solemn procession, extinguished a fiery eruption of Mount Vesuvius! Indeed, he attributes the preservation of Naples from being buried, like Pompeii, in the lava of its neighboring volcano, to its possession of the head, and blood, and bones of this old saint, whose holy history is a monkish fable. A less credulous person might ask, how Vesuvius could send its lava to Naples, without first making a bridge across the bay?

The following story, often published to the confusion of the priests, was confirmed to me in Naples, and by a Neapolitan, who, although avowing himself a Catholic, loved the priests just as much as if he were an American. When the French, in the days of Napoleon, occupied that country, the blood of St. Januarius refused to liquefy, as a token of his vast displeasure with the people for permitting the Franks to abide there. The awful news was spread in whispers from the confessionals through the city. The people, especially the Lazzaroni, were determined on another "Sicilian Vespers," and on the procession of the vials, which usually calls out the entire populace. The French commander was informed of all the plot. The day arrived. High mass was said. The old head of the saint was brought within sight of the old vials, but the blood refused to liquefy! A low murmur passed through all the streets. Two cannons were wheeled in a moment before the church, and other cannon were at the corners of the streets, ready to sweep them in an instant. Orders were sent to the priests in management of the juggle, that unless the blood liquefied in ten minutes, the church and city would be fired. In five minutes the saint changed his mind; he became alarmed, fearing the effects of a lighted match when placed in contact with gunpowder. The blood boiled up, and all the people rejoiced together. And the priests yet delude the people with this contemptible farce! The priests that performed Pagan ceremonies in the temple of Castor and Pollux would have given up this bungling fraud long ago.

You have no doubt heard of, if you have not seen, the church of Ara Cœli at Rome. It is a very ugly, barn-looking affair on the Capitoline Hill, and on the very spot, it is said, where stood the temple of Jupiter Capitolinus. It is in the possession of the Franciscan friars, a brotherhood, as I can testify, that stand sadly in need of washing. This church is less famed for its fine frescoes illustrating the life of St. Bernard, by Pinturricchio, than for its wonderful figure of the infant Savior, the "Sanctissimo Bambino," whose power in curing the sick has given it a world-wide popularity, and which receives more fees than any three physicians in Rome. "*Bambino*" is the Italian word for child; and this image is called *Il Bambino—The Child*, to mark its superiority to all others. The bare-headed monks, either bowing profoundly to the earth, or piously turning up their faces to heaven, call it "Il Sanctissimo Bambino."

I have seen this wonderful image, and yet I live! It is a wooden doll about two feet long, and not unlike, in form, to the Dutch dolls which are often given among us as a holiday present to children. It is wrapped in swaddling clothes after the custom of the Italians, so as to cover it all save its head and its feet. On its head is a royal crown, sparkling with brilliants; and from its head to its feet, it is covered with rubies, emeralds, and diamonds. This is the favorite divinity of the lower classes of the Romans, almost casting into the shade that of Mary herself!

As the good fortune which always attended me would have it, I entered the little chapel where this image is kept in state, just in time to see his little reverence go through a healing process. A monk opened for us the main door, and showed us into a small room, whence we were shown by another monk into the wonderful chapel. There were there, kneeling before the altar, three poor women with a sick child. The priest who acted in the affair was going through some ceremony before the altar. Soon he turned to the right, and with a solemnity which, because feigned, was laughable, opened a little cradle in which lay the glittering doll. He prayed over it; and then, taking it in his hands as if unworthy to touch it, placed it in an upright position on the altar. Here he prayed over it again. H then took it in his hands, and touched, with its toe, the head of the sick child, and crossed it with it. He then put its toe to the lips of the child, which was made to kiss it. And then each of the women, who were all the while upon their knees, kissed its foot. After a little more ceremony, Bambino was put back in his beautiful cradle, and the women withdrew. When the chapel was empty of Italians, we were invited inside by the priest. We were taken up to the cradle. He told us of the immense value of the jewels, many of them the gifts of kings; of the many miracles wrought by Bambino; and pointed to the many silver and gold hearts by which it was surrounded, in evidence. He gave us some items of its history, which were very rich. The cradle lies under a canopy; at one end of it is Joseph; at the other, the Virgin Mary; and over it is an image of God the Father! The priest was polite, communicative, but grossly ignorant. We paid him a few pauls, and retired, wondering more, and more, and more at the shameless, lying wonders of Popery; at the folly and wickedness of its priests; and at the stupidity of its people.

As the Bambino is among the most wonderful things at Rome, and is worth more than a mine of gold to the dirty monks of Ara Cœli, I will give you some account of it, as quoted from its authentic history, published with the permission of the Pope and cardinals, and for the edification of the faithful!

It was carved in Jerusalem, by a monk of St. Francis, from a tree of olive, which grew near to the Mount of Olives. The good monk was in want of paint, and could find none. By prayer and fasting he sought paint from heaven. On a certain day he fell asleep, and lo! when he awoke, the little doll was perfectly painted, the wood looking just like flesh! The fame of this prodigy spread all over the country, and was the means of the conversion of many infidels. It was made for Rome, and the maker embarked with it for Italy. But the ship was wrecked; and when all gave up the holy image as lost, lo! the case in which it was, suddenly and miraculously appeared at Leghorn! This wonderfully increased its fame and the veneration of the people. Thence it was soon transported to Rome; and when first exposed to the devout gaze of believers on the Capitoline Hill, their shouts of joy and their clamorous hallelujahs ascended to the stars! On a certain occasion, it is said that a devout lady took away with her the pretty doll to her own house; but, in a few days, he miraculously returned to his own little chapel, ringing all the bells of the convents as he passed! The bells assembled all the monks, and as they pressed into the church, behold, to their infinite joy, Bambino was seated on the altar! Did you ever hear of such a wonderful doll?

But this is not all. It is the universal belief among the lower classes of the Romans, that the laying of this doll at the foot of the bed of a woman in child-birth insures a safe deliverance! It is also the universal belief that this doll, by a change of its countenance, by becoming pale or flushed, infallibly indicates whether a sick person will live or die! And when doctors fail, the aid of Bambino is invoked for the recovery of the sick. It visits the sick in a splendid coach, and is attended by priests in full canonicals. As it passes along through the streets, every head is uncovered, and, however muddy may be the streets, the poor are on their knees for its worship. For these visitations, the monks, who have the doll in keeping, charge the most enormous prices. During my sojourn in Rome, it was sent for to the Vatican for the healing of somebody sick in the palace of the Pope! And this miraculous image is exposed to public veneration and adoration in a scenic representation of the stable at Bethlehem, from the 25th of December to the 26th of January of each year, during which time tens of thousands of people crowd the Ara Cœli and the Capitoline Hill for the purposes of its worship!

Now, Sir, here is a shameless imposture, palmed off upon an ignorant people by impious priests and monks. Nor is this thing done in a corner. This outrageous fraud is not perpetrated in Connaught, nor in Mexico, nor in Austria, nor down in deeply-degraded Sicily, but in Rome—on the Capitoline Hill—and under the eye, and by the sanction of Pio Nono and his cardinals! What epithets or adjectives does our language supply sufficiently strong to express our abhorrence of the enormous wickedness of Pope, cardinals, and priests, who would thus delude and degrade an ignorant and confiding people! And yet, Sir, the priests of Romanism, steeped in these vile, lying superstitions and wonders, come over here to tell us in America that there is no salvation for us so long as we refuse to submit our necks to the yoke of this Pope and his cardinals!

And will you, Sir—will any American citizen, in any form, give their countenance to the shaven-pated missionaries of such miraculous nonsense?

With great respect, yours.

LETTER XII.

Sham Miracles.—Holy House of Loretto—its History—Flight—Dimensions.—Miracles.—Litany of our Lady of Loretto.—Perpetrators of such Frauds, Impostors.

MY DEAR SIR,—I am not yet through with the sham miracles of Romanism, gotten up, and shamelessly advocated, even in our day, for the purpose of maintaining the terrible, the grinding influence of a wicked priesthood over an ignorant, deluded, and confiding people. Bad as is the bungle about St. Januarius, and base as is the conduct of the dirty Franciscans with the bandaged Bambino, there are other things of the same kind, if possible, worse than these.

Have you, Sir, ever heard of the once "Very Rev. P. R. Kenrick, V. G.," and now the Right Rev. Bishop Kenrick? He figures not a little among the Romish priests of this happy country. I have before me his wonderful work entitled "The Holy House of Loretto." It is published by Cummiskey, of Philadelphia. The title-page is without date—so is the preface; but the copy-right of it was secured by the publisher in the year 1841. And if you have any desire to see the miserable legends which these imported priests publish for the edification of the faithful, just glance at this wonderful book—I will not ask you to read its drivel. The authorship of such pages would subject any man, save a priest, to the charge or the suspicion of lunacy. But the world has become so accustomed to the lying wonders of priests, and knows so well the objects for which they are put forward, that now they excite little more than a smile of contempt.

This veracious book of the "Very Rev." and veracious "P. R. Kenrick, V. G.," proves to the satisfaction of all the credulous that the house in which the Savior was born became early an object of deep veneration; that Helena found it at Nazareth about three hundred years after the incarnation; that it was carried by angels through the air in May, 1291, and laid down by them upon a little eminence in Dalmatia, where it attracted wonderful attention, and performed wonderful miracles of healing; that when doubts arose as to its character, "the blessed Virgin, surrounded by angelic spirits," appeared to Alexander, then priest of a church near by, and sick of a violent fever, and informed him that in that house she was born, lived, received the message of Gabriel, and conceived the Son of God. This vision appeared to Alexander "between sleeping and waking," and when he had a violent fever. These, you know, are circumstances under which many besides "this respectable ecclesiastic" have strange visions. She moreover told him that the apostles had converted this house into a church; that Peter had consecrated its altar; that, because insulted in Nazareth by infidels, and neglected by Christians, it was carried over by angels to Dalmatia; and that, as a miraculous proof of all this, his health should be immediately restored. "On awaking, Alexander found himself immediately restored to health;" and his story was told and believed, and was proved true by the miracle of his restoration!

But the story is not ended. The Dalmatians were not long to enjoy this heavenly gift of an old house. For some cause, not discovered by the profound researches of the "Very Rev. P. R. Kenrick, V. G.," the house resolved to take another journey! So, on the night of the 10th of December, 1294, some shepherds, who were watching their flocks, beheld a house, surrounded by uncommon splendor, flying across the Adriatic, which separates Dalmatia from Italy. The shepherds waked up their companions to see the "mysterious object," and they all testified that "it was of a supernatural character." It pleased "the holy house" to rest in a district called Lauretum, either from its laurels, or from the name of the rich lady, Laureta, to whom it belonged; and hence the name, "the House of Loretto," which it retains even to this day! Soon it became very famous in its new location, and tens of thousands flocked to it for devotion and healing!

But the restless little house was not yet satisfied. The faithful, who sought to present, under its holy roof, their offerings to the Virgin, were often robbed by bandits. This greatly diminished the number of pilgrims, and, of course, the revenue of the priests. To remedy this evil, it walked off to a small hill near the road, where the faithful might approach it without fear of robbery. This new miracle greatly increased the public reverence for it, and the revenue. This hill was the joint property of two brothers, who quarreled about the rent they were to receive, when, in the language of "the Very Rev. P. R. Kenrick, V. G.," "most extraordinary to relate, this miraculous house was once more transferred, and placed in its present site, a very short distance beyond the property of the unworthy brothers." And there it remains "to this present." And to prove that all this is by no means incredible, he refers us, among other evidences, to the removal of a huge rock at the command of St. Gregory, as narrated by Alban Butler!! Now, Sir, I submit it to you, whether a priest who can write a narrative like this, in our age and country, is not entitled to wear a pallium made from the wool of holy sheep, or from the down of a goose?

This holy house, that can thus fly or walk at pleasure, is about thirty-two feet long, thirteen feet wide, and eighteen feet high, with a chimney and small belfry. The walls are of stone. There is in it a small altar, the one dedicated by Peter; and on it is an antique wooden cross. On the right of the altar is an image of the Virgin Mary, with the infant on her arm, with the hair of each divided after the manner of the people of Nazareth. This image is surrounded with gold lamps, by whose constant glare and dazzle it is somewhat concealed. The Virgin and Son are most gorgeously decorated, and are brilliant with precious stones. This holy image was carried to France in 1796, but it was brought back with pious pomp; and, welcomed by the discharge of cannon and the ringing of bells, it was borne to the holy house on a rich frame, carried by eight bishops, on the 5th day of January, 1803.

And the miracles wrought by this holy house are numerous and wonderful. It is hung round by "the votive offerings in gold, silver, wax, and other materials," presented by those on whom miracles were performed. Pietro Barbo was there miraculously healed, and was informed by the Virgin that he would be elected Pope! He was so elected, and assumed the name of Paul II. He issued a bull, dated November 1, 1464, in which he speaks of "the *great wonders* and *infinite miracles*" wrought by means of the Holy Virgin in this house. This house has been the pet of many a Pope, who have expended treasures upon it! And there it stands at the present hour, "the most celebrated sanctuary in Italy"—hung round by votive offerings of great value—visited by pilgrims from all parts of the world—and with a regular establishment of priests, sustained at an enormous annual expense, mainly collected from the beggar pilgrims. There also is the "holy porringer," in which pap was made for the infant Savior, and which imparts wonderful sanctity to every thing that is put into it! A small stone from this house has been sold for many dollars; and it is said that a poor little mouse caught there was preserved with great artistical skill, and was an effectual preservative against diseases!!

Now, Sir, permit me to ask you whether imported priests, one of whose bishops could write such a book as the "Holy House of Loretto," in which such ridiculous fables are gravely detailed for the edification of the faithful, are the men to whom the formation of the religious sentiment and the conscience of our country should be committed? When our people can believe such drivel, where will they be in the scale of civilization? Where will be the greatness and the glory of the country of Washington?

But as to this "Holy House of Loretto," there is a depth below any to which we have yet attained by the aid of the "Very Rev. P. R. Kenrick, V. G." I would gladly omit reference to it, because of its blasphemous superstition, and because of my reluctance to refer to a man who is daily proving himself more and more to be unworthy of confidence, and who is fast sinking to his true level in the estimation of Papist and Protestant; but it seems necessary to the completion of my picture of this "Holy House." In this flying house is an image of the Virgin, with the infant Savior in her arms. It is grown black with age; nor can you tell whether the person of whom it is an *exact picture* was black or white. Now, Sir, conceive of one of your own daughters prostrate on her knees before that old carved image, very far from being fashioned after a beautiful model, and with a Missal in her hand, praying to it, in a most devout manner, the following prayer:

"We fly to thy patronage, O Holy Mother of God; despise not our petitions in our necessities, but deliver s from all dangers, O ever-glorious and blessed Virgin.

Holy Mary,
Holy Mother of God,
Holy Virgin of Virgins,
Mother of Christ,
Mother of divine grace,
Mother most pure,
Mother most chaste,
Mother undefiled,
Mother untouched,
Mother most amiable,
Mother most admirable,
Mother of our Creator,
Mother of our Redeemer,

} Pray for us.

Virgin most prudent,
Virgin most venerable,
Virgin most renowned,
Virgin most powerful,
Virgin most merciful,
Virgin most faithful,
Mirror of Justice,
Seat of Wisdom,
Cause of our Joy,
Spiritual Vessel,
Vessel of Honor,
Vessel of singular Devotion,
Mystical Rose,
Tower of David,
Tower of Ivory,
House of Gold,
Ark of the Covenant
Gate of Heaven,
Morning Star,
Health of the Weak,
Refuge of Sinners,
Comforter of the Afflicted,
Help of Christians,
Queen of Angels,
Queen of Patriarchs,
Queen of Prophets,
Queen of Apostles,
Queen of Martyrs,
Queen of Confessors,
Queen of Virgins,
Queen of all Saints,
} Pray for us.

"We fly to thy patronage, O Holy Mother of God,

despise not our petitions in our necessities, but deliver us from all dangers, O ever-glorious and blessed Virgin.

"Pray for us, O holy Mother of God.

"That we may be made worthy of the promises of Christ."

This, Sir, is extracted from a book now before me, called "The Garden of the Soul, a Manual of Fervent Prayers, Pious Reflections, and Solid Instructions, calculated to answer the use of the members of all ranks and conditions of the Roman Catholic Church, etc. By the Right Rev. Dr. England, late Bishop of Charleston, with the approbation of the Right Rev. Dr. Hughes, Bishop of New York." And the above extract is from "The Litany of Our Lady of Loretto." Again I say, conceive of one of your own daughters praying this prayer from the Garden of the Soul, prostrate on her knees before that black statue of Mary. Does not your heart revolt from the thought? Would you not as soon see her bowing in a heathen temple, before a heathen idol? Wherein would be the practical difference? Would you not feel humbled at being the father of a child that could be reduced to the performance of such a miserably superstitious and vainly repetitious service by the arts of priests? And what would be your feelings of indignation toward a priesthood that could thus humble you by degrading your child? And it is to this low level that Romish priests, with all their appliances, and all their "deceivableness of unrighteousness," are seeking to reduce the youth of this land. One bishop writes the History of the Holy House—another bishop writes, or translates, the Litany of Our Lady of Loretto—and John Hughes, Bishop of New

York, approves the whole! Have you, Sir, any language by which to denounce the whole imposture as it deserves? I have none, and will not, therefore, undertake it. But the men in clerical garb who could countenance such fraud and superstition, should be esteemed and treated as we do the priests of Juggernaut, or the veriest impostors that live by defrauding the community. Such vile frauds, practiced by its priests, should sink Romanism as with the weight of a thousand millstones to the bottom of the ocean. Poor Dr. England has gone to the grave. Peace to his ashes. But Bishop Kenrick and Bishop Hughes are yet alive; and the greatest harm I wish them is, that when the "Holy House" resolves on another flight across the Adriatic to Dalmatia, they may be in it as passengers. Judging from their books, they will not add materially to its weight, nor will they be any loss to our country. In their flight they may responsively repeat the "Litany of Our Lady of Loretto."

With great respect, yours.

LETTER XIII.

Sham Miracles.--St. Anthony of Padua.—The Virgin of Modena.—Blood of Thomas à Becket.--Miracles of St. Patrick.--Miracles at Downpatrick.—St. Dagland's Grave.—The Boy exorcised.—Xavier's Miracles.—The wonderful Crab.—Priests not to be trusted.

My dear Sir,—I am not yet through with the sham miracles of Romanism. You know the Romish Church claims the power of working miracles; and the absolute working of miracles is put forth as an incontrovertible evidence of its being the only true Church. And to sustain the monstrous claim, no persons, save those who have waded through their lying legends, can have any conception of the stupendous absurdity of the miracles that are adduced. And if those already adduced—the blood of Januarius—Bambino—the Holy House of Loretto—patronized by popes, cardinals, bishops, kings, and nobles, and in the face of the world are so unspeakably absurd, how absurd must be those lesser miracles, palmed by wily priests on the lower classes of the people, and in the dark corners of the earth, where detection is not apprehended from the peering scrutiny of Protestant eyes! Let me state to you some of these.

St. Anthony of Padua was a giant in his day. Butler gives an abstract of his life, which has been the theme of more than one credulous biographer. He was a man of eloquence; and, while the rest of his body has returned to dust, his tongue was found, thirty-two years after his death, fresh, red, and incorrupt as when he was living, and is now kept in a most costly case in his church at Padua! An unbeliever said one day, "If this glass does not break on dashing it against that stone, I will believe in Saint Anthony." He dashed it down, and it did not break! The miracle was so obvious that he immediately believed! Another infidel said he would believe if the dry slips of vines he held in one hand would bear grapes enough to fill the cup which he held in the other. Immediately Saint Anthony caused the dry vines to bear grapes; they ripened in an instant, and produced as much juice as was required, and of the most delicious kind! This infidel became a most devout follower of the saint. And by narratives of miracles as contemptible as these, the monkish life of this saint is filled!

Amid the Alps in Savoy, and near to the town of Modena, there is an image of the Virgin that works many miracles, but nearly all of the same kind. It restores, on their presentation, dead-born children to life, just long enough to receive baptism, when they again expire! And there is abundant testimony to prove that such children, when presented to this image, open their eyes, stretch out their hands, and even sometimes make water! But when baptized, all signs of life pass away! What an image!

Who has not heard of St. Thomas à Becket? He was for ages the great Thaumaturgus of England, and wrought more miracles than did the Savior and all his apostles. His blood, on his being put to death, was carefully collected, and possessed astonishing efficacy.

It cured all diseases, and even restored the dead to life! When the blood was found insufficient for the demands of the faithful, it was mixed with water; and the least drop of water, if only tinged with the blood, possessed a healing efficacy. And water thus tinged with the blood of the rebel was sent out into all parts of the Christian world as an infallible cure for all kinds of diseases! You full well know, Sir, what miracles of wickedness this Thomas of Canterbury committed while living, who wrought such miracles of power after he was dead! But we hear little of him of late! Might not a revival of miracles at his shrine now greatly aid Nicholas Wiseman in subduing the iron obstinacy of the English mind in its resistance to the blessings of Romanism? Might not that remarkably acute and veracious historian, the "Very Reverend P. R. Kenrick, V. G.," in the exercise of his wonderful gifts as an antiquarian, bring something to light concerning Becket which, at this juncture, might have an effect of reviving the faith which in our land is so sorrowfully on the wane? Such a work, especially if published with the approbation of the "Right Reverend Dr. Hughes," might have a most happy effect in arresting the stream of converts from Romanism to Christianity.

The Irish, although a noble people in many respects, are peculiarly credulous and superstitious. The lower classes are generally Papists, and are exceedingly ignorant; and their faith in their priests, until within a few years, was unbounded. Hence sham miracles have been wrought there in greater numbers than, perhaps, in Italy itself. Jocelin's Life of Saint Patrick is now before me, as printed in Dublin in 1809, and in a cheap form for extensive circulation. It contains little more than a detail of the miracles he wrought, some of which are of the most astounding character. Here are a few of them. Gormas was born blind. He was informed, in vision, that if he would, with the hand of the boy Patrick just baptized, make a cross on the ground, a spring of water would rise on the spot, in which, if he would bathe his eyes, he would immediately see. He did as he was advised, and immediately saw! And the spring is there to this day! But which one of many springs it is, none can tell.

Patrick went out to play on a cold day, and brought home some pieces of ice and cast them down. His nurse told him, chidingly, that he ought to have brought home some dry wood for fire. He took the pieces of ice, and, putting them together, prayed over them, and soon the ice was in a blaze! Of course, the nurse was astonished, as she was in duty bound to be. Who would not be?

As he was playing one day, instead of minding his flock of sheep, a wolf carried off one of the lambs. In the evening he was scolded for his sloth and carelessness. But he bore all patiently, and poured out his prayers for the restoration of the lamb. On the next morning, when he led the flock to pasture, the roguish wolf returned with the lamb in its mouth, and laid it at the feet of Patrick, and then fled to the woods!

Patrick fell into the hands of strangers, who sold him to a certain man for a kettle! "How small a purchase for so precious a merchandise," exclaims Jocelyn. But the kettle would not boil when hung over the fire —the hotter the fire, the colder was the water in the kettle, until, in the midst of the flames, the water became ice! The kettle was returned, and Patrick was taken back, when the kettle boiled as usual, and the saint was set at liberty!

When Patrick was returning from Rome, where he was made a bishop, as he was about embarking at a British port for Ireland, a leper besought him to take him with him. He consented, but the sailors refused. So, casting into the sea "an altar of stone, that had been consecrated and given to him by the Pope," he ordered the leper to sit on it. And the stone sailed over the Channel as fast as the ship, and got into port with its passenger in perfect safety!

Rius was a very old man and a very great sinner. He promised Saint Patrick if he would restore him to the bloom, the freshness, and the joy of youth, that he would become a Christian. He prayed over him, and made the sign of the cross upon him, and he was restored to "beautiful youth," when he became a Christian.

A very wicked man, named Foylge, one day killed the coachman of Patrick. The saint struck him dead by a word, and his soul went to hell. But the devil entered into the body of Foylge, and it walked about. In a few days the saint was passing a house where the soulless body of Foylge was: he ordered the devil to depart from it, when the body fell down, alive with worms! It was immediately buried, as neither its sight or smell could be endured.

And with such silly fables as these a book of nearly three hundred pages is filled! And although the translator will not vouch for the entire truth of all these miracles, and the priests may deny its authority, yet it is abroad among the people, and its narratives are believed by multitudes. Nor do I see any thing in the book any more incredible or ridiculous than the lying wonders of the Bambino of Ara Cœli, or of the Holy House of Loretto, which are at this hour encouraged by the entire Papal court, and drawing vast revenues from every part of the Papal world. Can a priesthood which can palm such sublimated nonsense upon any people, have any object in view but their degradation? Can they be otherwise than a curse to them? Can such priests be a blessing to America?

But Jocelin's book is not authentic—its miracles are not articles of faith! Here is the door of escape for the priests. Why, then, not denounce it? Why do priests aid in its circulation, while they make bonfires of the Bible? And why permit things as bad, if not worse than any thing narrated in it, to be practiced under their eyes? The grave of St. Patrick is said to be at Downpatrick, in the county Down, in Ireland. There also are the holy wells of purification. On Midsummer eve of each year, the people resort to the grave, and fill their ears with its clay, and then rush to the wells, there to bathe, for the purposes of healing from all their maladies. And men and women, in perfect nudity, rush into the healing waters together! And priests are present to hear confessions, and to receive their pennies from the beggar pilgrims to these holy places! Is any thing in Jocelin worse than this?

The grave of St. Dagland is in Waterford. His stone coffin is filled with bones every year by miracle. On the 28th of June of each year, these bones are taken out, and are borne away as precious relics, and as preservatives against various afflictions and diseases. These miraculous old bones are, of course, sold! They have no miraculous power unless they are paid for, and that pretty liberally! Is any thing in Jocelin worse than this?

Within a short time, a poor boy, near Boyle, in Ireland, went to a Protestant school. His mother gave a reluctant consent. This boy was chilled almost to death in a bog during a stormy day, and went home violently sick. A numbness pervaded his body, which medicine and time only could remove. The poor mother, thinking it was a visitation of heaven upon herself and child for permitting him to go to the Protestant school, sent for the priest. He confirmed her suspicions, and offered to cast out the devil that possessed the boy on the condition that he should not go again to the Protestant school. The conditions were agreed to; and just as the boy was on the recovery, the priest exorcised the evil spirit, and he is now alive and well! And I saw the poor, bare-footed mother of that boy, who submitted to the locking up of the mind of her child in ignorance, to secure the muttering of a miserable exorcism over him by a contemptible priest! Is any thing in Jocelin worse than this?

Have you ever, Sir, read the life of Francis Xavier? It was one of the classics of my youthful days. If you have not, will you permit me to ask you to glance at it—I do not ask you to read it. He wrought prodigious miracles, far surpassing in number and power those of the Savior of the world. He foretold future events—spoke unknown languages—calmed tempests at sea

—cured various diseases—and raised the dead to life. And although all performed in India, Dr. Milner, in his wonderfully absurd book, "The End of Controversy," endorses them all. Permit me to narrate to you one of the miracles of this saint as a specimen of the rest. St. Francis had a most precious crucifix, which, in a voyage at sea, he lost overboard. He was inconsolable, and prayed for its recovery. Walking one day upon the sea-shore, he saw his lost crucifix coming toward him on the surface of the water! He went down joyfully to the water's edge, when a crab, holding the crucifix in his claws, paddled up to him, and most reverently laid it down at his feet! But the credit of this miracle is due, not so much to Xavier as to the crab; and, were I one of the court which makes dead men saints, who wrought miracles in attestation of their sanctity, I think I would find it difficult to decide between the claims of Xavier and the crab for a place in the calendar. Might there not be a St. Crab as well as a St. Viar? An old stone, much mutilated, was found with the letters S. VIAR upon it. It was immediately supposed to be the grave-stone of St. Viar, who was immediately placed in the calendar. The lost pieces of the stone were found, and, when put together, the inscription ran thus: PREFECTUS VIARUM, *overseer of the highways*. Yet St. Viar was not deposed. And what is in the way of having a St. Crab?

Now, Sir, are priests who practice such gross frauds as these—who, by sham miracles like these, seek to keep the yoke of Romanism upon the necks of the ignorant in all lands—are such priests to be trusted, or in any form countenanced? Are such priests fit to be intrusted with the formation of the character of our people? Is not every thing we hold dear in danger, just in proportion to the number and the influence of such jugglers and their adherents? If, Sir, it were possible for you to write a book advocating these sham miracles, like Milner, or like the "Very Rev. P. R. Kenrick, V. G.," I have no doubt but that you would die of the disease of self-contempt. And what respect can you keep up for the priests that advocate them, or for the system of Romanism, of whose literature and faith they form so conspicuous a part?

With great respect, yours.

LETTER XIV.

Relics.—Scala Sancta.—Sancta Sanctorum.—Relics of Santa Croce—of St. Proxede—of St. Peter's—in Milan—in Cologne.—Sanctioned by the Church.—Made to Order.—That they should be true, not essential.—Their Effects upon the People.—These Forgers of Relics unfitted to be our moral Teachers.

My dear Sir,—The spirit of Romanism is the spirit of human nature. Well considering the instincts of the fallen nature of man, it has built upon those instincts a system of superstition which towers to heaven, and which casts its dark shadow over all the earth. A regard for relics is a part of our nature. We cherish with fond affection any thing which serves as a memorial of parents, children, valued friends—of the great, the wise, the good, the heroic, who have adorned the race, and blessed the earth by their deeds. And upon this principle of human nature, in itself innocent, and, within due bounds, laudable, Romanism has built up a system of fraud, and falsehood, and imposture, which should unite the race in hissing it out of the world. Permit me to ask your attention, in the present letter, to the relics of Romanism.

Near to the Church of St. John Lateran, and within the same inclosure, is a little chapel which contains the celebrated *Scala Sancta*, or holy stair-case. It contains twenty-eight white marble steps; and the priests inform us that this is the holy stair-case which

Christ several times ascended and descended when he appeared before Pilate, and that it was carried by angels from Jerusalem to Rome. At certain times it is covered with persons crawling up it on their knees, with their rosaries in their hands, and kissing each step as they ascend. I called at this place several times to see the devotees, but in vain. I went up and down the lateral steps without any to molest me, save a fleshly old monk, who sat as sentry facing the holy stairs, and who never failed to jingle a money-box in my face. On one occasion, two beggars offered to go up the stairs for me, in due form, for a paul each, and to pray for me as they crawled up; but it would look like simony, and I declined the bargain. On another occasion, I ventured to place my Protestant feet on the three upper stairs, when my valet was frightened into hysterics lest the people should know it, or I should be punished for sacrilege. Resolved not to be cheated out of a sight I so long desired to see, I went there on a Friday afternoon, and the stairs were covered with people, mostly beggars, most devoutly crawling on their knees; and when the ceremony was ended, going away in the highest merriment. But not a priest was there. As I gazed upon the revolting and superstitious scene, my mind recurred to that memorable day in the world's history when Luther ascended these stairs. "While going through his meritorious work," says D'Aubigné, "he thought he heard a voice like thunder speaking from the depths of his heart, '*The just shall live by faith.*' These words resounded instantaneously and powerfully within him. He started up in terror on the steps up which he had been crawling: he was horrified at himself; and, struck with shame for the degradation to which superstition had degraded him, he fled from the scene of his folly." From that hour he walked forth a free man; and thus the fraud of the holy stairs, and the revolting, degrading superstitions there practiced, were promotive of the glorious Reformation. This grand incident gave those wooden-covered stairs more interest to me than all the legends of monkery and priestcraft concerning them.

There is a vast amount of mystery and sacredness thrown around the little building which contains these holy stairs. Here are several apartments which are kept locked, and to which I sought admission in vain. At the top of the holy stairs is a room called the *Sancta Sanctorum*, which is held in peculiar veneration. There is a picture of the Savior, by Luke, seven palms high, and an exact picture of him when twelve years of age! There is the pen of the seraphic doctor, brought by an angel from heaven, and with which he wrote his works! There is a feather from the wing of the archangel, which he dropped on the salutation of Mary! There is a bottle of the milk of Mary! There is a bottle of the tears which Jesus shed at the grave of Lazarus! And there is the cord which bound the Savior to the post when scourged! And in the church itself are the heads of Peter and Paul, which, on certain occasions, are exhibited with magnificent parade. Indeed, St. John Lateran is exceedingly rich in relics, as it ought to be, considering it is denominated "Mater et caput ecclesiarum."

The Church of Santa Croce, in Gerusalemme, is one of the great basilicas of Rome. It was built, it is said, by Helena, on the site of the residence of the brute Heliogabalus, and of his successor Severus. It derives its name from the fact, or fiction, that Helena deposited there a third part of the holy cross which she discovered on Calvary, and mixed with its foundation some holy clay from Jerusalem. This is the place where the "golden rose" of former days was consecrated; but it is now famous only for its large collection of relics. Near the chancel are two catalogues hung up for the perusal of all: one is a detail of the indulgences granted to all who there worship, and the other is a list of its sacred relics. The list I saw myself, and give it, as translated by Seymour. It is very rich, and worthy of all attention.

"Three pieces of the true cross, deposited by Constantine, and kept in a case of gold and jewels.

"The title placed over the cross, with the writing in Hebrew, Greek, and Latin.

"One of the most holy nails by which our Lord Jesus was crucified.

"Two thorns from the crown of our Lord Jesus.

"The finger of St. Thomas, which touched the most holy rib of the risen Lord Jesus Christ.

"The transverse beam of the cross of the repentant thief.

"One of the pieces of money supposed to be given for the betrayal of Christ.

"The bodies of St. Cæsarius and Anastasius.

"The cord by which our Lord was bound to the cross.

"The sponge which contained the gall and wormwood.

"A large piece of the coat of Christ.

"A large piece of the vail and hair of the Virgin.

"Some of the clothing of St. John the Baptist.

"Portions of the arms of St. Peter and St. Paul.

"Some of the ashes of St. Lawrence the martyr.

"A vessel of the balm in which the head of St. Vincent was dipped.

"Some earth from Calvary saturated with the blood of Christ.

"A vial full of the blood of Christ.

"A vial full of the milk of Mary.

"A piece of the sepulchre of Christ.

"A piece of Mount Calvary.

"A piece of the place where Christ was smitten."

To shorten this catalogue of wonders, I must omit the list of bits of stones from the various places mentioned in the history of Christ.

"Some of the cotton in which was collected the blood of Christ.

"Some of the manna which fell in the wilderness.

"Some relics of eleven prophets.

"A portion of the rod of Aaron, that budded.

"A part of the head of John the Baptist.

"Some of the skin and hair of St. Catharine of Sienna.

"A tooth of St. Peter.

"A tooth of St. Giordon."

And then follows a list of some bones of a hundred and one apostles, prophets, martyrs, widows, and virgins; and the whole closes up with "a hundred and thirty-seven cases of other relics of saints, both male and female, whose names antiquity has not distinguished." And those relics, Sir, are exposed, on certain occasions, by cardinals and bishops, for the worship and adoration of the vulgar!

The following are some of the relics in the Church of St. Praxede, taken from the catalogue engraved in marble, and near the altar, where all can read it.

"A tooth of St. Peter.

"A tooth of St. Paul.

"The chemise of the blessed Virgin Mary.

"The girdle of Christ.

"The reed and sponge given to our Lord with gall and vinegar.

"The swaddling clothes of Christ.

"The coat without seam, belonging to our Lord.

"Three thorns of the crown of thorns.

"The tomb of the Virgin Mary."

Then follows a list of the heads, arms, knees, thighs, cloaks of apostles, monks, martyrs, saints, and virgins, with which I will neither burden my page nor your memory.

Even at the risk of disgusting you and my readers with these miserable relics, I will name a few more of them. In St. Peter's they show you the very pillar against which Christ leaned in the temple at Jerusalem—portions of the cross—Veronica's image of the Savior—the head of St. Andrew, and the spear of St. Longinus, presented by Bajazet. In St. John Lateran is the table at which the Lord's Supper was instituted. In the Mamartine prison they show a curious stone, covered with a grating to preserve it. It has a hollow on its surface. A soldier knocked down Peter, and his head fell on this stone, and made that deep hollow in it. Peter's head must have been quite hard! At St. Pietre di Vinculo they show the chain that bound Peter, and which was miraculously broken by the angel! Filings from this chain have been sold at exorbitant prices, to be set in rings and breast-pins by the faithful! In another church is a square stone of white marble, which was carried by angels through the air from Jerusalem, on which the Savior stood when he met the apostles after his resurrection, and bearing the marks of both his feet! Around this stone beggars pray, and cover it with kisses! In Milan they show you the skeleton of Borromeo, gorgeously arrayed, and a vast supply of the teeth, nails, hair, and bits of skin of the apostles, put up in glass vials; as also the brazen serpent which Moses made in the wilderness, and which Hezekiah caused to be broken in pieces! These relics you find every where in Papal countries. In a box behind the altar, in the Cathedral at Cologne, they have the skeletons of the three kings that worshiped the Savior, and the bones of the Magi; and for six francs you are shown these old bones, by a jolly beadle, for the good of the Church! On the left, as you enter by a side door, and turn toward the altar, is a case containing Mary and Bambino, and, as is said, some most precious relics. This case I saw covered over with heads, and arms, and legs, and hearts, made of composition, as votive offerings for cures performed by the image and the relics. I saw a woman, and an old man, and a young girl diseased in the eyes, bowing before this case, while some females were scrubbing the stone floor and screaming at the top of their voice, and some boys were playing hide and go seek around them. But enough of this horrible wickedness of the priests, and gross ignorance and superstition of the people. I feel humiliated in even penning these terrible evidences of the enormous wickedness of Romanism and its priests.

But you will ask, Are these things sanctioned by the Pope and his cardinals? Sanctioned by them! Why, Sir, they glory in them. And on set occasions these relics are brought out by the Pope and the cardinals, and are exposed to the populace with magnificent pomp, who bow and prostrate themselves before these old bones, old coats, old wood, and old stones, more profoundly than they ever do before God! O, Sir, could you be present at the exhibition of relics in St. Peter's—or in St. John Lateran—or in Santa Croce in Gerusalemme, and witness the solemn pomp with which these relics are adored by Pope, cardinals, bishops, and the inferior clergy, you would never again think of the question whether or not they are sanctioned by the Pope and his cardinals!

But are these the true relics which they are represented to be? Impossible. Who can believe that the Holy House of Loretto—the blood and head of Januarius—the Bambino of Ara Cœli—the chemise of the Virgin—the bottle of her milk—the robe of the Savior—the bones of the saints, are what they are said to be? When you push the keepers of these relics, they will admit that there is no certainty as to them. And, as in the case of the bodies of Peter and Paul, which are said to be under the great altar of St. Peter's, when you seek to find many of them, they are not there. Multitudes of the old cases and boxes which are shown you as the sacred deposits of relics, contain nothing—or nothing like what is represented. The thorns from the crown of thorns are iron nails—and the bones of the saints are nothing but old bones collected from the Catacombs, and labeled for the market! The man who can believe that that old feather is from the wing of Gabriel—that that old cloth was the chemise of the Virgin—that those old bones were those of the persons to whom they are attributed, is almost fit to be a Papal priest! He certainly is, if the other necessary qualifications are as strongly developed as his credulity. Indeed, he is fit to be a true yoke-fellow of the "Very Reverend P. R. Kenrick, V. G."

But what motive can there be for such gross impositions? Motive enough for men who have no conscience, and who traffic in the souls of men. What would become of the monks of Ara Cœli without the wonder-working Bambino? They would starve. These relics attract multitudes to their shrines, all of whom pay for the sight, and pay the priests in keeping, to say masses for their friends in Purgatory. Even English and American Protestants spend tens of thousands yearly for a sight at these things, to laugh about them after they return home. And Rome is the great Relic market of the world. When a relic is needed for the sanctifying of a church in New York or Baltimore, an order is sent to the Holy City, and a relic is made to order. Nothing is needful but to take off an old label from an old bone, or a dry piece of wood, or from an old piece of stone, and to put on a new one. And Mr. Milner informs us, that if our devotions are honest, it makes no matter whether or not the relic is what it purports to be!! If you send for a finger of Peter, and you are sent the finger of Pilate, it is just as good, if you are only sincere!! And who doubts it? And when the boxes of acred bones in the Church of Santa Croce, to which antiquity has assigned no names, but to which priests now do, are exhausted, they are very easily supplied with bones just as old and as sacred. Indeed, these relics do more to enrich the Church of Rome, and to attract pilgrims and wonder-hunters, than any other scheme which the priests have devised. By means of relics, the priests have converted the Catacombs into mines of gold.

And what, you may ask, is the morale of all this? Just such as you might expect. If no good can be reasonably expected from worshiping the glorious sun—or the beautiful moon, with her attendant stars—or the magnificent river, that waters and fertilizes the earth—or the statue of an old hero, that, by his prowess in war, fought his way to a seat on Olympus to quaff nectar with the gods, what good can be expected from the veneration or worship of rotten bones from the Catacombs—of little splinters from the arms, the legs, the ribs, or the skulls of fabulous saints—of holy bits of skin—of the parings of holy nails—of little clippings of holy garments—or of pieces of old wood, or fragments of stones? To ask the question is to answer it. But are these venerated or worshiped, you ask? Go to Rome, and to the Church of St. Peter's, and you will see, at "the exhibition of relics," the Pope, cardinals, bishops, and priests kneeling and bowing before these things, with a reverence as profound as ever you saw manifested by a congregation of Irish Papists on what is called the elevation of the Host. The Pope and his entire court give, not merely an assent to the whole imposture, but are leaders in their veneration and worship, and for the purpose of giving eclat to the wicked thing with the populace. And the whole effect upon the minds and morals of the people is most disastrous. God is a jealous god, nor will he give his glory to another. Nor will he permit man, created in his own image, to give to the creature the worship which is his due, without causing the consequences of such wickedness to follow him. And the worshipers of those old bones, and stones, and spears, and holy feathers, are just as moral as you might expect them to be; and so are the cardinals and priests, who are the chief actors in the monstrously wicked farce. As I shall show you in the sequel, Rome is another Sodom.

Now, Sir, in view of all this, whose truthfulness no informed person will question, permit me to ask you, whether Romanism is the form of religion suited to our American people? Are these forgers of old relics, and promoters of their veneration, and who amass enormous revenues by their exhibition and sale, the best teachers of religion and morals for us? Is the unblushing effrontery of our imported bishop and priests to be quietly borne, who tell us that these forgers and worshipers of relics, and who, by the sale of old bones from the Catacombs as the bones of saints and martyrs, defraud the world yearly of enormous sums of money, are the vicegerents of God, and that there is no salvation for us but by submission to their teaching and authority? What! no salvation for you or me save as we submit to that old Pope who bows in reverence and adoration before a box of old bones! Monstrous! As well might they send you to learn patriotism from Arnold, or me to learn the religion of God from the priests of Baal.

With great respect, yours.

LETTER XV.

Legends.—Sabbath evening in S. Carlo.—Gorgeous scene there.—Legends from Butler—from Lives of English Saints.—Dr. Duff's Testimony.—Foolish Legends of the Dark Ages revived.—The Religion of Legends not fitted for America.

My dear Sir,—In the present letter I ask your attention to the *legends* of Romanism. Unless I greatly err in judgment, you will find in them another powerful reason for the utter rejection of a system which lives by fabricating and propagating them.

My first Sabbath evening in Rome was spent in the Church of S. Carlo, in the Corso. I was attracted there, with others, to witness a high ceremony in honor of a saint whose name I now forget. The house was full, and in this respect was an exception to all I witnessed in Romish churches in Europe. It has three naves, divided by Corinthian columns; the middle one was crowded with children of both sexes; the girls dressed in white, with white vails most gracefully pinned on their hair, and flowing down their shoulders. Each child held in her right hand a small stick, with a beautiful flower tied to it with a string, and in her left, a lighted candle. A forest of candles blazed on the high altar. The Litany was responsively sung by the choir and the congregation, and with grand effect. The appearance of the children, each holding their stick, flower, and candle, and all kneeling, rising, turning round at the word of command, like little soldiers, was most interesting. Indeed, the whole scene was a gorgeous one. At a pause in the music, a long, lean Italian priest—and, in these respects, an exception to his short and stall-fed brethren—ascended a desk, and, in a most furious style, poured forth a short address to the children. The music again struck up, and, at another pause, a fat and monkish-looking priest, from another part of the house, addressed them; and, by their winks and smiles, the children seemed to enjoy the scene very much. Soon a movement was made to the left, and a pussy-looking cardinal made his appearance, headed and followed by priests and servants, bearing candles, a crook, and a cross; and, puffing under the double weight of his fat and canonicals, he made his way to the high altar. Mass was soon said, for the evening was quite hot, and the congregation dispersed. "And what," said I to our attendant, "is the meaning of all this? What was meant by that stick, and flower, and those candles in the hands of the children?" "This is Saint ——'s day," said he. "The saint, when once going up a hill, was very weary, and he stuck his staff in the ground, and he leaned upon its top to rest. He prayed for some evidence from heaven that he was in the right way; and his dry stick instantly bore a beautiful blossom! To commemorate that miracle was the object of the stick and flower in the hands of the children. And the candle was an emblem of the light of holiness reflected on the world by his life." Not understanding Italian, "What," I asked, "said those loud preachers to the children?" "They told them of the many wonders wrought by the saint, and exhorted them

F 2

to venerate him and to follow his example," was the reply. Here is a foolish legend, that I myself saw commemorated by a cardinal and many priests; and such legends form a great part of the religious literature of Romanism. They are published by authority, and have a prodigious influence upon the ignorant Papists of all nations. Permit me to detail a few of them, remembering that "*a legend is a story told respecting the saints.*" Some of these I have already detailed in my letters to you on sham miracles.

A man who insulted *St. Agnes* was struck blind by a flash of light. On being brought to the young virgin, she immediately restored him to sight. She wrought many miracles. *St. Anthony* was often assaulted by the Devil in human form, was often beaten by him until almost dead, but always came off victor. He cured many diseases; but was especially famous for the cure of that disease which has taken his name, "St. Anthony's fire." *St. Gudule*, whose relics are in the church of that name in Brussels, lighted her candles by her prayers. Might she not have understood the process of making lucifer matches? *St. Theodosius* often miraculously supplied his many guests with provisions, and a woman was miraculously healed of a cancer by the touch of his garment. A general, going to war with the Persians, begged his hair-shirt, and, wearing it in battle, gained a great victory, "by the protection of the saint through the pledge of that relic." *St. Egwin*, going on a pilgrimage to Rome, put on his legs iron shackles, and threw the key into the Severn; but he found it in the belly of a fish in Rome, which enabled him to take off his shackles. The miracles of *St. Hi-*

lary fill a whole book. *St. Placidus* fell into a lake, and was carried out by a current into deep water; St. Benedict saw this in a vision, and sent out St. Maurus to save him; Maurus walked upon the water without sinking in the least, and drew him to shore. *St. Macarius* made a dead man to speak, to convince an unbeliever of the truth of the doctrine of the resurrection. The relics of *St. Francis* of Sales raised to life two persons that were drowned, and have cured the blind and paralytics. *St. Romuald* drove several devils out of his cell who were scourging him, by mentioning the name of Jesus, and calmed a tempest on the sea, and wrought many miracles. His order of monks wear a white robe, the idea of which was suggested to him by seeing them going up a ladder to heaven in white. He died in the year 1020 or 1030, and his body remained perfect as late as 1466. His relics have wrought wonders. *St. Richard* cured his son by laying him at the foot of a great crucifix, and his relics have wrought miracles. *St. Stephen* told others their secret thoughts, wrought many miracles, as also did his relics. *St. Scholastica* was the sister of St. Benedict. They met one day, and the sister insisted that her brother should spend the night with her. But the rules of his monastery forbade him, and he refused. She prayed the Lord to stop his going away, and immediately a most fearful storm arose, which compelled him to remain. The sister died in a few days after, and Benedict saw her soul from Mount Cassino going to heaven in the form of a dove! *St. John of Egypt* was a prophet, foretold future events, and did wonders. He gave eyes to a blind girl, and spent a night, *in vision*, with a lady who wished to see him in the flesh. He miraculously cured a man of the tertian ague by giving him a good vomit! Thus many are cured of the ague in our day, and by doctors who are not likely to have a name in the calendar.

There are, Sir, two huge volumes before me, containing, in double columns, about one thousand pages each. They are "Lives of the Saints," by the Rev. Alban Butler, and were printed at the Metropolitan Press, Baltimore, in the year 1845. The legends here quoted are taken from these volumes, which have received the highest approbation of the dignitaries of the Romish Church, and which are crammed with just such stories. There is a saint or saintess, or several of both, for each day in the year, and the object of the volumes before me is to furnish to the faithful a little devotional reading for each day, for the purpose of kindling their devotion, and exercising their faith! The latter effect their perusal will most certainly produce! And yet, for the sake of his English and Protestant readers, Butler omits many miracles of the saints exultingly narrated by the Bollandists, the Jesuit compilers of the Acta Sanctorum, which, without being completed, already consists of nearly sixty folio volumes.

To show you that, the greater the absurdity, the greater the faith, I will produce a few more of these legends, as quoted from the "Lives of the English Saints." If you or I disbelieve them, or smile at them, we are very gravely told that it is because "the natural man discerneth not the things of the spirit," or because of "the intellectual darkness caused by three centuries of heresy." This, Sir, is not the ravings of superstition with multitudes, however you or my readers may smile.

The saints were greatly tormented by demons. St. Frodobert was often stopped by one, when going to school. He drove him away with the sign of the cross. When at prayer one night, a devil put out his candle. Another used to steal the bread of St. Auratus. Another broke the bell of St. Benedict, with which, when living on a rock, he used to ring for bread. Another cast down part of a rock to kill St. Auratus in his cell; but the saint made it stop half way down the precipice. Many female devils used to tempt the saints to sin, but always in vain. What a pity their power of resistance was not transmitted, by a kind of apostolic succession, to the cardinals and priests of Rome. St. Julian, St. Tozzo, St. Gall, St. Maximin, slew dragons. St. Sampson killed several. St. Senan made a very small candle burn a whole week. St. Faro made instantly whole a cup broken by his servant. St. Aicardus hung up his gloves on a sunbeam. St. Fintan, expecting company, and having no flour for bread, ordered an old mill, which had neither wheat nor water, to supply him, and it went right to work and did so. St. Tillo, on finding that his monks had no wine to give him, filled their barrel by miracle. I wonder if this was the beginning of that strong relish for wine for which the monks are famous even to our day! The reapers of St. Geneviève were greatly incommoded by rain. She came out and ordered it away, and it obeyed. St. Gildas and his companions took up their abode on an island inconveniently small. It miraculously expanded to accommodate them. St. Mochua and his companions sailed over a river on his cloak. St. Cannera walked over the sea. St. Barras, sailing in a ship, met St. Scothinus walking over the

Irish Channel. He asked the saint on what he was walking. Scothinus replied, "On a beautiful green meadow." And when Barras denied this, he plucked a handful of fresh flowers, and presented them to him. But Barras turned his own logic against him, by thrusting his hand into the sea, and drawing it up full of fishes. And long before rail-ways, or telegraphs, or ocean steamers were invented, the above Scothinus usually went from Ireland to Rome in a day, transacted his business there with his holiness in the evening, and was back the next morning. The Holy Virgin appeared to St. Alphonsus Liguori in the Church of Foggia, and was seen by all with the beautiful face of a girl of fourteen; and so fervent was he once in praying to her, that he rose up in the air, where he remained suspended for some time. He must have been made of light material. St. Ita, finding a man dead, with his head cut off, put it on again, restored him to life, and sent him about his business. And St. Cronon caused a wild beast, which had killed and devoured a man, to cast him up, and then restored him to life. And with legends like these, which are published even in our day, for the edification of poor, hood-winked Papists, I could fill volumes. These, Sir, are taken indiscriminately from the piles of trash before me, and are by no means the worst of their kind. But the miracles of the saints, when living, dwindle into insignificance, both as to number and magnitude, in comparison with those performed by their old bones when dead.

And are these monstrous and contemptibly silly legends now out of date, and disregarded by the people and priests? Far from it. The report of the speech of the apostolic Dr. Duff, which I heard him make before the British and Foreign Bible Society, at its last meeting, is now before me, in which he makes the following statements: "There is circulating a work in India entitled The History of Christ. And what do you think it consists of? Ten thousand legends, more monstrous than what is to be found in the Talmud. And this has been circulated, in the name of truth, as the history of our blessed Lord and Savior. And it is a notorious fact, that when the great Emperor Agbad had, in his tolerance, invited men of all religions to come to him, the celebrated Xavier, the Jesuit, went to tell him what Christianity was. The emperor's mind was open to the reception of the truth from all quarters; and he was really dissatisfied with Mohammedanism. Xavier reasoned in this manner: 'Here is a Mohammedan; he must be saturated with Mohammedan legends. If I tell him the plain truth, according to the simplicity of the Bible, he will nauseate the whole thing, because of its simplicity; I must therefore fix up Christianity to suit his taste.' And he manufactured a New Testament for him, filled with all manner of Persian legends, and represented this to the emperor as the New Testament. The emperor read it, and, with the simplicity of heart and sagacity which belonged to him, returned it, saying, 'If this be your Shaster, I have enough of such legends already, without coming to you to get more.'" And, Sir, wherever the missionaries of Romanism go in the propagation of that faith—whether to the Indians of our own woods, to the islanders of the Pacific, to the savages of Africa, or to the more refined idolaters of India—they pursue the precise course of Xavier at the court of Agbad. Dr. Duff testifies that, among the converts to Romanism in India, not a leaf of the Bible has been circulated for three hundred years, while these utterly despicable legends are circulated there without measure or end.

And when, Sir, you hear an occasional sermon in a Romish church, what is the topic of discussion? Every day in the year is a saint's day; some days have many saints allotted to them. Is it not generally a harangue upon some saint—his wonderful miracles—and the whole twisted into an argument to prove that the Church of Rome is the only true Church, out of whose pale there is no salvation? Did you ever hear an Irish priest preach on St. Patrick's day? If not, embrace the first opportunity; and if you will not hear of St. Patrick sailing on a flag-stone, it is because the priest recognizes you among his hearers, and as one more afflicted with the terrific disease of judging for yourself than the rest of them. And I am credibly informed that the chief topics upon which the priests dwell in the chapels filled with the poor Germans and Irish, even in America, are the legends, not merely as found sifted out in the volumes of Butler, but as narrated, in all their grotesqueness, in the huge folios of the Bollandists.

Now, Sir, as one having as much at stake as any other man in this nation—as one adorning its present history, and as truly desirous of its future glory, permit me to ask you whether you think these legends form the best religious literature for our people? Is it that best calculated to instruct and to ennoble the mind? Does not such trash oppress the mind? Does not belief in it enfeeble its powers and debase the man? Will not the people that believe these things believe any thing? And can they be fit material out of which to make Republicans, and noble defenders of free institutions? Are the priests that write and circulate these legends worthy of trust? They can not believe them themselves, and they write and propagate them for the very reasons that Xavier wrote a New Testament to suit the Emperor Agbad. The volumes of Butler are printed in your city, by the Bishop's press. They are sold, as the illustrated title-page informs us, "by all the Catholic booksellers in the United States." If these legends are disbelieved by your bishop, why permit his press to print them? Why wink at their universal sale in the country? Why not raise his voice against them? That Romish bishops believe these legends themselves is impossible; but they amaze the ignorant, overwhelm them with wonder, foster their superstitious regard for nunnery and monkery—for bishops, abbots, and hermits—for signs of the cross, holy wells, and relics—and for those means devised by a wicked priesthood for the purpose of keeping the Light of Life from the minds of the people. When, Sir, the religion of the Bible is supplanted by the religion of legends—when the sturdy Protestantism, that thinks for itself, is supplanted by that religion that gives up all thinking to the priest—when the twenty-two or three millions of people who, in our happy land, will believe only on evidence, is supplanted by a people who will believe all the lying legends of Romanism—then the last rays of the glorious sun of our liberty are fading away on the summit of our mountains.

The midnight of liberty is the high noon of Romanism; and the deepest darkness of despotism is the paradise of the priest.

With great respect, yours.

LETTER XVI.

The Mass not the Worship of God.—A theatrical Exhibition.—Waldensian Church in Turin.—High Ceremonies of Rome all theatrical—Feast of the Nativity.—Visit of the Wise Men.—Procession of Palms.—Judgment-hall of Pilate.—Procession at Bonville.—Sabbath evening Service in Edinburgh.—Popish Plays and Play-actors not suited to America.

My dear Sir,—I hope that by this time your mind, and those of my readers, are prepared for the conclusion to which my own has long since arrived—that Romanism is not Christianity; and that its priests, whatever else they may be, are not the ministers of Christ, nor of his glorious Gospel. If this conclusion is just, another immediately follows: *neither is its worship the worship of God.* If not prepared for this conclusion now, you may be at the close of the present letter, in which I shall endeavor to establish its truth.

The Scriptures speak of various kinds of worship; as, the worship of God—the worship of idols—the worship of the dragon and the beast—and the worship of devils. And we find various kinds of worship in the world, and under various forms. Some truly worship God in spirit and in truth—some worship idols—some devils—some mammon—some are "will worshipers"—and some worship "they know not what;" but all is in vain, save that of "the circumcision, which worship God in spirit, and rejoice in Christ Jesus, and have no confidence in the flesh." Acceptable worship embraces the outward homage, and the inward feeling; but the external act is nothing, save as it expresses the sincere internal feeling; for they who worship God must worship him in spirit and in truth. True worship is not confined to places, occasions, or persons; wherever the heart bows in humility before God, for the purpose of exalting his glorious name and perfections, there he is truly worshiped. And, as God is the father of all men, all men have access to Him for themselves, through his Son. All this is plain.

The worship of Romanism consists mainly in the Mass. There are missals, and penances, and prayers for private use; and there are high ceremonies for certain feasts and great occasions; but the Mass—the mass mumbled over in the same way in Connaught, Paris, and Rome, and with the same sleepy, unvarying monotony, is that which makes up the public worship of the people. Now what is the Mass? is it worship? I unhesitatingly say it is not; that it has no more claim to be the worship of God than had the ceremonies of Pagan priests at the altars of Pagan Rome. At best, it is only a *theatrical representation* of the truths which it purports to exhibit. And hence, Bishop England, and other Papal writers, talk of the "performance of the mass," as we ordinarily speak of the performance of a tragedy or a farce. And the Mass holds precisely the same relation to the history of Christ which Richard III., Henry VIII., John II., or any other of the historical plays of Shakspeare do to the characters and times which they represent. This even a superficial anatomy of the Mass will render quite evident.

As the sensuous encroached on the spiritual in Christianity, and as the shades of that long night called "the Dark Ages" thickened over our world, all the tendencies of religion were to the outward. The Bible was soon confined to cloisters, and it became the interest of priests to keep it there. To keep up the great facts of our religion in some way before the people, portions of sacred history were dramatized, and acted before the faithful. And this system, somewhat modified in different countries to suit the different states of civilization, exists at the present day. To see the system in full operation, you must go to Rome, where the tragedy and the farce are performed in gorgeous style.

But I must return to the "performance of the Mass," in which, "under the appearance of bread and wine, the Redeemer of the world is offered up in an unbloody manner, as a true, proper, and propitiatory sacrifice for the living and the dead." According to Dr. England, the altar signifies Christ—the white cloth that covers it, "the purity which should accompany Christ"—and the vestments of the priests are to remind us of the passion of Christ. The *alba* represents the white garment in which Herod clad the Savior—the *cincture* reminds us that Christ was bound—the *maniple* hanging upon the left arm, reminds us of the weight of our sins as borne by Christ—the *stole* on the priest's neck and crossed on the breast, represents the obedience of the Son of God—the *chasuble*, or outward vestment, with a hole in the centre for the head, with a cross embroidered on the back, and two stripes representing a pillar on the front, reminds us of Christ bearing the cross. When the priest is thus dressed up, he is prepared for acting. The wafer and wine are then brought out—

they are turned into the body and blood of the Lord, by the priest—then, as real Christ, he is offered as a victim to God on behalf of the people—then the victim undergoes a destructive change, to show the death of the Redeemer—then the elements are separated, the real body is seen under the appearance of bread, and the real blood under the appearance of wine, and the priest eats the one and drinks the other. Then the people are dismissed, if true believers, wonderfully edified and instructed—if not, smiling at the credulity of those who can believe that there is any worship in all this! This is the Mass! Now, Sir, if this is any thing but a theatrical representation of the death of Christ, with little meaning and less sense, in which the altar is the stage, the priest the chief actor, the people the spectators, and the church the theatre, what is it? And when, as in high mass, the dramatis personæ are multiplied, and opera singers are brought in to give attraction to the various scenes, the conclusion is irresistible that, instead of being engaged in the worship of God, you are actually witnessing a theatrical exhibition.

Never did I feel this to such an extent as in June last, when, after weeks spent amid the mass-houses of France, and Naples, and Rome, I entered, on a pleasant Sabbath morning, the extremely plain and primitive-looking church of the Waldenses, in Turin. On looking around me, instead of pictures, and statuary, and frescoes, I found all the walls presenting to the eye some passages of Scripture. On looking before me, instead of an altar blazing with candles and gilding, I saw a neat pulpit, with a large open Bible, and a minister of God reading and expounding it. Instead of persons gazing around with guide-books in their hands, talking, and criticizing, and smiling, I saw a devout people, with Bibles in their hands, turning up the text, and the passages read, and most devoutly singing God's praises, and joining in the prayers that were offered! The sight and the scene were truly refreshing to a mind jaded, and a heart disgusted with all I had witnessed for the few previous weeks. The transition seemed like passing from Purgatory to Paradise. Here was worship in spirit and in truth, while the gorgeous and heartless ceremonies of splendid cathedrals were a mere acting, and by wretched actors, of truths and things which neither priests nor people understood.

And this theatrical aspect of the Popish ritual is yet more apparent, if you pass from the Mass to the ceremonies of some of the high days of the Church. Seymour, in his Pilgrimage to Rome, has made this quite obvious as well as ludicrous. In St. Maria Maggiore, in Rome, they profess to have the cradle in which the Savior was laid at his birth, and at the feast of the Nativity they bring out that cradle, before the dawn of day, and, amid processions of priests, monks, nuns, preceded by incense, accompanied by singers, and guarded by soldiers, it is placed on the high altar for the view and worship of the faithful! And, after all, the wonderful cradle is only a splinter of old wood, covered with silver, and in a case of glass, and said to be a part of the manger! And the theatrical acting of the Nativity attracts its thousands!

The visit of the wise men of the East to the Savior is acted out in the Church of Andrea della Valle with great scenic effect. Mary, with her son on her knee, is seated on a throne—the Magi, transubstantiated into kings, dressed with crowns and purple, are introduced to her, and, after acting the parts assigned to them, retire. And as a reward for their labor and homage, she gives them some of the milk on which the Savior was nourished, and which they carry away as a precious relic!

The feast to commemorate the strewing of the path of the Savior with branches of trees is yearly celebrated with great pomp at St. Peter's. The Pope, magnificently arrayed, is carried into the church on the shoulders of eight men, attended by his court. The priests bring him palm-trees, which he blesses and sprinkles with holy water. Then the cardinals, bishops, priests, and foreign ministers receive from his holiness a palm, some kissing his hand, and others his foot. Then the procession of palms commences, and the whole is ended by high mass; after which, thirty years' indulgence is granted to all who witness the ceremony! And from the beginning to the end of Holy Week, all the ceremonies, by day and by night, are nothing but representations, in a theatrical form, of the sufferings of our Lord, about whose true history the people know far less than do those of the history of England, who know nothing of it but what they learn from witnessing the actings of the historical dramas of Shakspeare!

If further evidence is necessary as to the theatrical character of the Romish worship, permit me to quote from Seymour his account of the ceremony of Holy Week, which represents *the judgment-hall of Pilate.* "The Gospel is read by three priests. One of them personates the Evangelist who wrote the Gospel; and his part is to read the narrative as detailed. A second personates Pontius Pilate, the maid at the door, the priests, the Pharisees; and his part is to read those sentences which were spoken by them. The third personates our Lord Jesus Christ; and his part is to read the words which were uttered by him on the occasion. To give the greater effect to the whole, the choir is appointed to undertake those parts which were the words of the multitude. The different voices of the priests reading or intoning their different parts—Pilate speaking in one voice, Christ in another, while the choir, breaking forth, fill the whole of the vast church with the shout, 'Crucify him! Crucify him!' and again with the cry, 'Not this man, but Barabbas!' produce a most singular effect. Accustomed as we are to look upon the Holy Scriptures with reverence, and to read the narrative of our Lord's sufferings with a profound feeling of awe, it has something repulsive to our tastes, if not to our judgments, to find a theatrical character given to so holy an exercise."

Upon this evidence, which might be multiplied to any extent, I rest, Sir, my position, that the ritual of Romanism, however splendid, and to some weak minds attractive, is not the worship of God; that, at best, it is only a theatrical representation of the truths which it purports to exhibit. Every thing that enters into the public worship of Romanism is only a continuation of the tawdry shows gotten up in the Middle Ages to satisfy the longings of the religious nature of man, from whom a wicked priesthood had taken away the Light of Life. And how can we measure the wickedness of ecclesiastics who, even amid the light of our advanced civilization, take away the Bible from the people, and seek to supply the vast void by theatrical forces like these? And is it any wonder that, in Papal countries, the few join the priest at the acting of the Mass on Sunday morning? and that the priest joins the multitude to witness the acting of the farce in the theatre in the evening? It is at least an evidence that, if nothing else is left to the people of Naples, they have left a little remaining taste, as, while the churches are deserted, the theatre is crowded. The least interesting actors that are seeking for precedence in the dramatic world are lazy and lubberly priests, and they are the least worthy of patronage.

On the 19th of June last, in company with others, I reached the little town of Bonville, within a few miles of Geneva, on my way to Chamouni. Crowds of people were in the streets, and branches of trees graced all the doors and windows. It was a fête day, but in honor of what saint I know not; probably the "Very Rev. P. R. Kenrick, V. G.," might inform us. I there witnessed a scene such as I had not seen before—quite theatrical in its way. At the ringing of a bell, a procession was formed at the church of the village. It was headed by women in white robes; these were followed by children bearing baskets of rose-leaves; these by children bearing censers; these by priests; these by a ruby-faced bishop, fat and stall-fed as usual, bearing the host under a canopy; and the bishop by a vast multitude of people. The day was very hot and very dusty. At certain signs, the whole mass of people knelt down, and rose up, and turned to the right and left. At the sound of a little whistle, the children scattered leaves for the bishop to walk on, or incensed the priests. The soldiers were in the streets in great numbers and in full uniform. They saluted the Host with volleys of musketry on its approach; and when the bishop stopped, as he did several times, and turned round the Host so as to face the soldiers, they all fell on their knees in an instant, save the officers, who leaned on their swords, with their faces to the earth. After parading the streets in this way for some time, the bishop and priests returned to the church, and the people and soldiers went to drink and to play. When the farce was ended, the town was a scene of revelry. And with such mountebank exhibitions as these, the Papal world is full! And these exhibitions are what they call worship; and a firm belief in their efficacy is what priests call faith in God!

Now, Sir, that you may see, in contrast with all this, the true worship of God, go with me on the first Sabbath evening I spent in Scotland to the Gælic chapel in Edinburgh, which is situated almost under the shadow of the Castle. The house was crowded in all its parts. In the hymns of praise the immense congregation united. Every worshiper carried a Bible, and turned to the Scripture read, and to the text of the sermon. When prayer was made, every person rose and took a devotional attitude. Dr. Candlish was the eloquent preacher; and for upward of an hour did the people hang with breathless attention upon his lips, while he expounded to them the faith of Abraham, and, with words that burned, exhorted them to the exercise of faith in God. And when the service was ended, the multitude quietly walked away, praying that the word of the Lord might dwell in them richly, and that they might be sanctified through the truth. Now, Sir, which looks most like the worship of God—this scene in the Gælic chapel, or the saying of mass by a priest? Which looks most like Peter at the feast of Pentecost, or like Paul in the synagogues of the Jews—the Scotch minister preaching the Gospel, or the Italian priest saying mass? Which of these teachers is best adapted to our people and our institutions? Which is most likely to foster those principles that never yield but to the right—that will live only for the true? Sir, the one is a teacher of the truth, the other is an actor of the truth dramatized. Italy and Naples have only Popish actors—Scotland and England have religious teachers; hence the difference between their people! Mexico and Peru have had only religious actors for their people—New England has had religious teachers; hence the difference between them! The priest seeks to bind you to the Pope; the minister seeks to win you to God. The priest hides the Bible, and seeks to satisfy you with the mass and the other ceremonies of the Church; the minister puts the Bible into your hands, and exhorts you to be satisfied with nothing less than a heart and life conformed to its teachings. The priest damns you unless you believe the Church, which means the Pope and his cardinals; the minister tells you that "he that believeth in the Son hath life," and exhorts you to believe in God—to fear him, and then to fear nothing else. Which are the men ordained of God, and best fitted to be the moral instructors of our great and growing country? Need I answer these questions to satisfy a person of your sense and comprehension? Sir, God is not worshiped in the mass. Romish churches are Sabbath-day theatres for the enacting of Popish dramas; and Romish priests are nothing more or less than actors in sacred dramas, and most of them miserable hands even at that. Neither the plays nor their actors are the things for our people, unless the Bible, with its institutions, and the freedom which they secure, are a curse; and unless submission to the priest and the Pope, and the slavery which they insure, are a blessing. From such play-actors and their plays may the good Lord deliver us. Could the prophets, apostles, martyrs, and saints, of all ages and climes, hear us, we would invoke the aid of them all to save our land from the curse of Romanism.

With great respect, yours.

LETTER XVII.

Romanism tested by its Fruits in Rome.—No personal Liberty there—two Cases in Proof.—No security of Property—two flagrant Illustrations.—No Religion there—no Sabbath—no Bible—no Preaching—no worshiping Congregations—no serious Devotion there.—Is Popery the best form of Religion for our Country?

My dear Sir,—If the work of framing a government for a people were committed to your hands, and if you were in doubt as to which form would best promote their highest and truest interests, what plan would you adopt to resolve your doubt? You would adopt the common sense one, of testing the various forms that presented themselves by the effects which they produce, where fully established. This would be walking in the light of experience. The best fruits of Despotism you would seek in Russia and Austria—of a Limited Monarchy, in England—and of a Constitutional Republicanism, in the United States. And as an honest man, you would decide in favor of that form which promoted, in the highest degree, the highest interests of the masses of the people. So in religious things. If desirous to know the influence of Episcopacy upon a people, you would go to England—or of Presbytery, you would go to Scotland—or of Independency, you would go to New England—or of Popery, you would go to Rome. As trees are known by their fruit, so are political and religious systems by their effects. By this test, to which none can object, will you permit me to try Romanism, that you and all men may see the multiplied blessings which we may anticipate from its full establishment in this land? But where shall we apply the test? Where, but in Rome, the seat of the Pope—the centre of unity—the paradise of the priest—where the heresy of the Reformation has never obtained a permanent or impressive influence, and where, for fifty ages together, Romanism has had the molding of the people, without let or hinderance, in her hands. If Papal priests could have their wish and their way, they would, of course, model America after the pattern of Rome, which Cardinal Wiseman denominates the "Holy City." Now, Sir, I have been to the "Holy City"—I have seen its Pope, cardinals, and priests—I sought there information as to its civil, social, and religious state—and from personal examination, and from testimony received from the most credible witnesses, both natives, and foreign residents, I am prepared to say that, from the extent of its population, there is not a worse governed, less religious, or more immoral people in Christendom. And, tried by its priests, where there are no obstacles to prevent its natural results, Romanism should be the abhorrence of all flesh.

There is, Sir, no personal liberty in Rome. Since the return of the Pope from Naples to the Vatican, the reins of despotism have been tightened by a powerful hand. The patriots that could escape have fled; and you find them in Genoa, Turin, Geneva, France, and Britain—homeless, yet hopeful exiles—strong in faith that the sun of liberty will yet rise, even over Rome. The suspected are in prison; and the prisons are crowded. Spies, by day and by night, surround those who show any lack of confidence in the priests. While I was there, the plan was completed of dividing the city into small sections of about twenty families each, and of placing a priest over each of these sections; nominally to look after their religious wants, but really to act as the spies of the government! And through the vigilance of these spies, and the information which they wring from wives and daughters, and servant-women at the confessional, the sigh breathed after liberty by the most obscure man in its most obscure and humble dwelling is reported in a few hours to the head of the police! And if a Roman desires to visit other countries, before he can get permission, he must first get a certificate from the magistrate of his district that he is a good citizen—then from the priest of his section, that he is a good Papist: with these he goes to the head of the police, and if there is no information lodged there against him, he receives a passport. Take one occurrence as an illustration. A young Roman, a few years since, went to Sardinia, where he married. Business failed him, and he returned to Rome to seek employment, leaving his wife and children behind him. He entered the employment of a person who, in the Revolution, took part against the government. Within the present year, that man wished to return to his family, and with the certificate of the magistrate of his district, and of the priest of his section, he presented himself to the head of the police, who, I learned, is a priest. And simply because he was recorded as having been in the employment of an enemy of the old government, instead of getting his passport he was ordered to prison; and where imprisoned none know but God and the priests!

Take another instance and illustration of the glorious liberty with which Romanism would bless us! The government holds a monopoly in tobacco, and this monopoly it farms out to the highest bidder. The more tobacco used, the greater the duties accruing, and the higher the Church can sell the monopoly. Of course, the more the Romans chew, smoke, and snuff of the vile weed, the greater will be the profits of the Church. Knowing this, and to curtail the revenues of the priests, those who bear no fervent love to them agreed to refrain from its use, and to induce their friends to do the same. One evening Peter Ercolo met his friend Luigi Geuanini in a coffee-room, smoking a cigar, and persuaded him to smoke no more. There were several by-standers; soon Ercolo was arrested—was tried before the Second Tribunal, and found guilty of the crime of persuading his friend to consume no more cigars; and for this crime a respectable man, between thirty and forty years of age, was torn from his family, and sentenced for twenty years to the galleys! And I read the sentence as placarded on the chief corners of the city of Rome, and as signed by Cardinal Antonelli! Such, Sir, is the civil liberty enjoyed by the dwellers in the "Holy City," amid the relics of the martyrs, and under the direct government of the vicar of Jesus Christ, and the infallible head of the only true Church! And this is the liberty with which Romish priests, were it in their power, would bless our country! It is from those Roman tyrants that our priests get their authority—it is to them they yield their conscience, and swear perpetual allegiance. Are they the men for our people? Ask the patriots in exile—ask the patriots rotting in the prisons of the "Holy City"—ask Ercolo, tugging at the galleys for persuading his friend to cast away the end of a wasted cigar, are the spies and tools of Italian priests the men for our country?

Nor, Sir, is there any security for property in Rome. It is constantly confiscated, on the merest pretexts, to the Church; and when not confiscated, it is alienated to the "Holy See" in a great variety of ways. Two instances, in proof of this, were narrated to me there, and by a man of high position. A Roman of wealth married a lady of foreign birth, and by whom he had a large family of children. After a life of love and harmony, he died, leaving his property to his widow and children, by a will duly authenticated. Although regardless of the priests in health, he sent for one when dying—who confessed him, and anointed him, and "fixed him off" for Purgatory or Paradise. A few days after his death, that priest swore before the tribunal having jurisdiction in such cases, that the dying man confessed to him a great sin, and to atone for which he wished his entire property, contrary to his will, to go to the Church. And, on the oath of that priest, the will of the deceased was set aside—his property was turned into the treasury of the Church, and his widow and children were turned out penniless on the world! Thus nothing is necessary to deprive any family in Rome that has lost its head, of its property, but the oath of a priest! And if you had seen them in crowds, as I have, you would conclude, as I have, that it would be an easy matter to get a priest in Rome that would swear any thing. Absolution from perjury that enriches the Church is easily secured.

The other instance is as follows. It would seem as if there is a law in Rome which gives all property to the Church which has no *lawful* heir. An old man, of large possessions, married a young and handsome lady, and died, leaving a son behind him, the heir of his possessions. Just on the eve of his majority, not many months ago, a suit was instituted to prevent his entering on his paternal possessions, on the ground of his illegitimacy. And the Church gained the suit—the mother of the boy testifying to her own shame, and confessing that the father of her child was a shaven-pated, crimson-capped cardinal! "And this," said my informant, as we turned out of the Corso, "is the palace in which the old man died, and of which his widow and repudiated child have just been deprived." And when men lose not their property by confiscation, or by the robbery of ecclesiastical courts, they are ground down into poverty by an enormous taxation for the support of a Church which only compensates them with swarms of monks and nuns, splendid churches, lying legends, gorgeous processions, French soldiers, and spies to dog them by day and by night. And are these priests the men for our country? Ask that widow and her orphans deprived of her property by the oath of a confessor—ask those groaning under the yoke of a government the most detestable that the earth knows, whether these are the men for our country! They will soon tell you.

Nor, Sir, is there any religion in Rome. I do not mean to say that, among its thousands of ecclesiastics, there are none that love God, nor do I mean to say that the Lord has no chosen ones hidden amid the chaff and the trash that are every where visible there; but I do mean to say, and to affirm as strongly as language can do it, that among the masses of the priests and people there is no fear of God, and no knowledge of the doctrines of our religion. And how could there be, in the absence of the means instituted by heaven to sustain and to extend religion among a people?

There is no Sabbath in Rome. The only apparent difference there between the Sabbath and other days of the week is, that the shops are more gayly dressed—the markets are more full—and more people are engaged in buying and selling. On my way to St. Peter's from the Hotel d'Angleterre, I saw monks and priests in all the shops and markets, buying, as on other days, and chattering like magpies. In Naples the shops are closed, and all business suspended on feast-days, but on the Sabbath all business is brisker than usual. Romanism knows no Sabbath.

There is no Bible in Rome. I made many inquiries there for a Bible, but without success. The people have no Bible. They know nothing about it. An intelligent man of fifty told me that he never saw one. Multitudes of the priests know nothing about it. And when asked why they have none for sale, the booksellers will tell you that it is prohibited. Captain Packenham, once a banker in the city, and a most respectable gentleman and devout Christian, is now in banishment for circulating the Scriptures there during the short existence of the Republic. Much of true religion consists in knowing God and Jesus Christ; and how can they be known by a people from whom the Bible is excluded?

There is no preaching in Rome. Now and then, a foreign priest or ecclesiastic visiting there, in search of a pallium, or of a cardinal's hat, may get up a brief course of lectures for the edification of the strangers wintering there; but these are usually vain and ambitious men, who seek in this way to gain favor at court, and to promote their self-interests. There is no preaching to the Italians; and when there is an occasional exception to the rule, it is not the Gospel that is preached: it is either a eulogy upon some Popish saint, or a vehement harangue against the Reformation and Protestants. Popery treats as a nullity the ascending command of the Savior, "Go ye into all the world and preach the Gospel to every creature." This one crime, Sir, is enough to subject it to the curse of "Anathema Maranatha."

There are no worshiping congregations at Rome ordinarily. Crowds attend the high ceremonies of "Holy Week;" on great occasions, when there are gorgeous processions, at which the Pope and the military attend, multitudes are drawn together by curiosity; but, on ordinary occasions, there are no congregations to witness the ceremonies in the churches. In this I was greatly disappointed. The only exceptions I witnessed were at St. Carlo, in the Corso, and around the image of Mary, in St. Augustin, as already narrated. On Sabbath day, and on every day of the week, I was at the great basilicas and churches, and very often myself and company were the whole congregation! I witnessed the mass in St. Peter's, St. John Lateran, St. Mary Maggiore, performed by a bishop and many priests, when not a soul was present to form a congregation but my own little company. My last Sabbath morning there was spent between the Sistine Chapel and St. Peter's; and while mass was going on at several altars in the church, it would be a liberal calculation to say that there was an average of five persons at each altar. This was in the morning; the masses and vespers of the afternoon are literally deserted, unless where singing is expected. Indeed, where there is any religion at all among the people, it is usually of a vicarious character. The faithful leave the care of their souls to the priests; as a man sometimes commits his business to an agent, with powers of attorney to act for him. And they think, and truly, that the masses offered at the altars will be as efficacious in their absence as if they were present. Hence there is often a crowd of priests engaged in a ceremony without a soul to witness it. And what struck me as more singular still, was to see priests in St. Peter's on Sabbath day entering the beautiful chapels during the ceremony of the mass at their altars with guide-books in their hands, and criticizing the works of art by which they are adorned! Could they do so if they believed that a brother priest was creating God before them?

And I was amazed at the manner in which those who attended performed their devotions. Two girls will enter, and kneel together, and cross themselves; and it is truly ludicrous to see them alternately praying, and talking, and laughing. Persons upon their knees, and their lips moving very rapidly, repeating their prayers, have often eyed me from head to foot, and gazed on me as I went around the church. Every thing I saw among priests and people was chillingly heartless, save in an old Spanish officer, who daily visited St. Peter's, dressed in half uniform, with his sword dangling behind him. I saw him a few times on his knees, and he seemed really to pray, and to beat his breast with his hand, as if he felt the weight of some awful sins pressing upon his soul. I felt an anxiety to say to him that the blood of Christ cleanses from all sin.

Now, Sir, in the absence of the Sabbath—in the absence of the Bible—in the absence of the preaching of the Gospel—in the absence of congregations even from the ceremonies with which the priests seek to fill up the void left by the prohibition of the Word of God, how could there be any religion in Rome? God has devised means to ends; and when the means are not used, the ends are not attained. Sir, *there is no religion in Rome*. There is there blind superstition—there is Jesuit cunning—there is solemn pomp and ceremonial observances—but there is no religion. Nor is there, as a rule, in any country where Popery obtains among the masses.

Is Popery, then, the form of religion best adapted to our country? The foundations and bulwarks of our institutions, are the intelligence, the religion, the morals of our people; can these remain to sustain and to defend our institutions if Popery becomes the religion of our people? Let the past answer.

With great respect, yours.

LETTER XVIII.

Fruits of Romanism.—Idolatry in Rome.—A Prodigy.—Pictures of Mary —her Names and Worship.—Immorality of Rome.—Scene at Naples. —Key to priestly Profligacy.—Experience of Luther.—Mass for the Soul of Gregory XVI.—Vespers in the Sistine.—Cardinals—their Character.—Feelings of the Romans toward the Priests.—A Chat at Civita Vecchia.—Romanism detested at Rome.

My dear Sir,—In my last letter I commenced the work of testing Romanism by its fruits *at home*, that you and all men might see whether its propagation should be encouraged among the nations and people yet beyond the circle of its influence. I have shown you that in Rome, where the system culminates, where it has every thing in its own hands, there is no personal liberty—no security of property—no religion. There is in Rome no Sabbath—no Bible—no preaching of the Gospel—no worshiping congregations—no serious devotions; and how can religion exist in the absence of these? But I am not yet through with the fruits of Romanism at home. There are a few other statements I wish to place before you.

There is, Sir, the most gross idolatry in Rome. On this point I need not dwell, after what I have said already about the Bambino of Ara Cœli, the Virgin of St. Augustin's, and the relics which are to be found every where. You meet there, wherever you go, miraculous pictures, and wonder-working relics, and statues that came down from heaven, and places rendered sacred by prodigies; and before these pictures, relics, and images, you see poor people bowing down with as profound a homage as ever the Hindoos render to their idols. The priests may disguise or excuse this as they may; it is, after all, no less than idolatry. "You are here on holy ground," said our guide, when walking through and round the church of St. Maria Maggiore. "What makes it holy," I asked. "Because," said he, "God showed where the church should be built by covering its site two feet deep with snow in summer!" And this he said with a stolid gravity which would make it a sin to suspect him of quizzing. I turned to my "Guide of Rome" to see if there was any allusion to this prodigy, where, to my amazement, I read the following passage: "This church was built in the year 352, under the pontificate of St. Liberius, in consequence of a vision that he and John the Patrician had the same night, and which was confirmed the following morning, the 5th of August, by a miraculous fall of snow, which extended over the space which the church was to occupy: for this reason it was called St. Maria ad Nives." And you can scarcely turn a corner without meeting with a place which has some sacred and prodigious history like this. May not this be the reason why it is called the "Holy City." For similar reasons, Mecca and Medina are "holy cities."

The pictures and statues that most abound, and to which most resort in prayer and prostration, are those of the Virgin Mary. Indeed, what the Prophet is to Mohammedanism, the Virgin is to Romanism. To her are given names which belong only to God. She is called "Mother of God"—"Advocate of Sinners"—

"Refuge of Sinners"—"Gate of Heaven"—"Most Faithful"—"Most Merciful." And in the Psalter of David, as reformed by Bonaventura, we find this sentence: "Come unto Mary, all ye that are weary and heavy laden, and she shall refresh your souls." Churches are built to her honor—her shrines are crowded with devotees, and are hung with votive offerings. Her name is the first which the infant is taught to lisp, and the dying are directed to look to her for mercy. The soldier goes to battle under her banner, and the brigand plunders under her protection. In Italy and Spain, robbers wear a picture of Mary hung round their neck by a ribbon. If overtaken suddenly by death, they kiss the image, and die in peace. And while apostles, martyrs, saints, and relics are not forgotten, Mary is the divinity of Romanism. The city of Lyons erected a pillar to Mary for saving it from the cholera of 1832. When Pio Nino fled from Rome, he threatened the city with the vengeance of Mary: finding her rather tardy in her movements, he prayed France for aid, which, being more propitious than Mary, sent him forty thousand bayonets! Why, Sir, while Mary is in the mouth of every body, the common people do not know enough about Jesus Christ even to swear by him. Mary is to the Romans what Diana was to the Ephesians. Rome, as a city, is given to idolatry.

Rome is, emphatically, an immoral city—probably the most so in Christendom; and that notwithstanding it has an ecclesiastic of some kind for every thirty inhabitants! There are some statements which I blush to make on this head, and which I only make out of an imperative sense of duty. I wish every American citizen to know the blessings to be expected from Romanism when the system is fully established and developed among us.

In the broad street opposite the post-office, in Naples, I saw a priest at ten o'clock in the morning at a gambling table! The sight astounded me, as I then witnessed it for the first time; but my guide soon put me to rest by stating that the priests were among the most expert and successful gamblers in the city! The theatre of St. Carlo, in Naples, was opened on the king's birth-day. Without entering it, I went with my traveling friend and our valet to the porch, to see the Neapolitans in their gay attire, and to have a glimpse of the royal family. Of the men that went to the ballet, for such it was, the largest number were soldiers, the next largest were priests. There is no mistaking a priest in Italy. He is known by his regimentals; and, if naked, his shaven crown would reveal him. I was again astonished! Soon, however, familiarity diminished my wonder; and when, on a more full information, I saw that the only relation of the priest to religion was that of a formal and official kind, like that of a magistrate to the laws, I also saw that there was nothing to bind him to a moral life, or to submission to the moral law, beyond that which binds a civil magistrate. This is the key to much of the priestly profligacy to be found in Papal countries. Boys are devoted to the priesthood from youth—they are brought up for it—the doctrine of moral fitness is unheard of. They enter it under but one restriction—not to marry; but they may do any thing else. As some magistrates are excellent men, so are some priests; but the priest can do with impunity any thing which a magistrate can.

It was the experience of Luther, that the nearer he got to Rome, the more wicked were the priests and people. And writing from there a few days after he entered it, and while saying mass at its altars, he said, "It is incredible what sins and atrocities are committed here; they must be seen and heard to be believed; it is usual to say here, 'If there be a hell, Rome is built above it;' it is an abyss from which all sins proceed." And although centuries have passed away since the noble Saxon penned these lines, I am persuaded that they give, so far forth, a true picture of Rome at the present hour.

You, Sir, will remember, that on the death of the late Pope Gregory, masses were ordered for the repose of his soul all over the Papal world. In many places, and, no doubt, in the cathedral of your city, these masses were celebrated with great pomp. The ordering of these masses gave rise to many questions among Protestants; I confess it staggered myself. The repose of the soul of the vicar of Jesus Christ! of the holy Pope Gregory! What should disturb the repose of his soul? What did he do to disquiet his spirit after it shot the gulf which divides time from eternity? "If you take five minutes' walk," said a friend of mine, long a resident of Rome, to me one day, "I will introduce you to two fine young girls, the daughters of the late Pope!" I then fully understood why masses were ordered for the repose of his soul! Perhaps you may not know, Sir, that it is quite a common occurrence for the Popes to leave behind them many "nephews" and "nieces," the names by which their illegitimate offspring are designated. But so it is. Their progeny is not counted by units. And the example set by pontiffs, the cardinals, and priests, are not slow to copy.

I went one day to the Sistine Chapel to vespers, when the Pope and nearly twenty cardinals were present. He who has once seen there the entrance of the cardinals, each with his servant untwisting his robe—their kneeling before the altar, and their servants adjusting their robes while kneeling—their bowing to the altar and to one another—their taking their seats with their servants at their feet, and assuming a most devotional look—their leaving their seats to salute the Pope, with their scarlet robes trailing behind them, can never forget the sight! O, Sir, how every idea of the infallibility of these persons passes away, like the hoar frost before the sun, on witnessing the silly ceremonies they practice in the Sistine! If you should see twenty children going through these ceremonies, you would conjecture that they were keeping holiday on the 1st of April. I sought to read the cardinals, and I think I did read some of them. "Who," said I, "is that youngish man, with that dark, penetrating, cold-looking eye?" "That," said my guide, "is the Cardinal Secretary of State." I need not name him here. He heads the horrible clique, in whose hands the present Pope is but a puppet, and will be probably his successor. Now and then these men in scarlet turned up their eyes, and moved their lips quite fast, and put up their hands after the manner of little Samuel in the picture; but all was obviously to be seen of men.

"What," said I to a friend, who knows them well, "what is the moral character of these cardinals?" His reply astounded me. "It is to me amazing," said he, "that some of these men can keep up even the form of devotion in the presence of one another, when each knows that the other keeps three, four, or five mistresses. Some of them are the greatest debauchees in Rome; they go, Sir, from the bed to the altar, and from the altar to the bed. I know what I say. I have mixed and mingled with these persons. I have heard wicked and loose young men talk in my day; but the most loose and lewd conversation I ever heard in my life was from these men." "And is this the general character of priesthood here?" said I. "I am persuaded it is," said he, "except the Pope, who is a pure-minded man, and who would do better, and make others do better, if he could." He then went on to state that the priests are the corruptors of the people, and mainly through the confessional and the women. "Noble Romans," said he, "have told me, with tears, that because of the lewdness of these priests, and their way of ferreting out every thing at the confessional, they have lost confidence in the virtue of their wives, their mothers, their sisters, and their daughters. Domestic love and confidence, as a rule, are unknown in Rome."

So emphatic and terrific was the testimony of this person, that I went away, feeling that something had chafed his temper, and that he condemned all for the known vices of a few; and it was not until I heard his testimony corroborated from all the sources at which I sought information that I could admit it to be true. Like sin and death, confession and seduction follow each other in Rome. The crimes are there rife that brought from heaven a rain of fire on Sodom.

While sitting in the veranda of the hotel in Civita Vecchia, waiting for the steamer from Naples to carry us to Genoa, I got into conversation with a most intelligent Italian, who spoke English with fluency. "Why," said I, "do you not drive out these French soldiers?" as a parcel of them marched along to the tap of a drum. He replied, "We are not strong enough to drive out the rascals. But if Louis Napoleon is not elected—if a true republic is set up in France, that will recall these men, then we will have freedom." "You have priests here, too," said I, as half a dozen of them were tripping along beneath us. "Plenty," said he, with excited emphasis, and gritting his teeth. "What good do they do you?" I asked. "Much good," he replied, with a scornful toss of the head; "they eat up a man's own property—they suck his own blood out of him—and they go with his own wife." And this, as far as I heard it, is the unbroken testimony of Italy as to the priest; with one exception, and that was an American doing business in Rome, and he only asserted that the above statements are too strong, and that things are better than they have been. "If we can only get these French away," said my friend in the veranda, "we will show you Americans what we will do." "And what will you do?" said I. He replied, in a most energetic under tone, "we will establish an Italian republic, and the first thing we will do will be to kill off these d—d priests, *for they are the enemies of the people, and the spies of despotism.*" The next revolution in Italy will be a terrible one for the priests. The people have a terrible retribution in store for them, and they know it. And hence the tightening of the chains of despotism, from the lines of Sardinia down to the Straits of Messina, and the stealthy meetings between the Pope and his most faithful friend, the King of Naples, the most cold-hearted and villainous despot upon earth, for mutual support, when the sleeping fires burst forth. And burst forth they will.

If the morals of the clergy in Rome are such as we have described, what must be the morals of the people? Depraved and low, according to all testimony, to the last degree. As by common consent, the marriage vows are disregarded; and while externally every thing seems moral and decent, yet underneath there is little else than rottenness and putrefaction. I repeat it, Sir, there is no morality in Rome. Instead of being a "holy city," it is a fermenting vat of corruption, and the priests supply the chief ingredients which produce the fermentation. A venerable professor of one of our American universities, with whom I traveled on the Mediterranean, stated that, but a few days previous to my meeting with him, a priest was taken up in Jordina, in Sicily, for having eight women in his harem, three of whom were married persons!

Of course, a state of morals like this among the priests, when connected with a grinding despotism, framed and executed mainly by them, must make them and their religion despicable in the eyes of the people. And they are so, as is obvious from the deserted churches that you find every where, and from the unanimous expressions of their sentiments by the people whenever they can whisper them. There is, Sir, not a spot on earth where Romanism is more detested than in Rome—there is not a spot on earth where the Pope and his priests are more supremely contemned. If the people of Rome could only have their way, the Pope would be to-morrow in exile—his priests would be in the dungeons where patriots are now rotting; and the fabled chair of St. Peter would be at the bottom of the muddy Tiber, or ascending to heaven in smoke. And it is one of the most unaccountable anomalies of the day to see men so despised at home so favorably regarded abroad—to see men who can only retain their places at home by the aid of Swiss and French soldiery, claiming a universal dominion over the people and nations of Christendom, and parceling out kingdoms among their spies and tools for Papal purposes.

Is it, Sir, desirable to have the morals of Rome transferred to New York and Baltimore? If not, is it desirable that the priests, and the system which produce these morals, should be patronized among us? I am far from saying—indeed, I do not believe—that Romish priests in this country are as immoral as they are in Rome. I believe they are worse in Italy than in any other part of the world. But may it not be owing to the fact that the keen eye of Protestantism is upon them? What will be their morals, or ours, when they have all things to their mind? The Chinese say they find here a fine market for their worst teas—the French for their poorest silks—and the English for their worst manufactures. When fashions are worn out in Europe, they are often in full credit here! Must it be so with its religion also? Is it to the credit of our country that she should be dressing herself up in the old, tawdry, moth-eaten garments of the old whore of Babylon, which even the down-trodden Italians are casting indignantly away?

With great respect, yours.

LETTER XIX.

Avignon.—Hotel de l'Europe—mine Host.—Captain Packenham.—Elasticity of Romanism—the Pope—Priests.—Despotism of Romanism.—Friends of the Pope.—Neapolitan Catechism.—Priests the Watchmen of Despotism—their horrid Use of the Confessional—it should be the Abhorrence of all Flesh.

My dear Sir,—On Friday, the 23d of May, I was landed in Avignon, famous in history as the old seat of the Popedom during the split that rent the Papal Church in twain. Myself and friend put up at the Hotel de l'Europe, a most comfortable and pleasant house. The attractions of this town to a traveler are the old Palace of the Popes, now a prison, with the old cathedral by its side, both built upon the top of a rock; and the Museum, which is a curiosity in its way. On the side of the old palace is a tower upward of two hundred feet high, the Tarpeian rock of Avignon, and from which multitudes have been cast down for summary death! It is frightful to look at—it is frightful to think of the inhumanity that would cast even a dog down the dreadful steep! And after seeing its sights, and looking out from its towering cliff upon the winding Rhone that washes its base—the vine-clad hills every where visible—and upon the snowy mountains that prop the sky in the distant horizon, we returned to our hotel.

Its keeper is a polite Frenchman, slender in person, with an intelligent eye, a thoughtful countenance, a pretty good knowledge of English, and quite chatty.

After a few minutes of general conversation, he asked, in a pleasant manner, "Where do you go, Sir?" "To Rome," I replied. "And be you a Catholique?" he asked. "O no," I answered, "I am a Protestant;" and immediately added, "there are not many Catholics in America, save those who go there from Europe —the Catholic religion does not suit our institutions." With that emphatic shrug of the shoulder peculiar to a Frenchman, and with a peculiar look and accent, which made me doubt whether he spoke in faith or in fun, he replied, "You do not understand in America the religion Catholique: it suits itself to all the institutions in the world." This was certainly saying much for its gum-elastic properties, and it is true, with certain restrictions. It makes perpetual war against the Bible and the simple institutions of the Gospel. With these exceptions, it literally becomes all things to all men, but with this one object steadily in view, that it may induce some to put on its yoke. But, because its devices are known, its power is broken.

I met more than once in Sardinia and Switzerland the well-known Captain Packenham, to whom I had received an introduction from Sir Culling Eardley, a Briton by birth, a man of family and fortune, a philanthropist and Christian, and an exile from Rome and Tuscany, where he resided many years, because of his distributing in those places the Holy Scriptures in Italian! But few men have had better opportunities of studying Popery at home, or of forming so true a judgment of its priests. And as we were walking together the streets of Lausanne, and as he was pouring forth the noble thoughts of his noble mind, and with all the ardor of a warm Christian heart, he uttered this memorable sentiment: "*Popery, Sir, is the police of despotism, and its priests are its watchmen.*" Never was the system and its priests more truly, briefly, or eloquently characterized. The sentence is worthy of a place among the proverbs of the wise and good; and you will permit me, in the present letter, to state to you a few things to prove and to illustrate the truth of the saying of mine host at Avignon, and of the exile of Rome.

The gum-elastic properties of Romanism are obvious every where. Look at it from whatever stand-point you may, and you can not fail to see them. See these properties as manifested by the Pope! He is now a temporal prince—now the vicar of Christ—now glittering from his throne—now washing pilgrims' feet—lauded in America as a liberal, in Austria as a despot—to-day he is a shepherd of the sheep, and to-morrow, like Peter, a fisherman; "determined," in the language of an English wit, "to live by hook and by crook." There is not a state of things existing, nor is there one likely to arise, save the spread of the true Gospel, and the putting up of free, civil, and religious institutions in Central and Southern Europe, to which he may not extend or contract himself. His gum-elastic properties are wonderful.

Look at its priests. They will multiply idols to suit a Chinaman—they will worship the Great Spirit to suit the Indian—they will preach up greegrees and charms to gain the Hottentot. They will synchronize with any form of error to make friends for themselves, or adherents to their system, or to raise barriers against the progress of the truth. They will laud the despotism of Tuscany—they will consecrate the trees of liberty in Paris—they will shout hosannas to democracy in New York, and to the most despicable despot that lives, the King of the Two Sicilies, at Naples. They will preach up liberty of conscience in Baltimore—no liberty of conscience in Rome; the freedom of the press here—no freedom of the press in Naples. They will flout the British ministry for protecting British subjects from their wiles, and they will curse the King of Sardinia for permitting a Protestant Church to be erected in Turin! Sir, it is my deliberate conviction, that if upon the face of the earth there is a class of men more destitute of principle than another, or less to be trusted than another, it is the priesthood of the Romish Church. They are a sacerdotal company, disconnected by the ordinary ties of humanity with their race, a close corporation, and with no principles but those which promote their interest. "You do not understand in America the religion Catholique," said my host in Avignon; and in the name of humanity, who can understand it?

And the despotism of Popery is equally obvious as is the elasticity of its principles. To prove this, I will not go back to the annals of the Dark Ages—to the claims of Hildebrand—to the wars waged concerning the right of investiture—to the terrible interdicts of the Vatican, nor to the despotic doctrines which form the chief material of the system. To prove true the sentiment uttered by my friend at Lausanne, I will call before you living witnesses, which you may cross-examine at your pleasure.

A proverb is a short saying or a moral rule deduced from an extended experience, and whose truth all experience unites to prove. Now, Sir, it has passed into a proverb, that "men are judged by the company they keep." Let us try the Pope by this rule. If sent out to select from all the crowned heads of Europe the veriest despots, who, Sir, would you select? If you have read Gladstone's letters, you would probably select the King of Naples first; and in view of the recent atrocities in Hungary, you would select the Emperor of Austria next. Now he of Naples is the bosom friend of Pio Nino, and is regarded by the father of the faithful as the most pious of all his children, while the sin of perjury lies heavy upon his soul, and the blood of his betrayed and murdered subjects stains all his garments; and he of Austria, in whom centres all the despotism, superstition, and cruelty of the house of Hapsburg, is the chief prop of his chair! What the two great pillars, Jachin and Boaz, were to the temple of Solomon, these two despots are to the present Pope. And the greater the despot, the higher he stands in the affections of the Holy Father. So far for the Pope.

Now, Sir, for the priests. The following are extracts from a catechism, written by a bishop, and taught to all the children in all the schools in the Two Sicilies, as quoted from Gladstone's letters to the Earl of Aberdeen, to which I have just alluded. I would recommend the pamphlet to your serious perusal, and to that of all men. More horrible doctrines it is impossible to conceive of, or to pen; and yet they are published under the vail of religion! O Religion, how often has thy purity been invoked to give sanction and currency to the "doctrines of devils," and to the cruel machinations of priests!

"Q. Are all liberals wicked in one and the same fashion?

"A. No; but, notwithstanding, they are traveling the same road, and, if they do not alter their course, they will arrive at the same goal." That is, all liberals in politics will be eternally lost! There is, then, no hope for any of us in America!

"Q. Can the people establish fundamental laws in a state?

"A. No; because a Constitution or fundamental laws are, of necessity, a limitation of sovereignty; and this can never receive any measure or boundary except by its own act.

"Q. If the people, in electing a sovereign, impose upon him conditions or reservations, will not these form the Constitution and fundamental laws of the state?

"A. They will, provided the sovereign grant them freely; otherwise they will not; *because the people, who are made for submission, and not for command*, can not impose a law upon the sovereignty, which derives its power, not from them, but from God.

"Q. If a prince has sworn to observe a Constitution, is he bound to maintain it?

"A. He is, provided it does not overthrow the foundations of sovereignty; *and provided it is not opposed to the general interests of the state.* When a sovereign finds a fundamental law is seriously hurtful to his people, he is bound to cancel it, because the duty of the sovereign is the people's weal. An oath can not become an obligation to commit evil, and therefore can not bind a sovereign to do what is injurious to his subjects. *Besides, the Head of the Church has author-*

ity from God to release consciences from oaths, when he judges that there is suitable cause for it." Here is the old power of absolving kings from their oaths, and turning them loose as blood-hounds among their people, revived!

"Q. Whose business is it to decide when the Constitution impairs the right of sovereignty, and is adverse to the welfare of the people?

"A. It is the business of the sovereign, because in him resides the high and paramount power established by God in the state with a view to its good order and felicity.

"Q. May there not be some danger that the sovereign may violate the Constitution without just cause, under the illusion of error or the impulse of passion?

"A. Errors and passions are the maladies of the human race; but the blessings of health ought not to be refused through the fear of sickness."

This catechism, teaching such horrible doctrines, was written by a bishop, is circulated by bishops to all their priests, and by the priests is taught to all the people of Sicily; its doctrines are more carefully taught to the young than are any articles of the Christian faith. With these extracts before you, will you hesitate a moment to believe that "Popery is the police of despotism?" And with doctrines like these it supports despotism in every country in Europe where it exists, and where the despots are Papists. And as it absolves a Papal king from his oath to his subjects, so it absolves Papal subjects from their allegiance to their Protestant king, when the good of the Church requires it. Are these catechism-makers the men for our country?

Should these spies of despotism receive any countenance from freemen ?

But is it true that the "priests are the watchmen of despotism ?" Never was a more true sentiment uttered ; and never was the sentiment more true than at the present hour. The system is struggling for its very life—its foundations are giving way in all lands—the waves of public opinion are dashing against the superstructure, and its priests are putting forth every effort to save it and themselves, as they well know that when their ship sinks they will have hard swimming.

Despotisms are always base, and will use any means to retain their power. They are public robbers ; and, like other robbers, have no conscience as to the means they use. They employ spies—use bribery—lay snares —get up plots—sow dissensions, and use all unrighteous means to find out and to kill off their enemies, and to consolidate their usurped power, and to put new rivets into the chains that bind people and nations to their thrones. And as the Papacy is the basest of despotisms, it has the base pre-eminence of using the most base means to accomplish its purposes. Other despotisms seek by spies to discover plots, and secret cabals, and overt acts ; but Popery has a plan by which not only to discover all these, with almost infallible certainty, but also the very thoughts of men. And this it does through the infamous confessional—"the slaughter-house of consciences"—an institution devised in hell, and set up on earth in the name of religion, that "the Man of Sin" may find out the secrets of all families, and of all hearts, and for the purpose of wielding them all to the maintenance of his bad dominion. All are obliged to confess on the pain of eternal death; no confession avails if any sin or secret thought is kept back; and these confessions, when necessary, are sent to head-quarters. In this way the court of Rome is invested with a kind of omniscience, as through the priests, its spies, its watchmen, who have their confession-boxes every where, they find out the secrets of courts, cabinets, and families, and even the very thoughts of men's hearts. And what is the effect of all this? A true Papist is afraid to think, because his conscience drags him to the confessional; and the priest who sits there, weaving webs to catch the unwary, as does a bottled spider to catch flies, will drag out his thoughts, and when these thoughts are drawn out, they are sent to head-quarters! I know the theory is, that confessions made to a priest are buried in his bosom; but has not "the Head of the Church authority from God to release consciences from oaths when he judges that there is suitable cause for it?" And what cause can be more suitable than the good of the Church, and the safety of the chair of St. Peter?

And what, Sir, must be the natural effect of all this upon families? Go down to Naples and see! Many is the Neapolitan husband, son, and brother, rotting in the prisons there on the information wrung from their wives, mothers, and sisters by the "watchmen of despotism" at the confessional. Go to Rome and see! Many is the noble Roman in exile, or in chains in the dungeons of Rome, on the information wrung from the female members of their families at the confessional. If a wife or daughter goes to confession, the husband and father can intrust no secret to either, can not repose any confidence in them. The sweets and the confidences of home are unknown—the sweet, confiding love of the family circle is broken up—not a word of freedom, or of dissatisfaction, or of complaint must be uttered—no suspected guest must be entertained—no private meetings must be held or alluded to, for all, all must be told at the confessional, sent up to the Vatican, and down to the police! Even in the heart of a fond wife there is no secret chamber which the priest, "the watchman of despotism," can not enter, and from which he may not bring forth its most secret and sacred deposits. Thus the mother, daughters, and sisters are converted by the infernal confessional into spies upon the conduct of their husbands and brothers, and are taught to believe that they are at once serving God and the Church, and saving their own souls—yes, and even doing the greatest good to their husbands and brothers, when revealing their thoughts and their conduct to these "watchmen of despotism." And is this, Sir, a fancy picture? Go and spend a month in Naples, or in Rome, and seek information from those who are competent and not afraid to give it, and you will say that the picture is not one half to the life. And I only wonder that the husbands, sons, and brothers of wives, mothers, and sisters, that go to the knees of Papal priests to confess, do not rise as one man, and pile up the confession-boxes for a grand bonfire, and drive their reverend confessors and seducers to Purgatory for purification.

Nor, Sir, are these pictures of these "watchmen of despotism" confined to Naples and Rome. Their character in those lands of Papal darkness, where the very light is darkness, is their universal character. Wherever the bishops or priests, the monks or the nuns of Romanism are found, they are only the spies, "the watchmen" of the driveling despot that lives in the Vatican, himself the victim of a clique of cardinal despots. Through their instrumentality the nations of the earth lie open to the eye of Rome; and she is enabled to judge of the best means of keeping them in her power, or of subduing them to her sceptre. Archbishops are the spies of the cardinals — bishops, of the archbishops—priests, of the bishops—and your poor Popish maid or coachman, the nurse of your children, or the waiter at your table, is the spy of the priest! And this vast system of espionage and tyranny is mainly conducted through the infamous confessional!

Are these watchmen of despotism the men for our country? I put this question to you, as its honored and honorable chief judicial officer, and upon whose ermine there is not a stain.

With great respect, yours.

LETTER XX.

Character of Priests.—A Walk in Turin.—Bishops in England and America Spies of Rome.—Ecclesiastical Preferments the Rewards of Spies.—When Priests and Despots are in League, no Hope for the People.—Examples of priestly Despotism.—Curse from the Altar.—Case of the Antrim Miller.—Priests the Curse of Ireland.—Can they be a blessing to America?

My dear Sir,—As I have a little more to say on the subject, I return again to the "watchmen of despotism." These watchmen have been permitted to wear the garment and the crook of shepherds long enough; it is time that their overcoats should be torn off, and that they should be revealed in their true livery.

Perhaps in no part of the world are the priests of Romanism putting forth more strenuous efforts to promote the interests of the despotism of Rome than in the United States. And while lauding our institutions, and at times almost eloquent in favor of liberty of conscience, there is not a feeling of their hearts, nor a sympathy of their nature, which does not cluster around the man of the triple crown. As with one voice, did they not denounce the Roman Republic, and hurl their anathemas against its leaders, and preach up a "Peter pence" contribution for to sustain the priests carousing at Gaeta? Did not bishops here, while playing into the hands of Whigs or Democrats to gain their ends, denounce the revolution in Hungary, rejoice over the bloody triumphs of the united forces of Russia and

Austria, and denounce the great Magyar even before he trod the soil, or breathed the air of our free country? How do you account, Sir, for this sympathy with tyranny abroad, and this eulogy of freedom at home? Their heart is in Rome, and so is their allegiance. Priests are here "the watchmen of despotism," and are bound to Rome by every tie that can bind a slave to his master. And if it would only confirm the dominion of Pio Nono, and tend to suppress the Bible and the awful heresy of "private reasoning," there is not a priest in this Union who would not rejoice over the ruins of our Republic to-morrow. The man who believes otherwise is almost fit to read without a smile, and with edification, "the History of the Holy House of Loretto, by the Very Rev. P. R. Kenrick, V. G."

As I was one day viewing with a friend the city of Turin, admiring the beauty of the surrounding scenery—the Superga, the snowy Alps, the winding Po, and the beautiful Colline, sparkling with villas from bottom to top, "Where," said I, "is the new Protestant church to be erected?" We were moving along at the moment a beautiful promenade, wide, and planted with trees, and destined at no distant day to be the finest street in that rapidly increasing city. "In this very street," was the reply. No finer or more prominent position could be selected. The question led to a most interesting conversation as to the progress of free institutions in that country, and as to the determination of the king, and nobles, and Parliament to secure freedom to all to worship God as they deem best. During the deeply-interesting and eloquent remarks of my friend, he gave utterance to this sentiment: "Our English and American friends come to Italy to see us. We are glad to see them. We give them often in detail what is doing to promote right views and right institutions; but they often, unwittingly, do us great injury. They go back and publish our statements to the world; and the first we know of the matter is by hearing of a most urgent appeal from Wiseman of London, or Hughes of New York, for the withdrawal of all privileges from Protestants, so as to check all progress toward freedom in these countries. What we tell here in private is published abroad, and is sent back here by bishops and priests, as information to these priestly despots." What a fact in proof of the allegation that Popish priests are the spies of despotism! You can not, Sir, close your eyes to the existing state of things in Britain. There is not an act of Parliament—from its inception to its passage or defeat—bearing in the most remote degree upon the education or moral instruction of the people, which is not known and canvassed at Rome; and on which the Papal party in the kingdom does not side with the Vatican. And in our own happy country, the mitre and the pallium are usually rewards of merit bestowed by the Pope upon those priests who have best performed their duties as his pimps or watchmen. These ecclesiastical baubles are not the rewards of piety, or talent, or of high virtue, but of subserviency to that politico-ecclesiastical power which claims to fetter the nations, and to think for the race, by the authority of God. And the winners of cardinals' caps are usually those most unscrupulous in principle, and most destitute of the cardinal virtues.

"Popery is the police of despotism," said my friend

at Lausanne. That it is the agency through which despots can best govern their people, is most obvious. When the people are Papists, and the priests are in league with the state, what hope is there for the people? If a man breathes at the confessional the aspirations of his soul after liberty, they are known to the police. Wives and sisters are made spies upon their husbands and brothers. Where can a spark of patriotism glow beyond the scrutiny of priestly eyes? It prohibits the circulation of the Bible; it forbids the religious tract; it anathematizes all works which vindicate the natural rights of man; it walls out all evangelical influences; it withholds all religious rites, as in the case of the bishops of Sardinia, from those who oppose its policy; it muzzles the press; it stimulates the faithful by promises of heaven, and terrifies the disobedient by the threats of sending them to hell, making them all to believe that the keys of heaven and hell hang by her girdle. With an agency like this in his favor among a people, and that can do all this under the sanctions of religion, and as the vicegerents of heaven, what has any despot to fear? And hence the natural inclinations of despotism to Romanism! Without Romanism and its priests, the government of Naples could not survive a day, nor could that of Austria a week. Where the people are Papists, the priests are their real governors, and it is the policy of rulers to court their influence. This explains some things very queer in the recent conduct of the King of Prussia; it explains the entire conduct of that puppet, "the Nephew of his Uncle," as he is contemptuously called, who now rules in France; it explains the unworthy conduct of some of our own farthing politicians, who flatter the priest to get the votes of the people he rides! And until the power of the priest over the people is broken—until thus the strong motive is removed from despots for protecting and paying the priest, I see no hope for the nations now bowed down under the double yoke of despotism and Romanism. As long as the vigilant police of Popery can be sustained by a despot among a people that will submit to it, for the freedom of that people there is no earthly hope. To be free, the despot and the priest must go up into the air, or sink down into the pit together! Hence, unless I greatly misinterpret the feelings of Papal Europe, and the signs of the times, the next war south, or even north of the Alps, will be a terrible one for the priests. "The watchmen of despotism" will be the very first victims; as far as they are concerned, it will be a war to the knife. They have sown the wind, and they will reap the whirlwind.

And it is astonishing to what a degree the ordinary priests partake of the spirit of the system, and act the despot within the bounds of their little parishes. Even in this free country, much of our emigrant population suffers under their despotism; and, although free to think and to act for themselves under our laws, they stand in terror of "the higher law" of the priest. I have known the life of a poor servant girl to be threatened by her own immediate relatives for becoming a Protestant, and since I commenced writing this letter, another has told me that her own mother threatened to shoot her dead because she has attached herself to a Methodist Church! So horrible is the system that, when it takes hold of an ignorant mind, it extinguishes even natural affection! And, if not exhorters to these brutal exhibitions of superstitious passion, the priests are no check to them. In many portions of the world, they excite to them by exhortation and example.

Not many months ago, a poor Irish widow, with eight or nine children, came to me to secure service for one of them. They all looked healthy, but not one of them knew a letter of the alphabet. "How came you," said I, "to bring up these children in such gross ignorance?" Her reply astounded me. "I lived," said she, "in Ireland, between two small towns, in each of which was a good Protestant school, and I wanted to send my children to them, but the priest said if I did, that he would curse me from the altar; and then nobody would speak to me; and they might kill me and my children." And the least acquaintance with the cruel despotism of the priests in the south and west of Ireland, will satisfy any body that this is only a favorable illustration of their general conduct. I have recently passed through the north, west, and eastern portions of that unhappy country, and I have learned things as to their conduct to their people which should brand them with the brand of infamy as indelibly as ever was Cain.

Why, Sir, it is no uncommon thing for these "surpliced ruffians," as they are called by the London Times, to go to a school collected by the philanthropy and supported by the charity of a few Protestant ladies, and to break it up by cowhiding all its pupils. This is a very common occurrence. The daughter of an old magistrate residing near Ballinrobe collected a school, in which they daily taught the children of the poor. The priest entered it a few months ago, and asked if the children were taught to read with a view of reading the Bible. On being informed that they were, he whipped every child out of the house. The priest denounced from the altar a school under the care of the lady of the High Sheriff of Galway, and whipped a respectable old man out of the chapel for permitting his children to go to it. These Bible haters are often seen flogging poor ignorant mothers in the streets and roads for permitting their children to go to other than a Papist school, and when no such school is within their reach!

One of these Irish priests residing at Ballahadireen, a few years since, had a quarrel with one of his poor parishioners; in this quarrel, the wife of the man sided with her husband, like a noble-minded and honest woman. Seeing her in church one day, the priest cursed her from the altar. Her reverence for the priest, and her superstitious faith in his ghostly power, gave to the curse an awful effect. From that hour she has been a crazed maniac. She yet lives to testify to the power of the priestly curse over an ignorant people; and as she meets her neighbors, she thus addresses them: "I have lost my soul; when the priest cursed me, I felt my head open, and my soul flew away. I have been seeking it ever since, but have not been able to find it. O, will you not help me to find my soul."

To illustrate the *priest's curse*, and to show you its terrific power over a Popish people, permit me to narrate a case. There lived in the glens of Antrim a plain country farmer, who, with a few acres of land, rented a mill. He was well versed in the Irish language, and was employed as a reader to his neighbors of the Irish Bible. He was a Papist. The priest sought to dissuade him from the blessed work, but he would not be dissuaded. He threatened him; but he disregarded his threatenings. He then announced that, unless he desisted from reading to his poor neighbors the Word of God, on a certain Sabbath he would curse him from the altar, with "bell, book, and candle." But the ravings of the priest were disregarded by the honest man, who had now learned to fear God, and to fear nothing else. On the eighteenth of August, 1844, the curse was pronounced by the Rev. Luke Walsh, priest of Culfeightrin, upon Charles M'Laughlin, and two others that he had associated with him, as follows: "My curse and God's curse on Charles M'Laughlin, Hugh Shields, and John M'Cay, and on all who shall hold any communion with them, or eat at the same table, or work in the same field with them." Then the bell was rung, the book was closed, and the candles on the altar were extinguished. This completed the fearful curse. And thus these men, with their families, were excluded from the society, the business, the charities of the earth, and consigned to eternal perdition, for the sin of reading the Scriptures to their neighbors, and by a man professing to be a minister of the Lord Jesus Christ!!

And what was the effect of this curse as to the chief offender, M'Laughlin? No person dared bring corn to his mill; he was shunned in the streets as if a leper; none would buy of him, or sell to him; his children were beaten in the streets; and on approaching a wagon in a market town to buy some meal for his family, the owner fled from his wagon and his meal, as if an escaped spirit from the pit were approaching him! And, were it not for the protection of some Protestants in the place, he must have fled from the home of his ancestors, or have fallen beneath the blow of the murderer, who, in taking his life, would feel that he was serving God; and that if he sinned, he could easily procure a pardon from Father Walsh. The priest was brought to trial for damages, and was sentenced to a fine of £70, with costs; and the above facts are taken from the report of the trial now before me. I believe this "surpliced ruffian," Walsh, is yet alive; I know M'Laughlin is, and that he is an humble Christian, laboriously and successfully engaged in the prosecution of the work of missions among the Papal Irish that are swarming in the Cowgate and around the Grass Market in Edinburgh. I had the pleasure of visiting one of his stations in that city, and found him surrounded with many, once Papists, but who were brought to the saving knowledge of Christ by the reading of the Bible. Now, Sir, conceive of three or four thousand of these Father Walshes scattered all over Ireland—the watchmen of despotism in every parish; finding out family secrets at the confessional; putting out every light that would expose their wickedness; when neither coaxing nor threats will win men to their will, thus cursing them from the altar; and then, if you can, conceive of the fact that eight out of every ten of all its inhabitants believe that these priests are the vicegerents of God; that they do all they do by the authority of Heaven, and you will not wonder that Ireland is what it is, nor that its people, who are swarming upon our shores, are what they are. Their deep ignorance, their low vices, their unbridled passions, their low civilization, their squalid poverty, are all, all the results of the despotism of priests, many of whom are the most ferocious, vicious, profane, and rollicking wretches in the country. They care not for the government of the land; strong in the superstitious reverence of the masses, they put it to defiance. They care not for the rights of landlords who are not subservient to them; many of them have fallen at noonday on their own estates, because of a hint from the altar in the way of a question like this: "Should such men live?" They care not for the people, only so far as to keep the yoke of bondage on their neck. The people may do what else they desire if they will not send their children to Protestant schools, nor read the Bible, nor become Protestants. These men, who every where look as if they far preferred prescribing to practicing penance, have but two masters, the Pope and their belly. To these they yield implicit obedience; blessing all that promote, and cursing all that oppose these masters. O, Sir, are these Father Walshes the men for America? If we encourage these missionaries of barbarism in our free land until they obtain the preponderance they desire, we will deserve to be treated as was Satan by St. Dunstan, who led him about by the nose with a red-hot pincers; or to be ranked with the devout donkey of St. Anthony of Padua, who, after three days' fasting, left his provender to worship the Host.

With great respect, yours.

LETTER XXI.

Ballenglen.—An Incident.—Persecution of Converts.—Thrilling Fanaticism at a Funeral.—The Way the Priests get Money.—An Incident.—Cursing from the Altar.—Hard Case of Donovan.—Doing Penance in Sheets.—Priests' Power giving Way.—Anecdote of a Girl.—The Milkman.—Taking the Bull by the Horns.—The Curse of Ireland.

MY DEAR SIR,—Even at the risk of taxing your patience and that of my readers, I will again return to the conduct of Papal priests toward the Papal population of Ireland. I do so for various reasons: to excite a feeling of compassion in the bosom of all Americans toward its swarming emigrants weekly landed on our shores; to expose the priests and their religion to the world; to encourage Popish emigrants here to assert their independence, where there is no priestly power to strike them down; and to place before you and all our people what blessings we may reasonably expect from the many priests sent from "the island of saints," trained and drilled in Maynooth to guard our institutions, to enlighten and Christianize us.

In company with Dr. Edgar, and of Dr. Andrews, of Queen's College, Belfast, and of Mr. Allen, of Ballina, names not unknown in Ireland, or Britain, or America, I visited the Scotch Mission School in Ballenglen. It was deeply interesting to see there upward of a hundred children, neatly dressed, under pious and competent teachers, taught "to learn and to earn," and, with few exceptions, collected from the surrounding huts of the Papal peasantry. "Do you see that girl on the upper seat, about twenty-one or two years of age?" said the noble Scotch lady at the head of the female department to me. I looked, and replied in the affirmative. "That girl," she continued, "has been here but a few weeks. She came here not knowing a letter, and scarcely any thing else. She is learning rapidly, and can now earn two or three shillings a week with her needle, and can do considerable for the support of her family. When going home from school yesterday, the priest met her at the road, and sought to horsewhip her for coming here, but she outran him. She told her grievance to her mother, who sided with the priest, and expressed her sorrow that he did not catch her; and yet she returned here this morning, but without sleeping a wink, or eating a mouthful since she left here yesterday afternoon." Amazed at the statement, I asked if there was no redress against such priestly barbarity. "What can we do?" was the reply. "We may indict them, but then nobody will peril their life by testifying against them; nor can you get a jury, on which there is a single Catholic, to convict them. A priest not long ago was indicted for flogging a woman terribly, and yet, when called to witness against him, she testified that 'his reverence did not hurt her at all.'" And this is but an illustration of what is now of daily occurrence in almost every portion of Ireland.

Until within a few years, it was at the risk of his life that any of the peasantry dared to leave the priest for the minister. The fury of the priest excited the people to fury, and the poor convert was every where an unsheltered, unpitied object of abuse, contempt, and violence. Even the mother cast out the child from the sanctuary of her heart, and mourned over the conversion of her child to God as a deep, dark disgrace to her family. Hear a boy tell of the ties through which one must break when he deserts the religion of the priest:

"O pity the state of a poor Irish youth,
Whose heart has been touched with a love of the truth;
By father and mother renounced and forgot,
Should he dare to be that which the priest bids him not.
Should he open the Book which to sinners was given,
To try to make out the right way to heaven,
The eyes will look cold that smiled on him before,
And hearts that once loved him will love him no more."

And within a few weeks the constabulary force of the diocese of Tuam, over which the vulgar and savage M'Hale presides, has been greatly increased, for the purpose of keeping the peace, which has been greatly disturbed by attacks of the mob, stimulated by the priests, upon converts from Romanism.

It is impossible to make Protestants in America, or even Papists who have been born here, to understand the deep degradation to which the priests have reduced the native Irish, or the extent to which they have steeped them in the most gross superstition. Ponder the following statements selected from a little pamphlet, entitled "The Trials and Triumphs of Irish Missions," by Dr. John Edgar.

"At the burial of a convert, his sister hastily gathered in her apron their parents' bones, and buried them in another part of the church-yard, lest they should be polluted by the cursed remains of an impenitent heretic."

"At the burial of a convert who died of hardships endured in shipwreck, his sisters created a great disturbance by their desperate efforts to have him buried as a Romanist; and some idea may be formed of the excitement created among the Romish crowd, when one sister sung to the wild Irish cry,

"'O would that thy grave were made under the billow,
And would that the wild shark himself were thy pillow,
Than thus on the bed in thy senses to lie,
And our Church and her priesthood so boldly defy!'

"And the second sister, taking up the plaintive wail, sang,

"'O Donagh! Donagh! can it be,
And hast thou left us so,
The gem, the flower of all thy race,
With heretics to go?
We lay thee in thy father's grave,
Beneath thy mother's head,
No parson o'er thee e'er shall pray,
No Bible e'er be read.'

"In the native Irish grave-yards the latest-buried coffin is put under the others." This explains a clause in the above wail.

"How very largely must a Romish priest draw on the superstition of his victim when he demands a fee for saying mass to drive away vermin, or for cutting the sign of the cross to cure a vicious mule. During the famine priests trafficked to an enormous extent on the gullibility of their people by blessing salt, for hire, as a cure for the disease of the potato. Half a dozen of crews are paying them at the same time for saying mass over their boats; and for five or six pounds they make a bargain with the people alongshore to bring an abundance of herring or mackerel into the bay.

"O what would not Ireland be if the power of the priests was employed for good, as, alas, it is for ill! A man-servant in a highly respectable family, being apparently near his death, sent for a priest, who refused to administer 'the last rites' until he would bind himself by an oath, in the name of the Father, the Son, and the Holy Ghost, that he would never listen to the Bible again. He refused, and the priest left him. On this a fellow-servant rushed into the room, and so placed before him the horrors of damnation if he died without the rites of the Church, that he took the awful oath. Unexpectedly, he recovered, and he still lives, with the vow to resist all Scriptural instruction on his soul. When asked whether he did not know that the Bible was the word of God, he replied that he knew it well, but that he knew also that he would receive only the burial of a dog if he died without the blessing of the priest."

And can we wonder at the ignorance, the superstition, the poverty, the servility of the peasantry of Ireland that are landed on our shores, when they and their fathers have been crushed for ages under a spiritual despotism like this?

I have given one instance in illustration of the priestly curse from the altar. I select another from the little pamphlet before me. A poor woman sent her children to a Protestant school, and, on the trial of the priest for cursing her, a witness thus testified under oath: "The priest put on a black dress; the clerk quenched all the candles but one, and that one the priest put out, saying, 'So the light of heaven is quenched upon her soul.' He then shut the book and said,

'The gates of heaven are shut against her.' Her neighbors immediately withdrew all intercourse from her. Shop-keepers refused to sell her even a bit of bread. All her children but one were included in the curse; her husband forsook her; and, had she not been taken into the house of a kind Protestant, she must have perished when on the eve of giving birth to a child, which the priest had also cursed, for he cursed the fruit of her womb!"

Now, Sir, with priests of this infernal character swarming in every part of Ireland, making here a "sick call" for a shilling—there "giving a communion" for two and sixpence—there saying mass for five shillings—there baptizing for sums varying from two to twenty shillings; marrying sometimes for twenty shillings and sometimes for twenty pounds; and every where carrying on a war to the knife against the Bible, and all its free, ennobling, and elevating influences, can you, can any man wonder that Ireland is so low in the scale of civilization—that its people are so poor, ignorant, and superstitious—that its sons and daughters in all the lands whither they wander are hewers of wood and drawers of water?

As illustrating the terrible tyranny of these "surpliced ruffians" as exercised in another way, permit me to state another case which occurred a few years since. A Rev. Mr. O'Brien, wishing to build a chapel in the parish of Clonakilty, drew up a subscription paper, and taxed his parishioners according to his estimate of their means. A baker by the name of Donovan was marked at sixteen shillings and threepence, which he paid. He was again taxed nine shillings, which he also paid, but under protest, because of his poverty. Soon a third demand came for sixteen shillings more, which he refused to pay. On the next Sabbath, as he was going to mass, he was asked by the priest whether he would pay that sixteen shillings or not. He replied, "I am not able." The priest replied, "I will settle you." Terrified by the remark, Donovan sent sixteen shillings by his wife to the priest, who then refused to take less than two guineas. On the following Sunday he cursed him from the altar, and all those who refused or neglected to pay what they were taxed. Donovan went on the next holiday to mass, where he was formally excommunicated, and all were cursed who would have any thing to do with him. So terrible was the dread of this curse, that he could not buy turf enough to heat his oven, nor could he sell any of his stock. Reduced to despair, he went in penance, in a white sheet, to the chapel, and asked pardon of the priest and of God. The priest took him to his house and demanded the two guineas, but the sheeted penitent told him he could not possibly make it up. The excommunication was continued; the man was compelled to shut up shop, and was driven to beggary. These facts were brought out in a trial for damages before a jury in Cork, which fined the reverend rascal fifty pounds.

This thing of doing penance, by going to chapel wrapped up in a white sheet, is quite a common affair in some parts of Ireland. Sometimes whole families are compelled to go thus dressed, to atone for the sins of one member; and when the sin has any squinting toward Protestantism, the penance is increased by compelling them to go barefooted and bareheaded. A family in Mayo had thus to do penance for the sins of one of their number. To the family belonged a *young* woman, who, although advanced in years, had not quite surrendered all hopes of matrimony. Her natural hair, which was not so dark as it once was, she sought to conceal by raven locks, which gave her an appearance quite youthful. But on the fated Sabbath her borrowed locks had to be laid aside; and she entered the church sheeted, barefooted, and, sad to narrate, bareheaded! Her gray hair, and short and thin at that, revealed her years, and gave her hopes of matrimony to the winds. She yet lives, but has never forgiven the priest the double injury which he inflicted on her, to uncover her gray hairs and destroy her market. Although a good Papist, it is rumored that she raves at his reverence whenever she thinks of the exposure of her thin gray hairs on that penitential Sunday. I give you the story as I received it from a sympathizing acquaintance of the deeply-injured spinster.

O, Sir, there is not a poor, ignorant, half-clad Irish Papist, man or woman, that comes to these shores, that is not sent here by Providence to be a protest against Romanism, and a witness against its mercenary and ruffian priests, and to warn us as a nation against a system which only blights, to the extent of its influence, all the interests of humanity. Nations recover from the wasting influences of war, famine, and pestilence; but for the people who wear and will bear the yoke of Romanism, there is no recovery.

But, Sir, it is pleasant to know that, even in Ireland, the people are beginning to see, and rightly to estimate this horrible despotism, and to assert their rights, even amid the dangers that threatened them when cursed and excommunicated from the altar. The wand of the priest is broken; and the peasant that once cowered before him as a chicken before a hawk, or as a lamb before a wolf, now dares to resist him to his face. The gentry that once feared him, because of his fearful power over their tenants, are beginning to treat him as he deserves. In spite of his altar curses, children are sent to school—in spite of his anathemas, the people by hundreds and thousands read the Bible and believe it, and are passing over to swell the ranks of Protestantism. Some amusing anecdotes are every where told in illustration of all this. "Do you pray to the Virgin Mary?" said a priest to a bright-eyed Kerry girl, the daughter of one of his parishioners, that he met near a schoolhouse with a Bible in her hand. "No, your reverence; and why should I?" was the reply. "Because she knows all things, and will hear and answer your prayers," said the priest. Quick as a flash, the girl replied, "Now it is singular, your reverence, that if she knows all things, that she did not know where her Son was when he was missed from the company that was returning from Jerusalem to Galilee; and see, here is the place," handing him the Bible, and pointing him to the second chapter of Luke. And he rode away, no doubt cursing the Bible, the girl, and the school in his heart.

An Irish milkman commenced reading the Bible; his priest heard of it, and was soon at his house. "I am informed that you read the Bible, John," said he; "is my information correct?" "Sure it is thrue, plase your reverence! and a fine book it is," said John. "But you know it is very wrong to read the Scriptures, and that an ignorant man like you has no right to do so," said the priest. "But you must be afther provin' that same before I can consint to lave it off," said John. The colloquy then proceeded as follows:

Priest. "That I will soon do; I will prove it from the book itself." And, taking the Bible, he read this passage, from 1 Peter, ii., 2: "As new-born babes, desire the sincere milk of the Word, that you may grow thereby." "Here you see," said he, "that you are wrong to read the Scriptures yourself; you are only a babe, and you are enjoined to desire the sincere milk of the Word; one who really understands what the sincere milk is, must give it to you, and teach you."

John. "Ah, but be aisy, your reverence, while I tell you. A little time ago I was took ill; I got a man to milk my cows, and to attend on my business, and what do you think he did? Why, instead of giving me the rale milk, he chated me by puttin' water in it; and if you get my Bible, you may serve me that same. No, no, I will keep my cow, and milk it myself, when I can get the sincere milk, and not, as I should from you, mixed with water."

Priest. "Well, John, I see that you are wiser than I thought you were; and as you are not quite a babe, keep your Bible, but don't lend it, or read it to your neighbors."

John. "Sure enough, your reverence, while I have a cow, and can give a little milk to my poor neighbors who have none, I feel it my duty to do so, as a Christian, and, saving your reverence, I will."

What became of the milkman, the little pamphlet,

"Ireland, its Curse and Cure," from which I quote the incident, does not state; but it suggests that he was probably cursed with "bell, book, and candle," as was another man for the same offense, and upon whom it fell most heavily. He had a little field from which he made a living. It was plowed and sown; but the curse of the priest would allow no person to hire him a horse to harrow it. And, at dead of night, he was compelled to yoke himself and wife to the harrow, and thus to cover his seed!! And with such priests of barbarism swarming in the island, and thus every where governing and grinding the people, is it any wonder that the emigrants from Ireland are as ignorant and superstitious as we find them? They deserve our pity and commiseration; and the scorn and contempt with which they are often visited, should be poured upon the religion and its priests, which have been, and are, the chief causes of their degradation.

To show you the manner in which the gentry, so many of whom have fallen victims to curses from the altar, begin to treat the priests, permit me to narrate a circumstance. There resides at Clogher a family by the name of Holmes. The present head of the family, a large proprietor and humane, was denounced, and, to save his life, he fled to Dublin. The outrage became known to a younger brother in the army, who was greatly excited by it. He hastened home from London, and, on the eve of a feast-day, called on the priest, and requested him to ask the people, after mass on the succeeding day, to remain behind in the chapel, as he had something to say to them, to which he assented. Suspecting something, however, the priest commenced mass earlier than usual — hastened through it — and when young Holmes came to chapel, the people were dismissed. He invited them back to the chapel, and sent for the priest; but the messengers could not find him. "I will find him," said he; and left the chapel, but soon returned with his reverence. With the priest by his side, he thus addressed the people from one of the steps of the altar. "My fathers have long resided in this place, and have they not always been the kind friends of your fathers?" "Yes, yes, your honor," resounded from all parts of the chapel. "My brother has succeeded to the estates here, and has he not always been a kind landlord?" The same reply echoed from every part of the house. "And now what is the reward for all his, and all our fathers' kindnesses, which you are about to give him? There are those eating at your tables, sleeping in your beds, and sheltered in your houses, who are pledged to murder him; and, to save his life, he has had to leave the home of his birth. He will return in a few days; and I stand here before you, to warn you, that if my brother goes down to the grave a murdered man, there is one man in this parish that will soon follow him, and that man is this priest, who has denounced him from this altar." He turned round and looked the priest full in the face, who cowered before him. He left the chapel, the people making way for him, without insult or molestation. His brother returned in a few days to his family and to his home, where he resides at the present hour, as safe a man from assassination as there is in Ireland, as long as that priest and his brother live! I was entertained at the hospitable house of Clogher, and stood on the altar step on which that young Holmes stood, when, by his bold and manly bearing, he struck with a salutary terror the priest and his parishioners! As a sense of guilt always renders men cowardly, denunciations of landlords from the altar have greatly diminished since the hero of Clogher taught them how to put a stop to them.

Romanism and its priests have been, and now are, the curse of Ireland; and the only cure for Ireland lies in their removal. And can the curse of Ireland be a blessing to any land? Can it be, Sir, a blessing to America? Are these Father Walshes and Father O'Briens, these reverend and right reverend altar-cursing "watchmen of despotism," the men to Christianize and civilize Americans—the men to teach our people the Gospel of Christ, and the true way to heaven? From these ministers of barbarism and missionaries of darkness, may the Lord deliver us and our posterity!

With great respect, yours.

LETTER XXII.

Deceivings of Priests.—Nunneries.—Taking the Vail.—Stories about Luther and Calvin.—Case of poor Bruley.—The Vaudois Monsters.—Bridge of Purgatory broken.—Father O'Flanagan.—Why these deceivings?—Priests deserve Purgatory.

My dear Sir,—You can readily glean, from my preceding letters, my estimate of the general character of Papal priests. While there are exceptions to the rule, yet I believe, as a rule, that they are, like the Pharisees of old, " a generation of vipers;" that, as a class, they are dishonest traffickers in the souls of men. The trade of a priest, and especially when a priest becomes a bishop or an archbishop, is an exceedingly lucrative one. What may not a priest squeeze from a people whom he makes believe that he carries in his pocket the keys of heaven and hell, and that he can, at pleasure, admit them to the bliss of the one, or shut them up amid the eternal miseries of the other? And hence it is that these men so easily draw gold from the coffers of the rich, and extract silver and coppers even from the rags of the most wretched beggars. What will not a man give to save his soul? And all their worldly interests are involved in keeping up their delusions, and in keeping their people from contact with every thing that would in the least degree tend to dissipate them. And it is to their ways of blinding and deluding the people, so as to stimulate their faith, and to protect their frauds and deceivings from exposure, that I ask your attention in the present letter. Is there a thing peculiar to Popery which is not intended to delude?

How much Popery makes of nuns and nunneries, to fire the imagination of young, romantic girls, and to induce them to seek seclusion from the world within monastic walls! The abbess is a lady of rank, beauty, and exquisite taste! The nuns are all damsels of beautiful face and form, the history of each marked by some romantic incidents which strongly excite our interest. And then the sacred inclosure is such a charming spot in which to cultivate holiness, and where happiness is enjoyed by every inmate, but little below that of paradise itself! And then the pomp, show, and ceremony of "taking the vail" are so arranged as to exalt the heroism and piety of the maiden that takes it, and as, if possible, to induce other maidens to do likewise. How the true history of any existing nunnery would give all these delusions to the winds—would prove them to be the prisons of confiding girls—the houses of refuge for delinquent or disappointed lasses, or for daughters fleeing from domestic tyranny—and their parlors to be the lounging-places of immaculate priests! And how a true narrative of those "taking the vail," would dissipate all romance concerning them!

Seymour, to whose "Pilgrimage" I have already alluded, gives a very funny account of a "taking the vail," witnessed by him in Rome. It was in January. On approaching the monastery, the street, and vestibule, and church were strewed with flowers. The high altar was loaded with artificial flowers. The cardinal-vicar took his seat; soon the Princess Borghese entered, leading a beautiful female, and presented her to the cardinal. Her beautiful chestnut-colored tresses fell like a vail around her; her dress was white satin, richly damasked in gold; on her head glittered a crown of diamonds; her neck was covered with precious stones, flashing through her ringlets; her breast was gemmed with brilliants, set off by black velvet; so that she sparkled and blazed in all the magnificence of the richest jewels in Rome! All took her, of course, to be a youthful princess of vast wealth, renouncing the world for the cloister! And yet this beautiful young woman was only a servant, and the daughter of a servant, of the Borghese family; that splendid hair was only a wig; the jewelry belonged to her mistress, who took that occasion to display it; and the sweet, lovely-looking girl in her dress, when divested of her robes, was a vulgar, clumsy, and unlettered old maid of forty! And such are usually the nuns of Popery. And the whole scene was gotten up to gratify the vanity of the woman who wished to display her jewels, and to induce those not behind the curtain to believe that another rich heiress of a noble house had renounced the vanities of the world for the seclusion of a cloister!

And this is only a specimen of the way and manner in which priests delude the people every where! Take away the clothes in which they dress their mummery, and it would be only revolting. Go, Sir, on Christmas day, or any high day, into your cathedral, and, after blowing out all the candles, and sending the boys with censers and incense to their seats, and taking off the robes of the priests, and putting to silence the professional singers, cause the priests to go through a high mass! Why, Sir, you would laugh at the barren foolery; and "the awful, mysterious, and holy ceremony of the mass" would appear to you just as attractive as did the withering old maid, who was made a nun, to Seymour, when divested of her robes, her crown, and her jewels. Romanism is a corpse, and its ceremonies and canonicals are dresses put on to hide its putrescence, and to induce belief in the vulgar that it is a living body. Sure am I that if any sensible mother would find her children, at the close of a summer's day, going through the senseless rounds through which I have seen about twenty cardinals go, dressed in their scarlet skullcaps and robes, at vespers in the Sistine, she would be disposed to whip them and send them to bed.

To deceive and delude their people it is that priests and monks have fabricated the most false and ridiculous stories about the great and good men that have led on the blessed Reformation, and that have achieved the civil and religious liberty which we enjoy. If they have made their own adherents demigods, they have made the reformers demons. Who is ignorant of the Popish narratives of Luther's conferences with Satan—of the diabolical agencies which he wielded—and of his soul, on his death, flying away, leaving something like a smell of brimstone behind it? The monkish legends of the days of Luther are as full of stories to prove his Satanism, as is the life of St. Patrick of ridiculous miracles to prove his sanctity. And down to the present day an ignorant Papist will turn away horrified from the name of Luther, as it is said a demon will turn away from the sign of the cross, or from a sprinkling of holy salt or of water.

And similar stories are fabricated and circulated about the scholar and logician of the Reformation, the great Calvin. Here is the substance of a comment on Exodus, vii., 11, taken from the Douay Bible, printed in 1635, as quoted entire by Capper. Calvin, by words and money, persuaded a man in Geneva, by the name of Bruley, to feign himself dead, in order that, by a kind of Popish exorcism or fraud, he might bring him to life. But, alas for poor Bruley! when he feigned to be dead, he absolutely died, and by a direct visitation of Providence! And all Calvin's efforts could not restore breath to his body! O, if the reformer had only a toe-nail of St. Anthony, or an old tooth of St. Dominic, or some shreds from the garments, or some parings from the nails of some of the holy martyrs or virgins, poor Bruley might have lived again! Good Mrs. Bruley consented to the agreement; but when she found that Calvin could not restore her husband, she was in a violent passion, and called him a false apostle, and "a secret theefe, and a wicked murderer that had killed her husband," so that all Geneva knew, on the testimony of the hysterical Mrs. Bruley, that Calvin killed Bruley, but could not restore him to life! And stories like these against the reformers, and the great and good men who have opposed Popery, are scarcely less numerous than are the miracles of Mary and Bambino. And all for the sake of prejudicing the vulgar mind against their character and writings.

You, Sir, can not be ignorant of the history of the Vaudois or Waldensians, who kept the light of truth burning for so many ages in the valleys of Piedmont, when it had gone out in nearly all the earth besides! Their history is a thrilling one, and is full of blood—of blood shed by Romish priests, and by orders from the Vatican. And the question arises how or why the house of Savoy could turn its arms so long and so cruelly against a people so loyal, so moral, and so unoffending? It was because of the horrid representations made by Popish priests to the court. On a certain occasion, a prince of Savoy determined on a journey among the valleys of this wonderful people, of whom the burning bush, as seen by Moses, was a fit emblem. Standing by the first Vaudois house to which he came, he saw a fine, healthy, well-formed boy, whose appearance excited his astonishment. He sent for the parents, who, with their other children, came around him. His astonishment increased. He spoke with them, and found them intelligent, well informed, and loyal. "And are all your people formed like you?" said the prince to the peasant. "Yes, all," was the reply. He made them open their mouths, that he might see their teeth, when there was an increase of his wonder. "How is this?" said he, turning to his attendants; "we have been always informed by our priests that these people were monsters—that they had but one eye, which was in the middle of their foreheads—and that they had double rows of teeth; and, instead of finding them the horrible creatures which we have been informed they were, we find them in form, and fashion, and mind like ourselves."

Here, Sir, is the secret of the barbarity of the princes of Savoy to the Waldensian people. That people refused to bow their necks to the Papal yoke; they would not surrender the Bible for the Missal; with hearts as firm as the towering Alps, amid whose valleys they reside, they resisted every effort to induce them to surrender their ancient faith; and hence the baffled priests represented them as monsters—as the descendants, perhaps, of the Harpies, so intolerably disgusting, as sung by Virgil. Nor have I a doubt but that the princes who sent their armies into those peaceful valleys, with orders to spare neither age nor sex, were deluded by wicked priests into the belief that they were seeking to extirpate a race of monsters from the earth, instead of slaughtering a race of Christians, as simple, as pious, as harmless, as steadfast, as heroic as any which the world has ever known. And as I recently wandered along the banks of the Po, whose waters were once crimsoned with the blood of slaughtered Waldensians, and rode along the valleys through which the minions of the Pope so often carried fire and sword, I almost imagined that I could hear the blood of the slain crying to Heaven, and saying,

"Avenge, O Lord, thy slaughtered saints, whose bones
Lie scattered on the Alpine mountains cold;
Even those who kept thy truth so pure of old,
When all our fathers worshiped stocks and stones.
Forget not—in thy book record their groans—
Who were thy sheep, and in their ancient fold,
Slain by the bloody Piedmontese, that rolled
Mother with infant down the rocks."

Nor, Sir, has this method of deluding the people been surrendered by the priests. It is practiced, where it can be, in all shapes and forms in our own day. "I was traveling up to our valleys in my char-à-banc," said the interesting Vaudois pastor of Turin to me, "and took in a plain man that I overtook on the way. I soon found that he was a Papist. After some conversation, he asked me where I was going? I told him I was going on a visit to our people. He asked me if I was a Waldensian; and on telling him that I was, he eyed me from head to foot with astonishment. Seeing no deadly weapons about me, and as I treated him in the kindest manner, he became somewhat composed; but he finally left my carriage, preferring to walk rather than to continue in so doubtful, if not dangerous a position as that of riding with a leader among a people respecting whom the priests told him so many monstrous stories." Indeed, one of the chief duties of the priests is to sow jealousies and hatred among their people toward all who are not Papists. To what an awful extent this is carried in Ireland, where, until recently, the Papist regarded the Protestant as his deadly enemy! See how Protestant ministers are denounced, and Protestant books forbidden, and Protestant schools abandoned—see how, even in our free and happy land, the priests teach their people to look upon every thing Protestant as white with leprosy. How soon do our Protestants see, in the altered demeanor of their servants, the bad influences of those "father confessors," who go prowling after silly Irish men and women through the country, scaring them up to confess their sins, and to pay for the privilege!

Nor are even their own people exempt from the deceivings of the priests, who feel that they have a divine warrant to fleece their flocks as they can, and to pardon one another when they sin. I will not vouch for the truth of the following story, but I will give it to you just as I received it from the lips of one of the most honored and eloquent ministers of Britain, whose name is known and revered on both sides of the Atlantic. He asserted its entire truth. There lived a poor man, in one of the cities of Britain, who made his support by selling beer. He was honest, and punctual in his payments, and won the entire confidence of the brewer. He died; and, as the priest stated, his soul went to Purgatory. His widow carried on the business, and sent for one barrel of beer after another, until she was in debt to the brewer about one hundred pounds. The brewer, who was a Papist, went to make inquiry as to the cause of this large indebtedness. "And have you not heard of the terrible accident that has happened?" said the woman. "What is it?" asked the brewer. "The bridge of Purgatory is broken," was the reply, "and it takes a deal of money to repair it; and Father O'Flanagan is very faithful in collecting money to repair it, bless his soul; and when the bridge is finished, so that my poor husband can get across, then I will strive to pay you all."

The brewer did not like to be thus swindled through the priest, and laid his plans to get his money. He made a large dinner party, to which he invited the bishop, several priests, among whom was Father O'Flanagan, and a few other friends. After the punch began to work a little, he rung a bell, which was the signal for the introduction of the widow from the beer-shop. "Have you heard, your reverence," said the brewer to the bishop, "of the awful accident that has occurred?" "What is it?" said the bishop, with excited interest.

"Father O'Flanagan, will you tell the bishop about the breaking down of the bridge of Purgatory?" said the brewer. Father O'Flanagan blushed, looked at the woman, and then into his tumbler of punch, and was silent. The fraud was revealed; there was the poor woman to prove its truth; and the brewer declared that unless the one hundred pounds were paid down, he would expose the whole affair. The bishop gave his check for the amount—the old beer-woman was glad — the party broke up; and the breaking of the bridge of Purgatory cured the brewer of his Popery. I confess to you, Sir, that the story seemed to me incredible when I heard it, and I was for placing it on the same shelf with the monkish stories about Luther and Calvin; but after seeing what I saw, and hearing what I heard in Naples, Rome, Sardinia, and Ireland—after a more extended acquaintance with the profligacy of priests, their want of principle, and their love of money, I see no reason, in the nature of things, to doubt the story of the Rev. Father O'Flanagan. Sure I am that the fiction of Purgatory is made to yield millions every year to the priests, and in ways no more justifiable than that adopted with the poor widow that sold beer.

Such are the ways and the manner in which the priests of Romanism seek to deceive, to delude, and to prejudice the minds of their people; and all for the base purpose of continuing their own bad dominion, and of preventing the people from coming to the knowledge of the truth. No Gospel truth is left unclouded —no good man is left unabused—no good book is left out of the Index—bonfires are made of Bibles—no seed that can bear the fruit of discord is left unsown—fables are manufactured without end—miracles are made to order—history and philosophy are libeled—Bacon is made a dunce—Luther a devil—and Cranmer a knave, when required to keep the people in shackles, to oppose the influence of Protestantism, or to make people pass to heaven through the toll-gate of the priest. I have just charity enough for them to believe that they will stop at nothing that promotes their ends—that they will respect no law of religion, humanity, or propriety that will cross their path. This will seem to you, and to many of my readers, very uncharitable; but I appeal to the history of Romanism in all lands for its correctness. I appeal to the events now transpiring in Naples, Rome, Florence, and Ireland, to sustain me. If you, Sir, with your high reputation, should, on the perusal of these letters, openly declare yourself Protestant, they would serve you here, as they have done the Duke of Norfolk in England on his recent renunciation of Popery. There is not a priest or a Protestant renegade that can scribble a line, from the Atlantic to the Pacific, that would not be out upon you; and if they would not transfix you, as is the man in the Almanac, into whom the signs of the zodiac are pouring their arrows, it is because, like Achilles, you were baptized in the Styx.

And why is it, Sir, that Papal priests resort to these frauds and deceivings? Why is it they seek to prejudice their people against all other people, and to separate them from all the humanizing influences of religious and social intercourse? Why is it they prevent their people from thinking—from examining for themselves truths and topics which demand our belief? They know the feebleness of their position, and the weakness of their cause; and that, unless they hedge up their people on all sides, their craft is gone.

I would not do these priests evil. Were it in my power, I would convert them all. But if there is a class of persons living that deserve a good long residence in Purgatory, they are the men. And should they go there, and should the bridge break down, I would not give Father O'Flanagan a penny to build it—at least for one year.

With great respect, yours.

LETTER XXIII.

Rome Intolerant.—Persecutions sanctioned.—Bishops sworn to persecute—Deposed if they do not.—Wiseman's reply.—Proofs of Intolerance—Waldenses—Castelnau—Bezières—Morland's Address—St. Bartholomew—Edict of Nantes revoked—Irish Massacre of 1641—other Evidences.—Two Skins.

My dear Sir,—I desire in the present letter to ask your attention, and that of my readers, to the spirit which Romanism cherishes and manifests toward all who deny its claims and reject its dogmas. Unless I mistake the character of your mind, you will agree with me that it is only cruel in principle and in action.

But you will meet me at the threshold with the statement that Romanism has greatly changed in these latter days, both in its principles and conduct. If so, where is her infallibility? If so, her main foundation is gone. No, Sir; her infallibility places her beyond the reach of improvement, and stereotypes equally her truth and her falsehood, her divinity and her demonism. Nor will she thank you, or any body else, for excusing her on the ground of a change of principle, as such an excuse stultifies her boast, and subjects her pretensions to the ridicule of all men. I admit that in this, and many countries of Europe, she can not indulge her ferocious spirit, or even openly avow her principles; but is forced quietness any evidence of a change of principle? Do you not know that opinions are often cherished which can not be defended, and that a wicked spirit often rages the more intensely because it can not give vent to its fury? I assure you that even among ourselves the heart of an inquisitor lies concealed under the long coat of many an imported priest; and that, should circumstances permit, we would have our Dominics and Torquemadas in New York as in Rome, in Baltimore as in Seville, and on the banks of the Ohio and Mississippi as on the banks of the Tagus or the Duero. Because burning stones are not shooting upward from its summit, and rivers of burning lava are not flowing down its sides, we must not conclude that the internal fires of old Vesuvius are extinguished.

The vengeful and persecuting spirit which Rome has exhibited is characteristic, and is founded on her principles. This spirit has received the sanction of Popes and councils, and is therefore among the things upon which the Church has pronounced its infallible decisions. If Pius IX. pronounces against persecution, what becomes of the infallibility of Lucius III., who issued a bull authorizing it and exhorting to it? If a council should now pronounce against persecution, what becomes of the infallibility of the famous Lateran Council of 1215, or of the Council of Trent, or of the many other councils that sanctioned it? Indeed, the priest that would assert that Romanism has changed her principles on the subject of persecution, would be sent by his bishop to Jericho until his beard or his brains grew.

This spirit of persecution is taught in the Canon Law of the Church, which is made up of the decrees of councils, the bulls and decretals of Popes, and the writings of the Fathers—a law under which every Papist is placed, and which the officers of the Church are bound to administer. And this law, as you must know, is based on the assumption that the Pope's authority extends over all nominal Christians, and that none of us, by any dissent, can place ourselves beyond his jurisdiction, or beyond the reach of this law! So that all of us who call ourselves Christians, and who submit not to the Pope, are to be dealt with as heretics, and in the way and fashion which this law prescribes! And as bishops are the chief police-officers of the Pope for enforcing the Canon Law, and for inflicting its pains and penalties, before they receive the mitre or the pallium, made from the wool of holy sheep, they are obliged to swear as follows: "Heretics, schismatics, or rebels against our lord the Pope, or his successors, I will persecute and fight against to the utmost of my power." And lest an oath should be disregarded, it is provided, "that if a bishop shall have been negligent or remiss in purging his diocese of heretical pravity, as soon as this is made apparent by sure evidence, he shall be deposed from his episcopal office, and in his place shall be substituted a fit person who will and can confound the heretical pravity." The effects of this oath, and of this threat to keep up its remembrance, the world knows. Bishops have been the butchers of heretics—that is, of Protestant Christians. To prove their fidelity to their oath, and to retain their mitre upon their brow, they have in cruelty out-Heroded Herod, and out-Neroed Nero. They have stained all their garments in blood, and have pronounced the benedictions of Heaven upon men who have shed the blood of their fellow-men, and for no earthly reason but their rejection of the frivolous, and contemptible, and unreasonable dogmas of the priest.

To this oath, taken by bishops when receiving their badges of office from their lord and master, some attention has been recently excited in England. Cardinal Wiseman has been catechized in reference to it; and although the policy of bishops is to answer no questions, yet he was so questioned as to compel a reply. And what, think you, was his reply? He did not deny the taking of such an oath, for the oath itself could be produced; but he asserted that, when administered to British bishops, the above clause was omitted! The veracity of Nicholas of Westminster on this point has been called in question by some, but with that you and I have little to do. If the fact is as he states, it is a full admission that the clause is in the oath. And, if possible, I should like you to find out whether the grace extended to England by the Holy Apostolic See has also been extended to us in this heretical land; whether slippery John of New York, and the "Very Rev. P. R. Kenrick, V. G.," author of the wonderfully erudite book, "The Holy House of Loretto," were so kind toward us as to ask to have that clause omitted when they renounced their manhood, and swore allegiance to the despotism of Rome. Is the oath upon their souls "to persecute and fight against us to the utmost of their power?" I firmly believe it is.

So that Rome persecutes on principle, and swears all her bishops "to persecute all heretics to the utmost of their power;" and when she renounces the principles of persecution, she ceases to be an infallible Church. To sustain her character, she is bound to persecute whenever and wherever she can. To amend or reform her principles will be her death, and without benefit of clergy. How fearful the position in which her infallibility places her; her only alternative is death or intolerance, and the dilemma of her bishops is perjury or persecution. Horrible system!

And what a mass of testimony does the history of the world furnish to prove her fidelity to her principles, and the sleepless perseverance of her bishops in "persecuting and fighting against heretics, schismatics, and rebels against our lord the Pope!" She has set up a system of belief not merely differing from, but in opposition to that of the Scriptures, and has imposed it on the world as of divine authority. While she has forbidden the Bible to the people, she commands subjection to her own system, which the vast majority of men can not comprehend. Without their consent, she has subjected to her authority all living within the shadow of her sceptre, and has subjected to the severest penalties all who refuse her obedience. Romish persecution of those who could not receive as doctrines of God her awful assumptions and silly ceremonials, have been the most bloody and savage which the world has ever witnessed. And where, in proof of this, shall we commence our historic evidence?

Shall we begin with the Waldenses? The history of this people lies before me. Cooped up in secluded valleys, at the foot of the Alps, they are supposed to be the descendants of Christians who sought refuge from the barbarian hordes that ravaged Italy during the decline of the Roman empire. They were a people simple, industrious, pious, scriptural in their faith and worship, and most unoffending in their conduct to all men. In two things they were as immovable as the Alps: they would not give up their Bibles, nor acknowledge the claims of the Pope. These were their only offenses, and for these they were declared heretics, and the bloodhounds of Rome, the bishops and inquisitors, were let loose on them. Two vagabond and brutal monks were sent from Rome to see that justice was meted out to the heretics. They deposed the kind bishops of the district for permitting the heresy, and substituted wolves in their place. Castelnau, a man of cruel heart, was sent as legate. Raymond of Toulouse was excommunicated because he refused to join in the bloody crusade, but was made finally to consent by the cruel treatment of the Pope and Castelnau. About three hundred thousand men were let loose upon this people, to punish them for the sin of worshiping God as did their fathers and the apostles. The first outburst of their fury was on the town of Bezières, containing about sixty thousand persons. The legate gave up the people to slaughter, and the town to pillage and flames. "But how," said an officer, "can we distinguish the Catholic from the heretic?" And what was the reply of the atrocious legate, Castelnau? It is known, to the confusion of Rome, in all the earth: "*Kill all; the Lord will know his own.*" And every being was slain, and the town was consumed by fire!

And this was only the beginning of sorrows. For nearly fifty years was this carnage continued. Battle followed battle—city was burned after city—valley was entered after valley, until the rugged yet fair heritage of this pious and simple people was converted into a howling wilderness—until a million of their number, under the sabre and tread of the minions of Popery, were made to bite the dust! After reciting a list of barbarities, Morland, the high-minded envoy of Cromwell to Turin, thus addressed the Duke of Savoy: "What need I mention more, though I could reckon up very many cruelties of the same kind, if I were not astonished at the very thought of them. If all the tyrants of all times and ages were alive again, they would be ashamed when they should find that they had contrived nothing in comparison with these things that might be reputed barbarous and inhuman. Heaven itself seems astonished with the crimes of dying men, and the very earth to blush, being discolored with the gore-blood of so many innocent persons." And all the guilt of this enormous barbarity lies on the soul of the Papal Church. O, Sir, if you have never read, do read the history of the Waldenses. It has more than the interest of fiction, and is a fearful argument against Popery.

Shall we next consider the Massacre of St. Bartholomew, in France, and the Revocation of the Edict of Nantes? Every thing had been arranged by the perfidious Catharine and her son Charles IX. for the slaughter of the Huguenots. A royal marriage was arranged for the purpose of collecting in Paris the chief Protestant nobility of the kingdom. Coligny lay in his chamber, wounded by the hired assassin of the court; Mauravel, surrounded by his friends—the houses of the Protestants were all marked—the badges of the murderers were all arranged—the houses of Papists were supplied with torches—arms were supplied to the assassins, and at midnight the alarm-bell was rung from St. Germain. At the concerted signal, the Palais, the Tuileries, the banks of the Seine, the public places, the streets, the large edifices, sacred and profane, became illuminated as if by magic. In almost every window there was a blazing torch. And this sudden blaze was to illumine the path of the murderers to the houses of their victims. The noble and wounded Coligny, and up to his death caressed and flattered by the queen-mother and her son, was the first victim. He fell under the sabres and daggers of Besme, Petrucci, and Sarlabous. Tired of waiting the result, Henry of Guise called from below, "Besme, have you done?" "It is done," was the reply; and then, taking the dead body, they threw it out of the window, that Henry might judge for himself. The shouts of the murderers urging each other to blood, and the wailings of men, women, and children, as they were falling beneath their blows, were heard in every street and lane of Paris. The bright sun of the 24th of August, 1572, revealed the city converted into a vast slaughter-house. The massacre continued seven days in Paris. From the capital it extended to the provinces; nor for two months was the murderous sword returned to the scabbard; nor until, according to Sully, seventy thousand, or, according to Péréfixe, one hundred thousand Protestants were slain. And how were the tidings of this bloody sacrifice to the Moloch of Popery, which spread consternation through the world, received at Rome? With thanksgivings to Heaven, and with the roaring of cannon from its walls. A *Te Deum* was sung, at which the Pope and his court attended; a medal was struck to commemorate the event; and a picture of the massacre was added to the embellishments of the Vatican, to commemorate to all ages the triumph of the Church over her enemies! Upon that picture, Sir, I have gazed with mine own eyes in the ante-room of the Sistine; and if Rome has changed her principles on persecution, why permit that picture to perpetuate her shame?

The Massacre of St. Bartholomew was followed by fearful civil wars, in which it is supposed that one million of men were slain. These were brought to a close by the Edict of Nantes, published by Henry IV. in 1598, and which secured to the Protestants the free exercise of their religion. But Henry was murdered; and his illustrious minister, Sully, was exchanged for the priest, Richelieu. The Jesuits got the ear of Louis XIV., and soon clouds of portentous aspect were seen rapidly collecting over the Huguenots. They were removed from office. Their churches were torn down. They were prevented from assembling for worship. Their children were torn from them at seven years of age by the priests, to be educated as Papists. These cruelties drove them to despair. They emigrated in great numbers. Soon they were prevented from leaving the country; their ministers were executed; booted and spurred missionaries were every where among the people; the sick, who recovered after refusing the sacraments of Romanism, if men, were sent to the galleys, and if women, to perpetual imprisonment and to penances; and if they died without submission to the Church, their dead bodies were to be drawn on a hurdle and cast upon a dung-heap! These awful severities soon reduced the Huguenots to the verge of total extinction; and from beginning to end they were instigated, and in great part inflicted by Romish priests. In the funeral oration of Flechier for Le Tellier the Jesuit, he ascribes to him the high honor of being the author of that "work of God," the Revocation of the Edict of Nantes, and of the bloody cruelties that followed!

Shall we next consider the Irish St. Bartholomew of 1641? The chapter is a bloody one. Fired by their priests, and by the Popish gentry whose property had been confiscated during preceding disturbances, a plan was concerted, to which the perfidious Charles was no stranger, to cut off the Protestants of the island. A chief actor in the bloody tragedy was Ever M'Mahon, Romish bishop of Down, who was true to his oath "to persecute and fight against heretics to the utmost of his power." Bad as was that of France, the Irish Bartholomew was worse. I shudder while I quote from histories before me some of the narratives connected with this tragedy. On the Sabbath before the commencement of the massacre, the priests gave the wafer to the people, and sent them out with an exhortation to kill the Protestants, and to seize their property, as a certain preservative against the pains of Purgatory! A company of nearly one hundred, men, women, and children, were driven upon the ice on Lough Erne; having pushed them as far as they could go in safety, they flung the infants, torn from their mothers' arms, toward the point where the ice was weakest, and, in seeking to rescue them, all perished save two. Women were stripped naked, and sent into the woods—to perish.

Many were sportfully drowned; many hung; many stabbed to death; many boiled and roasted; many were hewn to pieces; many had their bellies ripped up, and their bowels torn out; many were driven into houses, and were burned in them; many were torn to pieces with dogs; and in some cases, one end of the intestines was tied to a tree, and the person was driven round the tree until his bowels were all torn out! The account of the numbers who thus cruelly perished varies; but some judicious historians say that it could not be less than 200,000. Of this awful massacre, Sir William Jones says, "If we look into the sufferings of the first Christians under the cruel tyranny of the heathen emperors, we shall not find any one kingdom, though of a far larger extent than Ireland, where more Christians suffered, or more unparalleled cruelties were acted within the space of the first two months after the breaking out of this rebellion." Eastern barbarians never inflicted upon the most base wretches such execrable cruelty. And all the blood there shed lies upon the soul, if soul it has, of the Papal Church.

But, Sir, the time would fail me, as would your patience and that of my readers, to give, in testimony, the persecutions of Italy, of Spain, of Poland, of Austria, of Bavaria; or, coming down to our own times, of Zillerthal, of Madeira; or, coming down to our own day, of Florence, of Naples, of France, of Ireland. The principles of Popery are unchanged, and so is her conduct where she can wisely carry out her principles. Did she not put up the Inquisition as a slaughter-house for heretics, and is not the Inquisition vindicated in a work dedicated to yourself, and does not the Papal Church now send the whole Protestant world to perdition? And what better is this than making a great *auto da fé*—piling up the dry stubble as mountains, binding millions of Protestants upon the pile, and then commanding the God of heaven to apply the torch, and consume them all! Why, Sir, the cruelties of the French or of the Irish St. Bartholomew are mercy when compared to this! It is the very sublime of the horrible!

I would not be guilty of the unfairness of making the children accountable for the sins of their fathers when they reject their principles and abandon their practices; but when they hold their principles, and excuse their practices, and walk in their footsteps where and when they can, then there is no letting of them off. The most barbarous cruelty on record is that perpetrated in the name of God, and under the sanction of religion. Has Rome changed her principles? She can not. Have bishops and priests changed theirs? They dare not. See how, in Rome, Naples, Austria, they fetter the press. See how, in Ireland, they oppose the Bible and the education of the people. See how, in France, they sympathize with Louis Napoleon to shackle the press, to drive Protestants from all places of trust, and to monopolize the education of the people. See how, in Mexico and Cuba, they wall out all liberty of conscience, and prevent freedom of worship. With us, Sir, they are shy of avowing their principles. Here every thing is against them; but where they have the power, they are as intolerant as was Hildebrand. These priests from Maynooth and St. Omer's carry, in the same bag with their vestments, two skins, that of a lion and a fox. For the present, like slippery John, they wear that of the fox; but when the fit time comes, it will be soon doffed for that of the lion. Are these priests the men for our country? Should they be trusted?

With great respect, yours.

LETTER XXIV.

Bad influence of Popery on the Nations.—Results from its Principles.—No exceptions.—Naples.—Rome.—Sardinia.—Female Degradation.—Ireland.—Protestant and Papal States compared.—Spain.—Colonies of Papal States.—Is Popery the best Religion for our Country?—Protestantism has made the United States what they are.—What will they become if surrendered to the Jesuit and the Priest?

My dear Sir,—Up to this point I have sought to place before you what I consider to be the true character of the Romish Church, of its priests, its ceremonies, its impostures, and spirit. And my object in all this is avowed—to demonstrate to you, and to the entire American people, so far as I can arrest their attention, that nothing but evil—unmingled evil—can be expected from the spread of Popery in this land. Whatever may be its guises, or promises, or honeyed words, it has but one object in view, and that is its own elevation, and at whatever expense. And wherever it has reached its desired elevation, it has shed the deadly shadow of the upas tree upon all the highest and dearest interests of humanity. And as confirmatory of the statements already made, and of the just inferences from those statements, I wish, in the present letter, to ask your attention to the influence of Popery on Papal nations. Unless I greatly mistake, you will find here an argument of overwhelming power for its rejection.

Its baleful national influence we might infer from its principles, and from their bearing upon individuals. It banishes the Bible from society. The Church does all the thinking; the people have only to believe. It brands "private reasoning" as heresy, and, unless abandoned, as a damning sin. God is the source of truth; but he has committed it to his Church, and the Church has committed it to the priest, and the people must go to the priest for it, and unless they do, they are damned! Thus it brings every person to the knee of the priest, to receive, as the truth of Heaven, whatever sense or nonsense he may utter in the name of the Church, without any right to question it, and without any means to authenticate it! It subjects the people to the priest, the priest to the bishop, the bishop to the Pope, and it makes no matter what may be the character of the Pope—whether he be a tyrant, like Hildebrand—a bloody wretch, like Julius—an infidel, like Leo—or the very pink of lechers and incarnate devils, with Borgia—he is the vicar of Jesus Christ, and the infallible head of the Church! The course, from which it has never turned aside, save to recruit its strength, is to involve the people in darkness; to create and to increase a superstitious reverence for the ghostly power of the Church; to render the masses subservient to the priest; and to bring all the powers of the individual and of the state into obedience to the power which she claims to exercise by divine right. And as Popery rises to the heights of its aspirations, the people sink into darkness and degradation. If there is an exception to this rule, where is it to be found?

Is it to be found in Naples? Would that I could

place before your mind the moral picture of Naples, as it now lies before my own. There Popery has all things to its mind. The king, the queen, the government, the people, the press, the army, the navy, all the appliances of education, are under its control. And never did you see a peacock flirting its gaudy feathers on a summer's day with more ostentatious pride than do the priests of Rome their regimentals along the sunny highways of Naples. Their very tread shows their consciousness of the firmness of the ground on which they stand, and their air testifies to their feeling of security. You meet them every where in numbers beyond number, fat, sleek, and well dressed, and testifying by their hearty laugh, their lordly port, their satisfied look, that they are at home. And if for priests there is an earthly paradise, it is Naples. Rome is nothing to it in this respect. But when you turn to the people, alas! what a sight! Poverty, wretchedness, rags, lazzaroni, beggars, soldiers, mountebanks, and donkeys, meet you every where. The masses of the people are ignorant, superstitious, and immoral beyond your conception. And as you pass from the cities and large towns through the country, the most astounding evidences meet you every where, that you are among a semi-barbarous, superstitious, illiterate, and most degraded people. And the despotism of Russia, or of Turkey, is American liberty in comparison with the horrid despotism of Naples! If Popery, as a system, is a blessing, as the "Very Rev. P. R. Kenrick, V. G.," would have us believe, judging from Naples, it reserves its blessings for the priests, and showers its curses on the people. Popery, like the sun in midheaven, has all Naples to itself; and intolerable despotism, abject poverty, stupid ignorance, gross superstition, and priestly arrogance, are the gifts and blessings which she confers on the people. Apply the rule where you may, and you will find that Popery and poverty, priests and beggars, always go together.

Is the exception to be found in Rome, or the States of the Church? Will you turn to my seventeenth and eighteenth letters, and read them again, with a view to answer this question? We read here at home of "old Romans," "brave," "noble," "generous Romans;" our conceptions of them are large, generous, and manly. Their generals are Cæsars; their patriots are all Cincinnati; their soldiers are all like those of the seventh legion; and their women are all Cornelias or Julias. But on entering Rome, or in riding through the States of the Church, these dreams all vanish, not leaving a wreck behind. And you can scarcely imagine that the ignorant, servile, poverty-smitten, deceiving, lying, superstitious people that you every where meet, can be the descendants of the men who planted the eagles of victory at the extremes of the world. Indeed, I felt like turning my valet out of my room when, on paying him his wages, he bowed his knee servilely before me, and impressed his kisses on my hand. Can this fawning dog, said I, be a descendant of the old Romans? Next to the Neapolitans, the subjects of the Pope are the most degraded people in Europe; and why the Neapolitans should have the pre-eminence in degradation, I know not, save on the principle that the filth and feculence of a mountain are usually washed to its base, whence they send up their putrid exhalations. If the Popish system is a blessing, what prevents it from bearing the richest fruits in Italy? And what are its fruits there at this hour? Swarms of priests, monks, nuns, and beggars; poverty, ignorance, superstition; the press shackled; no liberty, civil or religious; no security of property; no Bible; no Sabbath; splendid churches converted into opera-houses, with no congregations; and lying wonders without number or end.

Is the exception to be found in Sardinia? You feel, on entering Sardinia, that you are beyond the shadow of the sceptre of Pio Nono, from the improved condition of the people, and the evidences of growth which every where present themselves; but yet you feel that you are in a Papal country, where Popery is the religion of the people, and where, save amid the valleys of Piedmont, Popery has had for ages an open field. And yet the degradation of the masses is most striking. They are tunneling the Appenines for a rail-way from Turin to Genoa, and, in June last, I saw an army of women performing the work of horses, carrying on their backs, in baskets, the stones and clay from those tunnels, and depositing them in the valleys, over which they are raising embankments. I saw women carrying limestones from the quarries to the kilns in which they were burned! This is a sample of the civilization which Popery has conferred on Sardinia. While there is an improvement upon Rome and Naples in this country, yet the fruits of Romanism are mainly the same. Unless the present current of affairs is checked by Rome and Austria, who are exerting all their power to do it, a better day is dawning upon the dominions of the house of Savoy. The exiles from Florence and Lower Italy, the persecuted for conscience sake, find refuge there. Because the liberty of thinking and of worship are secured there, Turin is rising like an American city. But the blessings it possesses beyond Rome or Naples it owes to the fact that its Popery is less intense.

Is the exception to be found in Ireland—poor, degraded, yet beautiful and noble Ireland? There you find a warm-hearted, generous, imaginative, impulsive, and noble people, and, as the world knows, capable of the highest improvement, and what is their state? Go to their holy wells and holy places—to their fairs, their villages, their cabins, and what is their state? Visit them wherever in other lands they congregate, as in the Cowgate at Edinburgh, and what is their state? See them, as in their native dress they are landed on our shores, and follow them to their places of carousal, and what is their state? The Papal population of Ireland are greater Papists than the Pope himself, and are more under priestly influence than the people of Rome —far more—and what good has Popery done them or their island? The curse of Ireland has been, and now is, its Popery. Its lands are fertile—its climate is genial—its people are industrious; but the influence of the priest, like the breath of the sirocco, has blighted the land—has debased its people—has made them a by-word in all the lands of their dispersion.

The battle between Popery and Protestantism, as to their doctrinal basis, has been often fought; and, when fairly fought, has been always lost by the priest. Nor can it be otherwise. If the Bible is true, Popery is a false system—and, unless the senses of man are made to deceive, it is a system of lying wonders. If there is any moral position on which the mind of this age is satisfied, it is that Popery is the mystery of iniquity. And now, for three hundred years, these two systems have existed side by side; and, as if on trial before heaven and earth, they have each been exerting their influence for the purpose of manifesting their legitimate effects. And what, Sir, are the results? What is the effect of each on human liberty. Compare Naples, Rome, and Austria, with England, Prussia, and these United States, and see! What, upon commerce? Compare Spain, Portugal, and Austria, with Britain, and see! What, upon intelligence? Blot out the Papal nations, and what is lost to the intelligent world? A few stars only would be missed from the sky. Blot out the Protestant nations; and the effect would be like the sun setting at noon-day. Even the "Very Rev. P. R. Kenrick, V. G.," author of the "Holy House of Loretto," would feel that the darkness was increasing around him. What are their effects upon thrift and industry? Compare Ireland with Scotland, or Connaught with Ulster, or Cork with Belfast, and see! What, upon morals? Compare Italy with Scotland, France with England, and see! The facts in the case are very plain, and beyond mistake by an honest inquirer. Protestantism educates the mind, frees the spirit, extends the circle of thought and action, expands the affections, stimulates to independence, puts the Bible into the hands of all men, and teaches them to fear God, and to fear none else. Hence its effects, every where visible, on the people and nations that embrace it. On the other hand, Popery seals to man the

Book which the Lamb died to unseal, shackles the spirit, forbids reasoning on religious truths, shuts up the affections to its own adherents, and seeks only the extension of its power and the submission of the people. The high noon of its prosperity was the period known as the "Dark Ages;" and it seeks now to put all things on the back track for those ages. It has no Sabbath —no Bible—no preaching—nothing, nothing to elevate —nothing but a silly round of ceremonies as unmeaning as they are absurd. Hence, as Wylie says in his recent excellent work on the Papacy, "Wherever we meet Popery, there we meet moral degradation, mental imbecility, indolence, improvidence, rags, and beggary. No ameliorations of government—no genius or peculiarities of race—no fertility of soil—no advantages of climate, seem able to withstand the baleful influence of this destructive superstition. It is the same amid the exhaustless resources of the New World as amid the civilization and arts of the old—it is the same amid the grandeurs of Switzerland and the historic glories of Italy, as among the bogs of Connaught and the wilds of the Hebrides." And the testimony of Macaulay, in his eloquent History of England, is to the same effect: "Throughout Christendom," he says, "whatever advance has been made in knowledge, in freedom, in wealth, in the arts of life, has been made in spite of the Church of Rome, and has every where been in the inverse proportion to her power. The loveliest provinces in Europe have, under her rule, been sunk in poverty, in political servitude, and in intellectual torpor; while Protestant countries, once proverbial for their sterility and barbarism, have been turned, by skill and industry, into gardens, and can boast of a long list of heroes, statesmen, philosophers, and poets." Again, he says, "Whoever passes, in Germany, from a Roman Catholic to a Protestant principality—in Switzerland, from a Roman Catholic to a Protestant canton—in Ireland, from a Roman Catholic to a Protestant county, finds that he passes from a lower to a higher grade of civilization."

A few months ago I was enabled to verify this picture of the eloquent and philosophic historian. I passed from Genoa to Turin, and from Turin to Geneva through Chambery. About three or four miles from Geneva, you pass through a gate, leaving Sardinia behind you. In five minutes you are persuaded, by the style of building, the appearance of thrift, the evidences of taste, of wealth, of intelligence, by the altered appearance of the people, the tillage, the mode of dress, that you are in a Protestant country. After spending a few days in Geneva, I passed through Bonville and Sallanche to Chamouni. A few miles from Geneva, you pass through another gate, and enter the kingdom of Sardinia; and the exchange of decent houses for huts—of neatly-dressed people for rags—of a self-sustaining people for beggars — and the appearance of crosses, priests, and pictures of the Virgin, soon convince you that you are within the dominions of Popery. And so it is every where.

But if you wish to see at a view the gigantic national wreck which Popery can make, look at Spain. Washed by two seas, with splendid harbors—penetrated by noble rivers—with fertile plains extending from the Pyrenees to the Straits of Gibraltar—with a climate proverbially genial, and a soil proverbially productive—with the key of the Mediterranean by her girdle, and thus with power to command the trade of all Western Asia and Southern Europe, she holds a position on Europe's map which should make her its great power. And she was so once. Under the Moorish kings, Spain was the garden of Europe. And why are her harbors without ships—why her mines unwrought—why her national poverty—why her featherweight influence among the nations—why her little exports—her decaying cities—her internal feuds—why has she fallen from a position once so high to one now so low? The history of the infernal Inquisition, of the bloody bigotry of her bishops and priests, and of the superstition of her kings and queens, will answer these questions. Popery has ruined Spain, and sown all its fields with salt.

And the national ruin that Popery achieves at home, she propagates abroad. Where have Spain or Portugal planted a colony that has not manifested in its development the evils of Popery? Not in Mexico—not in Brazil—not in Chili or Peru—not in India, nor on the islands of the Pacific. If you wish to see, and within the reach of your own eye, the different effect of the two systems upon national prosperity, compare Papal Mexico, with its genial climate, its rich lands, its mines of gold, with New England, with its sterile soil, its cold climate, and barren hills. Sir, the striking difference, and under circumstances so favorable to Mexico, can only be charged to the difference in religion which has obtained among the people. And this parallelism holds equally true, whether applied to nations, states, cantons, counties, cities, commerce, intelligence, morals, habits, or individuals.

Now, Sir, in view of all this, whose substantial truth you, at least, will not question, permit me to urge upon you the inquiry, Is Popery the best form of religion for our country? If it is the best form for one, it is the best for every citizen; and would it be for the future glory and happiness of this country for us all to give in our allegiance to Pius IX.—to give up our Bibles—to give up preaching for the Mass—and Christ for Mary—and the only Mediator for an army of saints and nuns—and all our religious books for Butler's Lives of the Saints—and the history of Jesus for the devout perusal of the "Holy House of Loretto," by the "Very Rev. P. R. Kenrick, V. G."—and for all of us to come to the conclusion that the claims of our long-coated priests are all right, and to submit to them? I am sure that you, even you, to whom was dedicated a work containing a vindication of the infernal Inquisition, would go against all this with a vengeance. You love your country, and its institutions, and its future glory too ardently to place it under the care of the Jesuit and the priest, and thus to make it a mere tributary to the rickety despotism of Rome, which is only kept in existence by French bayonets.

But what would work evil to the mass can not be good for the individual; and the question returns, Is Popery the best form of religion for the individual? There is but one answer to the question; it admits of but one. It is by debasing individuals it debases the masses, and lays its ax at the root of all national greatness. There is not a living person that is not the worse for being a Papist; nor can a man or woman embrace it without mental and moral injury.

Protestantism, Sir, has made our land what it is. It originally colonized these states—it laid the mental and moral training of our people at the foundation of our institutions—it put up our school-houses and colleges—it nerved the hearts of our sires to resist the encroachments of power—it fought and won the battles of our independence—it has made us an enterprising, law-abiding, and industrious people—it has founded our governments—framed our laws—given integrity to our judges—and has made this the home of the exile from all lands. It has built our cities—whitened the ocean with our canvas, and has sent our ships to every bay, yes, to every creek of the ocean. It has extended loyalty, and thrift, and enterprise, and wealth, and security, and happiness from shore to shore—from the Atlantic to the Pacific, where the west is lost in the rising east. Nor can you or I indulge any vivid hopes for our country, save in its Christianized, that is to say, spiritually-Protestantized futurity. Let the Pope and the priest reign here as they do in Naples, Austria, and Rome, and then New York will be as Naples, and Baltimore as Rome, and our great and growing country like unto the empire of the house of Hapsburg, the Sleepy Hollow of the world; and our active, industrious, and thriving people, as lazy, as poor, as stupid, and as vicious as are our neighbors of Mexico, or as wicked and avaricious priests can make them. When the priest gains the ascendent here, the last rays of the sun of our glory are dying away on the summit of our Rocky Mountains.

L

What, then, you will ask, is to be done with the Papists and priests that are rained down upon us from the old nations of Europe? This question I will answer in my next.

With great respect, truly yours.

LETTER XXV.

Emigration—must increase—mostly Popish.—What to be done for them —Liberty—Conscience—American Spirit.—Tide stayed until now. —Right of all Men to the Bible—Wickedness of withholding it.— Differences between Protestantism and Popery.—Edinburgh Irish Missions.—Rev. Mr. King.—Character of Priests.—Pilgrim of Struel. —Treatment Priests deserve.

My dear Sir,—There is, as all the world knows, a vast influx of emigrants from all the states of Europe to our shores. Upon the wharves of all our great commercial cities you see the garb, and you hear the tongue peculiar to all the nations and people extending from the North Cape to the Island of Sicily, and from the Black Sea to the western shores of Ireland. And yet they come. They are penetrating our interior—they are to be found in the city, in the town, on the prairie, in the woods, in the shop of the mechanic, breaking up a virgin soil into which a plowshare has never entered, and carrying with them their language, their customs, their morals, and their religion, to the foot of the Rocky Mountains, and from both the oceans that now bound our great country. And there is a buzzing stir amid the old nations of Europe, like unto that which may be heard in a bee-hive previous to its swarming, which clearly indicates that what of emigration we yet have seen here is but as the few ripe grapes when compared with the overflowing vintage, or but as the little rise in our great rivers, caused by a few summer showers, when compared with our spring freshets, caused by the dissolving of our snows upon our extended mountain ranges. The masses of Europe are tenants, and they are beginning to feel the oppression of their landlords, and that from it there is no way of escape save by revolution or by emigration; and as the chances of revolution are at present against them, they prefer to emigrate. "Our gentry," said a noble Scotch clergyman to me, "are beginning to think more of sheep than of men, and are sending off their tenants to make room for their sheep and black cattle. Our people must go to America." "You will not find a healthy person any where that is not thinking of going to America," said the guard of a stage-coach to me, as I was riding through Ireland. Soon we came to a stopping-place. A fine, rosy-cheeked girl, with health in all her movements, came with a message to the guard; and determined to put his saying to the test, I said to her, "My fine girl, do you think of going to America?" "I am going next month, your honor," said she, her face radiant with smiles. The people of Europe are waking up to a sense of their wrongs; and the more they manifest that they see and feel them, the more oppressive are their civil and ecclesiastical rulers; so that, in the nature of things, great as the emigration now is here, it must be vastly increased.

And as the majority of emigrants for some years past have been Papists, so it must continue to be. The Papal nations are the poorest, the worst governed, and the most oppressed; and the Papists of Protestant nations, as of Britain, Prussia, and some of the minor states of Germany, are the least thrifty, and are those to whom a change of country would seem to offer the most inducements. So that for years to come there must be a vast yearly accession to our population of those educated under Popish institutions, and, of course, of Popish priests. And if Popery and its priests are what I have described them to be—if Popery in all lands, and to the extent to which it obtains, is a national curse, the question with which I closed my last letter is a very grave one, "What is to be done with these Papists and priests?" Will you permit me to indicate what I consider the true answer to the question?

Not a feeling must be indulged or manifested other than that of permitting them to enjoy, to the utmost extent of our institutions, a free and full liberty of conscience. Ignorant, superstitious, and semi-civilized as they may be, when naturalized they are citizens. Our Constitution knows neither Jew nor Gentile, Papist nor Protestant. All good citizens it treats as does a kind father his children. Nor must we show any jealousy of placing a fitting man in a place of trust or power simply because he is a Papist. I rejoice, Sir, that you, a nominal Papist, are at the head of the judiciary of this great country, and that you were placed there by a thorough Protestant, who hated the Pope far more, I fear, than he hated sin, because of the advantage it gives us, if, for no other reason, of contrasting the two systems. Think you that a Protestant, if pure as Marshall, if learned as Blackstone, if eloquent as Webster, could be made chief justice of Cuba, or Mexico, or Naples, or even Belgium? Would not the taint of Protestantism countervail all other qualifications, and tend rather to secure his expulsion than his elevation?

And then we must teach them the rights of conscience, and to respect those rights—that God is the only lord of conscience. It is hard to learn them this, when their very conscience has been educated into the opposite belief, that the Church and the priest give laws to conscience, and that we are bound to persecute those who refuse compliance to those laws. It is a great lesson for us to teach, and for them to learn; and when truly learned by them, the power of the priest is gone. If you, Sir, are conscientiously a Papist, I am conscientiously a Protestant, and to our God we are only accountable. Within the domain of conscience no Pope, prelate, or priest has a right to place his foot; and the intruder within that sacred inclosure should be as unceremoniously expelled as were apostate angels from heaven, who were driven pell-mell over its battlements, and cast down into everlasting chains and penal fire. The supremacy of conscience and the supremacy of the Pope are in the opposite scales; as the one rises, the other sinks. The man who enthrones God in his conscience is lost to the priest. He has no longer any use for confessions, penances, or extreme unctions—for holy water or holy chrism. He is a subject of the perfect law of liberty. We must then teach them to assert their own rights of conscience, and to respect those of others. Then the priest will have lost all power to foment the people to such riots as have occurred in New York, St. Louis, and Milwaukie, and which have so clearly demonstrated that a change of country or climate does not soon change the nature of the hyena

We must also seek to imbue them with the true spirit of our country. It is among the greatest of the many blessings of Heaven to our land that our present tide of emigration was held back until our people became sufficiently numerous, and our institutions sufficiently established, to be unaffected by it—until our people acquired a character of their own, and power to impress it upon those who seek here an asylum for themselves and their posterity. Had our present emigration taken place one hundred years ago, it would be substantially a transference here of Ireland and Germany, and of the other European nations, with their language, and religion, and social institutions. But now it affects us but little more than do the fresh waters of the Hudson, the Susquehanna, or the Mississippi, the salt water of the ocean. Indeed, as the Atlantic takes these and other rivers into its bosom, and assimilates all their turbid waters to itself, imparting to them all its color, and salting them with its salt, so may our country receive into her arms the multitudes fleeing to her for refuge from the despotisms of the old world, and mold them all into the American form. Nothing here lives by divine right, but the true. We permit men to swagger as they see fit, and to put forth what claims they please; but the moment they attempt to enforce claims by divine right, they soon learn their latitude and longitude. When priests claim to think for us, we only think the harder. The more they seek to induce us to sing hosannas to the Pope, the louder we proclaim him to be the anti-Christ. The more they oppose the Bible, the more we print, circulate, and read it. And the more they circulate such books as "The

Garden of the Soul," "Butler's Lives of the Saints," and "The Holy House of Loretto," by the erudite and philosophic P. R. Kenrick, V.G., to revive the drooping faith of their flocks, the more we claim and exercise the privilege of laughing at them from one end of the land to the other.

The fact is, that we, Sir, have a character peculiarly our own. Our fathers taught us to think for ourselves; and this spirit is fostered by all our institutions. The prevalence of education makes the masses intelligent; and before our general intelligence, and the Protestant atmosphere that covers the land, ignorance and credulity are fast disappearing. Indeed, the tendency is less to faith than to infidelity. Nothing is now taken for granted, however venerable for years, or however intrenched behind authority, without examination. Whether right or wrong, this is the American peculiarity. And if we only rightly and truly impress it upon the emigrants swarming here from other lands, it will be the death of Popery. The Irish, English, French, Scotch, Germans, Italians, Hollanders come here, not to propagate their national characteristics, but, like different ingredients thrown together, each yielding, in a chemical process, their peculiarities, and all uniting to form a new substance. The British emigrant gives up his queen—the French his king, president, prince-president, or consul—the German his king or emperor—and why should the Papist cling to the Pope? Why should he fling from his body the chains of civil despotism, and hug the chains of spiritual despotism, which are eating into his soul? Why should he not seek a spiritual as well as civil emancipation? He is here beyond the reach of the arm of despotism; and, imbibing the true American spirit, he should think, and read, and act for himself. The men that wear the fillets made from the wool of holy sheep, and their priests, may rage, but their rage, like the thunders that are sometimes heard in the distance of a fine morning, reminding us of the storms of the night, excites no terror. When the bear is within bars, he may rage until he is willing to stop.

And this American spirit is so contagious, that there are but few emigrants who are not in some measure affected by it. Even the priests feel it. However they may feel about it, they have to yield to it. "Why do you attend our worship and read our Bible?" said I to a Papist, on my outward voyage, who was going home to Ireland on a visit. "O, I have been some years in America," was his reply. He had caught the spirit of our country. And while the exceedingly illiterate, and those advanced in life, who emigrate here, may, with few exceptions, retain their Popish prejudices, and may be proof against the contagious spirit of our country, it will not be so with the young and intelligent, nor with their children. In the nature of things, it can not be so, as a rule. The son of an Irishman will neither wear his father's breeches nor brogues, nor will he kneel to his priest. The son of an Irishman, a Frenchman, or Italian is an American, and he will not be a Romanist. We have a mill, of which the common school is the nether, and the Bible and its institutions the upper stone; into this mill let us cast the people of all countries and forms of religion that come here, and they will come out in the grist Americans and Protestants. And the highest wisdom of our country is to keep this mill in vigorous operation.

We must also teach them that it is the inalienable right of every man to read the Bible. As prophets and apostles spoke "the words of this life" in the hearing of all that composed their audiences, and to the end that all should understand them, so their messages, when committed to writing and to the press, are for the perusal of all, and that all may understand them. And what right has the priest to obtrude himself, and to take from you the Bible, or to compel you to receive its teachings only as he interprets them? When a boy, and absent from home, had you not a right to take your father's letters from the post-office, and to read them, and to find out their meaning, without going to the priest? And is not God the father of us all—and is not the Bible his paternal counsel to us—and what right has the priest to take it from us? What if some parts are omitted that he deems inspired, why not permit you to read the rest? What if some passages are not translated to suit him? these are but few in comparison with those to which no objections are made. There is no excuse that can be made for the opposition of the priest to the Bible. If I could not get a copy of the Bible without having annexed to it the history of "The Holy House of Loretto," I would take it; if I could not get it save with the minor prophets omitted, I would yet take it. Protestant ministers are not afraid of their people reading the Douay Bible, and never burn it; and why should Popish priests wage so deadly a war, not only against the Protestant Bible, but against the unrestricted circulation and reading even of their own authorized versions? Their wickedness in all this must be exposed—their object, which is to keep their people in ignorance of their horrible deceptions, must be every where proclaimed. We must not compel any to read the Word of God, but we must see to it that none are prevented from reading it. We owe, Sir, to a free, unrestricted use of the Bible all we are, and all for which we may reasonably hope. And Bible-hating, Bible-burning priests are the men who, more than all others, are placing the ax at the root of the tree of our liberty, under whose branches we now so quietly and securely repose. When the Word of God is read by all our people, the craft of the priest is over—to use a figure of Luther, a big hole is made in the head of his drum. And, like unto the "Holy House of Loretto," when deserted in Dalmatia, he may take up his line of march for Italy.

We must also wake up the mind of our Papal population to discussions upon the great topics on which Popery and Protestantism differ. There is a kind of controversy which is greatly to be deplored—there is another kind which is greatly to be desired, and which is absolutely necessary as long as error exists to oppose the truth. There was once a feeling that inveterate drunkards were beyond reclamation; and there was a prevalent sentiment in the Protestant world that Papists were beyond the influence of truth, and the hope of conversion; but abundant facts prove both to be groundless. Many priests, and people in multitudes, have and are yearly deserting and denouncing Popery. I spent a part of two Sabbath evenings in the Irish Mission Chapel in Edinburgh, in which the Rev. Mr

M'Menomy, once a Papist, presides. It was crowded to an overflow with Protestants and Papists. Subjects were selected for discussion, and they were discussed freely on both sides. The Bible was the standard to which every thing was brought. I heard there shrewd Irish Papists, with remarkable dexterity, advocate the dogmas and customs of their Church; and the good results could be seen in the benches crowded with converts from Romanism, and in the multitudes inquiring whether the religion of the priest was or was not the religion of the Bible. I attended another meeting, where, in a more quiet way, M'Laughlin, "the miller of the glens of Antrim," who was cursed from the altar, is doing also a noble work among the Papists of Edinburgh. They meet and discuss the claims and doctrines of the priest; and the result could be seen in an upper room filled with plain, humble, but yet intelligent people, who were rescued from the wiles of "the man of sin," and who could give an intelligent reason for the hope that was in them. And it is in ways like these that priests, and the people by tens of thousands in Ireland, are passing over to the religion of the Bible. What the people need is light. Romanism has kept them in darkness, and has filled their minds with fables, prejudices, and monstrous superstitions; let the light of Heaven into these minds, and these fables, prejudices, and superstitions are seen in their true character, and are at once abandoned. Hence the awful dread of discussion—and of the Bible—and of good books—and even of common schools, by the priests, save where their own tools are the teachers. Nothing suffers by right discussion but error; and, as in Ireland, so here, all right means should be used to wake up the mind of our entire Papal population to an examination of the claims and doctrines of their Church, to the despotism of the priest, and to their duty to assert their Christian liberty in a land of freedom. One man like the eloquent and warm-hearted King, of Dublin, whose name will not soon be forgotten among us, would be of incalculable benefit to all our great cities. Familiar with the controversy, courteous in his demeanor, brilliant in debate, ready at repartee, full to an overflow of Irish humor, and with a heart catholic in its instincts, and under the guidance of the law of love, he is the terror of the priest and a favorite of the people. Copying the example of his magnificence of New York, Father Ignatius, a predestinated dolt, fled to Halifax before him; and the right reverends and the honorables, who head the Papal gatherings at the Rotunda, decline his invitations to fair discussion. And thus the eyes of multitudes are opening to a perception of the errors of Romanism, and to the wickedness of its priests.

And, above all, we must seek to place before the people the true character of their priests. What, Sir, was their character before the Reformation? What was it at the time of the Reformation, as drawn by Papal writers? To the last degree wicked. And what is it now in Rome? "Rome, in its priests and people, has not been, for a thousand years, such a sink of corruption as it is at this hour," said a gentleman to me in Rome, who has resided there for years, and who has had every opportunity to know it well. And if such is the character of her priests at the very seat of her power and her infallibility, what must be their character in her distant provinces? Better, I think, than in Rome, but yet bad. While I am far from saying that no Popish priests are pious or sincere, and would not limit the mercy of God, who sends his rain upon the just and the unjust, I am yet free to say that they awfully impose upon their people, and for no object but gain.

In addition to the testimony already adduced to support this opinion, permit me to state another, as narrated at length in Hardy's little volume on the "Holy Wells of Ireland." A gentleman found a young man performing *stations* at the Well of Struel, near Downpatrick, and held with him the following conversation:

"What is your name?

"John Lalley.

"Where are you from?

"The county of Galway.

"What induced you to come so far to do stations at this place?

"Last November, a spirit in the shape of a man appeared to me every night for three weeks, near the house in which I lived in the county of Galway; and one night I took courage and spoke to it, saying, 'In the name of the Father, Son, and Holy Ghost, do me no harm, nor any one belonging to me, and tell me what it is that troubles you.' The spirit then replied, 'I am glad you spoke, for this is the last night I would have appeared to you. I have been dead these nineteen years, and you were but three and a half old when I departed. Before my death I promised to do stations at Struel, but never performed my vow; and because I did not do them, I can not rest.'

"Did you inquire what was his name?

"Yes; his name was Paddy Brady.

"Where did he say he lived when he promised to do the stations?

"In the neighborhood of Downpatrick, near Struel.

"What was his calling when living?

"A carpenter.

"Where did he say his spirit had been for the last nineteen years?

"For the first five years he was up to his neck in water, under a bridge in this county; and for the last fourteen he has been in a sand-pit in the county Galway.

"Are you certain that no person ever attempted to impose upon you in this affair? Were you ever inclined to doubt about it?

"No, never; for the night he was going away, he took hold of my hand, and left a black mark on it, and went off in a flash of light.

"Have you been in a bad state of health lately?

"No.

"Have you felt your head very uneasy or in pain?

"Never in my life.

"Where do you believe the spirit is now?

"In Purgatory.

"And was he in Purgatory at the time he was under the bridge and in the sand-pit?

"Yes.

"Why did you not come sooner to do the stations?

"Because he told me that the proper time to do them would be from May to Midsummer.

"Have you ever spoke to your parish priest respecting this strange affair?

"Yes, I have.

"What did he advise you to do?

"He advised me to do the stations.

"What is your parish priest's name?

"Coyne.

"Has the Bishop of Galway ever heard of the matter?

"Mr. Coyne is the under-bishop of the diocese.

"Were there any masses said for the soul of this man after he died?

"Yes; his mother got two masses celebrated, for which she paid.

"And could not the masses get him out of Purgatory?

"The masses will hold good; and if he had not promised to do the stations, they would have fully answered.

"Have you seen the priest of this parish since you came?

"I have.

"Have you told him all about the matter?

"Yes.

"Did he say any thing against your doing these stations?

"Oh no.

"Did he say he would write to your priest about you?

"Yes.

"Has he done so?

" Not yet.

" Have you brought any letter from your parish priest to the priest of this parish ?

" No.

" How long have you been here ?

" To-morrow will be the tenth day.

" What time do you begin your stations ?

" About six o'clock in the morning, and I do six stations before I break my fast. I have not done until seven o'clock in the evening.

" I see you are taking a smoke ; do you never take a drink of water through the day ?

" No, neither bite or sup till the six stations are finished.

" Do you believe that you will get any benefit of your own soul in consequence of your doing these stations for the spirit you supposed you have seen ?

" Yes, I do ; for the spirit told me if I would do this for him, that he would do five hundred times as much for me when he would be happy.

" If you had not engaged to do these, what do you think would have been the consequence ?

" The spirit said that if I would not consent to do this for him now, he would have to remain in the *sand-pit fifty-five years longer.*

" Could he get no one but you to do the stations for him ?

" I was the person fixed on since I was three years and a half old.

" Have you made any agreement to see the spirit when you go back ?

" No ; for as soon as I am done he will be happy.

"Do you believe that he is now in pain?

"I bless my Lord that he is not now in pain, but he is in total darkness.

"Do you think that the Lord Jesus Christ could have saved him without either masses or the stations?

"To this he made no reply, but, in a hesitating manner, expressed a persuasion that the masses and stations were really necessary.

"Can you read?

"No.

"How do you earn your bread?

"I am a brogue-maker.

"Is your father or mother alive?

"My mother is alive.

"Have you walked from the county of Galway here?

"I have, barefoot.

"How do you support yourself while here?

"I have no means of support but what I get from the poor family of this house; they are very good to me.

"Will you go home as soon as you have done all the stations?

"I will not be able, my feet are so sore.

"He then showed his feet; they were very much bruised, and, when he pulled up his drawers, his knees were nearly in a state of complete ulceration."

Here, Sir, is a picture of the degradation produced by Popery, and of the superstition encouraged by its priests at the present hour. And this is not an exception to their influence, but an illustration of it. And black and bad as it is, it is sense when compared with things and scenes of daily occurrence under the eye of the

Pope himself. And if they do better in this country, it is owing, not to their principles, but to the civilization amid which they live. Romanism is heathenism extended, and its priests are no more Christian ministers than were the priests of Jupiter. So I believe, and believing, I so declare. And their influence, through all its extent, is only evil, as to the temporal, social, intellectual, spiritual, and eternal interests of men. Their grasp upon the mind and conscience of their dupes is like that of the priests of India upon the poor Hindoos, and is retained in the same way. To break that grasp, the true character of the priest must be unfolded; and, when truly seen, the people will desert them, and leave them here and every where, as in Rome, to parade their vestments, and go through their senseless ceremonies, within the sacred inclosures of empty churches.

Such, Sir, is my answer to the question, What is to be done to our Papists and priests? We must give light to the people. But, from the Pope to the most illiterate Irish mass-monger, the priests are impostors, claiming a divine right to exercise their impositions, and to damn us all, unless we submit to them. Whatever they may receive at the hand of God, they deserve nothing at the hand of man but to be treated as impostors.

With great respect, truly yours.

LETTER XXVI.

Strictures on Popery ended.—Popery to be extirpated—its End hastening.—Friends of Freedom Enemies of Popery.—Suspended Wrath.—Religion essential to national Greatness.—What true Religion is.—Nature of the Church of God—its Object and End.—Tendency to vicarious Religion.—Great Curse of Christendom.

My dear Sir,—I have concluded all that I originally intended to say to you on the subject of Romanism, and all that I now deem necessary to expose it, in its theory, its government, its practices, its frauds, its fruits, and its priests. Believing it, as I do, to be a system of huge iniquity, framed like that of Hindooism, which in so many points it resembles, by the cunning of ages, and solely for the benefit of the priest, I have spoken plainly and honestly. While I know that, in the estimate of the priest, my sin is mortal, of so deep a dye as to defy the cleaning influence of holy water or holy oil, I yet believe that from you, and multitudes of others in this land, my statements will be candidly examined, and my motives duly appreciated. If statements such as I have made in these letters against Romanism could be made as truly against any one branch of the Protestant Church, they would be fatal to its existence. All the world would unite in hissing it to Purgatory. And, unless I read backward the indications of Providence, the time is not far distant when Popery will be thus treated by the nations and people which have been so long crushed beneath the weight of its intolerable exactions. In this opinion I am aware I differ from many Protestants, who look upon Popery as extending its alliance with the despotisms of Europe for mutual support. But this only tends to hasten the event for which the earth is groaning. The men are every where multiplying whose ardent souls are thirsting for freedom as does the hunted hart for the water-brooks; and wherever found, whether in Rome, Naples, Tuscany, or Austria, the moment they see that the priest and the despot are united to crush them, they will fling to the winds the banner of revolt against both. Indeed, they are now doing so by tens of thousands. The tighter Popery now screws on her fetters, the better. The flesh will quiver where the pincers tear — the blood will follow where the knife is driven; and the more the victims of its cruelty are multiplied, the nearer the hour when the Lord will destroy it with the brightness of his coming. We never so feel like crushing a serpent as when it claims the right of casting its slimy folds around us, and of injecting its deadly poison into our veins. Over Romanism and its ministers the wrath of God and the wrath of man are alike suspended; and their unblushing claims, their monstrous pretensions, their wicked deceptions, their alliance with despotisms, their readiness to use the powers of heaven or of hell, as may best suit their purpose, and without the least compunctions, are only hastening the hour when that suspended wrath shall fall upon them and grind them to powder. Indeed, it is among the darkest enigmas of Providence that they have been permitted to continue so long.

Will you permit me, Sir, in this concluding letter, to say to you, and to the thoughtful and educated minds of this land, a few things which I could not so well say any where else, and whose bearings you will readily see upon our individual, national, temporal, and eternal interests. I ask for them the consideration which their essential importance demands. For the sake of distinctness, and to prevent all confusion of thought, I will present what I have to say under a few heads.

1. I wish you well to consider the importance of true religion to national greatness. Although the Christian is the religion established in the minds of the American people, we have no religion established by law. And for this, our great peculiarity, the Christian has far more reason of thankfulness than the infidel. It places the religion of God on a vantage ground among us, which it has nowhere else. While, in the eye of our law, the Jew, the Christian, the Atheist, the Pagan, are on the same level as to all civil rights, we are not, therefore, an irreligious people, nor should our men of education and position therefore regard all forms of religion or irreligion with the same favor. Man is laid under a constitutional necessity to have a religion of some kind; and if he does not embrace the true, he will a false system. Some men may be Atheists, and assert that ours is a fatherless world —some may be infidels, and deny a divine revelation —but the masses of the people will be neither Atheists nor infidels; unless instructed into a knowledge of the Christian religion, they will be the dupes of gloomy superstition or of burning fanaticism. The evidence of

all history proves this statement true, as does also the present state of the nations. Mere negations can not satisfy the religious longings of our nature; and if we know not the true God, we will have many gods—if not the only Mediator, we will have many mediators—if not the way of true worship, we will have will worship—if not the Bible, we will believe in lying legends, old wives' fables, or any spiritual frauds which crafty and wicked priests may invent. And the influence of their religion upon individuals and nations must be known and read of all men, and has already been illustrated in these letters.

These things being so, can you, Sir, can any man, be indifferent as to the form of religion which shall finally obtain among the masses of the people which shall crowd this great confederacy of states? The religion of this country will give form and direction to its destiny. The Bible is the Magna Charta of human liberty, and hence the bitter hatred of it by despot and priest. Alexander of Russia and the Popes of Rome have sent out their bulls to bellow every where against it. As the religion of the Bible obtains in this land, the passions of men will be subdued, their principles will be formed and strengthened, our laws will be just and humane, our people will be intelligent and industrious, the national mind will be stimulated, commerce and the arts will flourish, and God will make our officers peace and our exactors righteousness. If forms of religion not sanctioned by the Bible obtain, the reverse of all this must be the result; the chapters of our heroic history will soon come to an end; and however protracted may be those which shall record our decline and fall, decline and fall we must. If Romanism prevails here, nothing on earth can prevent us from sinking as low as the Romans. By motives, Sir, like these, I would urge upon you, and upon all men of character, position, and influence in this land, to cast the entire weight of their influence in favor of the extension of the religion of the Bible among all our people. It is the true and the cheapest way, if not the only one, of perpetuating our institutions; and to send them down, unimpaired, to bless our posterity, as they are blessing us.

2. I wish you and all men to form a definite idea of what true religion is. Because so often used as synonymous with sect, or with an adjective designating some sect, untaught minds are very liable to mistake in reference to it. We speak of the Papal, of the Protestant, of the Jewish religion—of the Presbyterian, Methodist, Baptist, Episcopal religion; and when many consider it at all, they consider it objectively, or in the light of sectarian controversy. Now true religion exists apart from all this, and is independent of all sects, parties, and controversies. *It is a right disposition of mind and heart toward God, exercising itself in all appropriate ways.* There never was, nor will there ever be but one true religion in the world. Whether existing in the bosoms of angels or of men, it is the same in substance. It is independent, as to its essence, of all priestly interferences, and of all social relations. It is not assent to certain theological opinions—nor is it zeal for certain peculiarities—nor is it a rigid adherence to ritual observances; it is a right disposition toward God, manifesting itself in ways of beneficence toward man.

Wherever that right disposition exists, and is truly manifested, there true religion exists. That right disposition is of God; and the person that possesses and manifests it, by whatever name called, within whatever temples he worships, is a child of God. And all church privileges and sacraments belong to such a man, by right of the new disposition wrought within him by the power of God.

This, Sir, is the Bible and the Protestant view of true religion. Its seat is in the heart—its author is God—its end and life are to do good to men and to glorify God. I need not tell you how opposite is all this to the fundamental doctrines of Romanism, which resolves religion into submission to forms, sacraments, and ceremonies, and to the influence of priestly interferences, and which persecutes and anathematizes none so severely as those who worship God in spirit and in truth, having no confidence in the flesh, and no faith in the priest.

To what a fearful extent has this view of true religion fallen out of the minds of men! The heathen will return from the most exhausting pilgrimages, and from oft-repeated ablutions, to lie and steal, and to commit all sin with greediness. At the canonical hour the Arab will bow in prayer before Allah, and will then rush upon his victim and drive his spear through his heart. The Papist will rush from the Carnival to the austerities of Lent, and from the humiliations of Good Friday to the frolics and festivities of Easter. The Spanish buccaneer will devoutly kiss the picture of the Virgin which he carries in his bosom, and then, for the sake of a few dollars, plunge his stiletto into the bowels of his victim. And the priest will go up the steps of Ara Cœli, praying the Virgin as devoutly to bless him with a prize ticket in the lottery, as to intercede with her Son to secure for him mercy. And even, Sir, in the Protestant world, the tendency of the human heart is too obviously manifested in the multitudes who resolve true religion into a mere formalism. The forms and ceremonies of religion are but little worth when its power and truth are absent; and when the form and ceremony not only take the place of, but array themselves in hostility against its power and truth, they are only evil, and that continually. Well will it be for the future of America if these truths are understood and carried out by its mind and its men.

3. I wish you to form a true and definite opinion as to the true nature of the Church of God. In the light of Scripture and reason, such an opinion is easily formed, although, amid the fogs of schoolmen, Papists, and High Churchmen of all kinds and creeds, to find the Church is as hopeless a task as to find the quadrature of the circle, or the inextinguishable lamp. A Christian Church is a company of believers in Christ met together for worship. The entire Church of God, in its visible form, is composed of all who profess the true religion, and their children—in its invisible form, of all who truly believe and manifest a right disposition of mind and heart toward God and man. As the grains of gold exist amid heaps of sand, so the true people of God are found amid those who make a profession of his name. It must be quite obvious that those who profess the true religion are not separated from the visible Church by any peculiarity which they may adopt, not

affecting the great principles of truth; and that, though different branches of the visible Church may take unto themselves distinctive names descriptive of their peculiarities, they are not therefore separated from the great body of believers. As the various tribes of men, though called by different names, and speaking different languages, and possessing peculiar habits, belong to the human family, so the various denominations of men who profess the true religion, though differing in many things, form component parts of the visible Church. So that the true Church is not confined to the domains of Popery, Prelacy, or Presbytery; it is composed of all who receive and practice the truth. Pascal and Fenelon, though Papists—Rutherford, and Chalmers, and Wesley, and Robert Hall, and Leighton, and Wilberforce, and Gurney, though Protestants, differing on minor topics, all belonged to it; and their true fame and name should be equally dear to the entire Church These views, which might be expanded into a volume, must be here compressed into a paragraph; but I hold them as of vital importance to all the great interests of this land. The Papist confines the Church to those who submit to the claims of the Pope, and sends all others to perdition. The Prelatist of the Oxford stamp confines the Church to those who believe in the divinity of the order of diocesan bishops, and receive ordinances from them, and gives all others over to uncovenanted mercies. While yet others would confine the visible Church to those who enter it through the ordinance of baptism by immersion. In my view, Sir, these sentiments are all false and schismatical. And the mind and the men of this nation should rise in open opposition to these schismatics, whether they hail from Rome or from Oxford, and who are here seeking, for no good end, to sow the seeds of dissension among believers in the Gospel. There is a great principle of Christian charity that underlies all sectarian differences, and which is of more importance than all of them together; and when that principle rises to its due importance, the priest, who never turns his back to the altar, or ascends the pulpit but to flourish his scalping-knife, will find that he is driving a poor business.

The most simple and beautiful institution in the world is the Church of God; to it God has committed the truth as contained in the Bible, and with the command to make it known to all men; and its great object and end are to bind men to God and to one another, by the diffusion of the truth, by inducing men to obey it, and by teaching all men, where they can not see alike, to exercise toward each other mutual charity. It is deeply to be deplored that the Gospel, which is the perfect law of liberty, has too often been made a yoke of bondage; that the Church, designed to be the joyous residence of all those made free by Christ, has been so often converted into a fortress of priestly intolerance. Judaizing views of the Gospel, which confine its blessings to certain tribes—which give efficacy to ordinances only when administered by certain hands—low and narrow views of the Church, which confine its existence and privileges within certain lines, and which shut up all admission to it save by the doors opened and guarded by certain porters, have too often dashed the waters of life with a strong infusion of wormwood and gall. But this is all the bitter fruit of

Romanism; and where these things exist in Protestant churches, they are simply proof that the old leaven has not been all cast out—that some of the bitter roots of the old tree remain.

The priests, ministers, or people who cut off from the Church of God all but themselves, and who exclude from heaven all but those who enter by their gate, are those to whom the least tolerance should be shown. The man who truly repents of sin, and believes on the Lord Jesus Christ, is adopted into the family of God; and to expel such a man from the Church for refusing submission to our claims, is like a servant expelling a child from the house of his father for refusing to comply with his low whims. Such men may do for Italy or Oxford, but they should receive no countenance in the country of Washington.

4. Permit me, Sir, in closing, to say a word on the tendency of human nature to a vicarious religion. Truth is revealed for the benefit of the individual mind —and true religion has to do with the individual heart, and its graces are to be manifested by the individuals who possess it. The object of the ministry is to preach the truth, and to exhort all men to believe and practice it. Neither the priest nor the minister can repent for others—nor believe for others—nor secure meetness for heaven for others. Nor can any man employ them as his attorney to transact his individual business with the court of heaven for him. And yet to all this there is a tendency in human nature; and upon this tendency Romanism has built up a vast system of fraud and falsehood. "Why," said a friend of mine to a highly-cultivated man and eminent politician, who had

been educated in the Romish faith, and yet held it in a waning regard, "why do Papists trust so much to their priests, and pay so little attention to what so vastly concerns their eternal welfare?" His reply was characteristic. "We have," said he, "but little time to think about religion—and it is hard to know much about it—and we let the priest do the thing up for us, as he has nothing else to do—and then, when we come to die, we send for him to fix us up to meet God." Here is the whole matter revealed in a sentence. The priests transfer the merits of one man to another—they transfer the benefit of devotional exercises from one man to another—indeed, they are the hired proxies through whom the masses of the people seek to serve God. And they make the people believe that if they only cling to the Church of Rome, and leave all with them, all will be well. This, Sir, is what I mean by a vicarious religion, and through which Papal priests have ruined generations, and filled the world with the fame of their pious frauds.

In the great work, Sir, of saving the soul, neither you nor I can do anything by proxy nor by a priestly attorney. We sin for ourselves—none can sin for us; and the soul that sinneth, it shall die. So we must repent and believe for ourselves—none can repent or believe for us; and he that believeth in the Lord Jesus Christ shall be saved; he that confesseth and forsaketh his sin, shall find mercy, and none the less readily if all the priests on earth were in Paradise or Purgatory.

Such, Sir, are my views, very briefly, but yet freely and frankly expressed to you on the importance of religion to national greatness—on the nature of true religion—on the nature of the Church of God—and on the tendency in human nature to a vicarious religion. I believe them worthy of your attention, and of that of all the educated and influential minds of this land. If correct, all good men should unite in supporting and extending them. If adopted by all our people, they would extend the benign influence of true religion over them all—they would make all true believers in Christ to feel and act as brethren—they would destroy the trade of the priest, a result most devoutly to be desired—they would extinguish all sectarian jealousies, and induce all men to live unto God for themselves—they would make our land a mountain of holiness, and the dwelling-place of righteousness. They would prevent for evermore the transplanting here of the upas-tree of Popery, under whose baneful shade nothing flourishes but despotism, superstition, priestly intolerance, ignorance, beggary, and moral and social corruption.

My work, Sir, is done. My letters are ended. I cast them as bread upon the waters, with the hope that they may be found after many days. Should you be induced by them to re-examine the system of Popery, and to reject it, and to set yourself in a cordial opposition to it, as have multitudes of the greatest men that have ever adorned our race, you would write your name high up on the pillars which support the temple of our freedom, and you would do much to save our land, in all future time, from that mystery of iniquity which, viewed in whatever light, is at this moment the great curse of Christendom.

With great respect, yours.

THE END.

Layard's Discoveries at Nineveh.

Popular Account of the Discoveries at Nineveh. By AUSTEN HENRY LAYARD, Esq. Abridged by him from his larger Work. With numerous Wood Engravings. 12mo, 75 cents.

Lectures on the History of France.

By Sir JAMES STEPHEN, K.C.B., LL.D. 8vo, Muslin, $1 75.

Wesley, and Methodism.

By ISAAC TAYLOR. With a new Portrait. 12mo, Muslin, 75 cents.

A Lady's Voyage round the World.

By Madame IDA PFEIFFER. Translated from the German, by Mrs. PERCY SINNETT. 12mo, Paper, 60 cents; Muslin, 75 cents.

Sixteen Months at the Gold Diggings.

By DANIEL B. WOODS. 12mo, Paper, 50 cents; Muslin, 62½ cents.

London Labor and the London Poor,

In the Nineteenth Century. A Cyclopedia of the Social Condition and Earnings of the Poorer Classes of the British Metropolis, in Connection with the Country. By HENRY MAYHEW. With numerous Engravings, copied from Daguerreotypes, taken, by Beard, expressly for this Work. Publishing in Numbers, 8vo, Paper, 12½ cents each. Vol. I. ready, Muslin, $1 75.

Chalmers's Life and Writings.

Edited by his Son-in-Law, Rev. WILLIAM HANNA, LL.D. 4 vols. 12mo, Paper, 75 cents per Volume; Muslin, $1 00 per Vol.

Pictorial Field-Book of the Revolution;

Or, Illustrations, by Pen and Pencil, of the History, Scenery, Biography, Relics, and Traditions of the War for Independence. By BENSON J. LOSSING, Esq. With over 600 Engravings on Wood, by Lossing and Barritt, chiefly from Original Sketches by the Author. Publishing in Numbers, 8vo, Paper, 25 cents each. The work will be completed in two vols. Vol. I., handsomely bound in Muslin, is now ready, price, $3 50.

Moby-Dick;

Or, the Whale. By HERMAN MELVILLE. 12mo, Muslin, $1 50.

Travels and Adventures in Mexico:

In the Course of Journeys of upward of 2500 Miles, performed on Foot. Giving an Account of the Manners and Customs of the People, and the Agricultural and Mineral Resources of that Country. By WILLIAM W. CARPENTER, late of U. S. Army. 12mo, Paper, 60 cents; Muslin, 75 cents.

A Dictionary of Practical Medicine;

Comprising General Pathology, the Nature and Treatment of Diseases, Morbid Structures, &c. By JAMES COPLAND, M.D., F.R.S. Edited, with Additions, by CHARLES A. LEE, M.D. Part XXII. now ready, price 50 cents. In 3 large 8vo vols., Muslin, $5 00 per Vol. Vols. I. and II. now ready.

A Manual of Roman Antiquities.

From the most recent German Works. With a Description of the City of Rome, &c. By CHARLES ANTHON, LL.D. 12mo, Muslin, 87½ cents.

A Manual of Greek Antiquities.

From the best and most recent Sources. By CHARLES ANTHON, LL.D. 12mo, Muslin. (*Nearly ready.*)

Forest Life and Forest Trees:

Comprising Winter Camp-life among the Loggers and Wild-wood Adventure. With Descriptions of Lumbering Operations on the various Rivers of Maine and New Brunswick. By JOHN S. SPRINGER. With numerous Illustrations. 12mo, Paper, 60 cents; Muslin, 75 cents.

Elements of Algebra,

Designed for Beginners. By ELIAS LOOMIS, M.A. 12mo, Sheep, 62½ cents.

Analytical Geometry and Calculus.

By ELIAS LOOMIS, M.A. 8vo, Sheep, $1 50.

Nile Notes of a Howadji.

With Engravings. 12mo, Paper, 75 cents; Muslin, 87½ cents.

The Fifteen Decisive Battles of the World,

From Marathon to Waterloo. By E. S. CREASY, M.A. 12mo, Muslin, $1 00

A Latin-English Lexicon,

Founded on the larger Latin-German Lexicon of Dr. William Freund. With Additions and Corrections from the Lexicons of Gesner, Facciolati, Scheller, Georges, &c. By E. A. Andrews, LL.D. Royal 8vo, Sheep extra, $5 00.

Lamartine's History of the Restoration

Of Monarchy in France. Being a Sequel to the "History of the Girondists." By Alphonse de Lamartine. Vol. I., 12mo, Muslin, 75 cents.

Robinson's New Testament Lexicon.

A Greek and English Lexicon of the New Testament. A new Edition, Revised, and in great part Rewritten. By Edward Robinson, D.D., LL.D. Royal 8vo, Muslin, $4 50; Sheep, $4 75; half Calf, $5 00.

Buttmann's Greek Grammar,

For the Use of High Schools and Universities. By Philip Buttmann. Revised and Enlarged by his Son, Alex. Buttmann. Translated from the 18th German Edition, by Edward Robinson, D.D., LL.D. 8vo, Sheep, $2 00.

The Nile-Boat;

Or, Glimpses of the Land of Egypt. By W. H. Bartlett. With Engravings on Steel and Illustrations on Wood. 8vo, Muslin, $2 00.

Comte's Philosophy of Mathematics,

Translated from the Cours de Philosophie Positive of Auguste Comte, by W. M. Gillespie, A.M. 8vo, Muslin, $1 25.

History of the United States.

By Richard Hildreth.——*First Series.*—From the First Settlement of the Country to the Adoption of the Federal Constitution. 3 vols. 8vo, Muslin, $6 00; Sheep, $6 75; half Calf, $7 50.——*Second Series.*—From the Adoption of the Federal Constitution to the End of the Sixteenth Congress. 3 vols. 8vo, Muslin, $6 00; Sheep, $6 75; half Calf, $7 50.

Louisiana:

Its Colonial History and Romance By Charles Gayarre. 8vo, Muslin, $2 00.

The Lily and the Bee:

An Apologue of the Crystal Palace. By SAMUEL WARREN, M.D., F.R.S. 16mo, Paper, 30 cents; Muslin, 37½ cents.

The Queens of Scotland,

And English Princesses connected with the Regal Succession of Great Britain. By AGNES STRICKLAND. 6 vols. 12mo, Muslin, $1 00 per Volume. Vols. I. and II. ready.

A New Classical Dictionary

Of Greek and Roman Biography, Mythology, and Geography. For Colleges and Schools. By WM. SMITH, LL.D. Edited, with large Additions, by CHARLES ANTHON, LL.D. Royal 8vo, Sheep extra, $2 50.

The English Language

In its Elements and Forms. With a History of its Origin and Development, and a full Grammar. By WILLIAM C. FOWLER. Designed for Use in Colleges and Schools. 8vo, Muslin, $1 50; Sheep, $1 75.

Harper's N. Y. & Erie R. R. Guide:

Containing a Description of the Scenery, Rivers, Towns, Villages, and most important Works on the Road. Embellished with 136 Engravings on Wood, by Lossing & Barritt, from Original Sketches made expressly for this Work, by WM. M'LEOD. 12mo, Paper, 50 cents; Muslin, 62½ cents.

The English in America.

Rule and Misrule of the English in America. By the Author of "Sam Slick the Clockmaker," "The Letter Bag," "Attaché," "Old Judge," &c. 12mo, Muslin, 75 cents.

The Literature and Literary Men

Of Great Britain and Ireland. By ABRAHAM MILLS, A.M. 2 vols. 8vo, Muslin, $3 50; half Calf, $4 00.

A Greek-English Lexicon,

Based on the German Work of Passow. By HENRY G. LIDDELL, M.A., and RICHARD SCOTT, M.A. With Corrections and Additions, and the Insertion in Alphabetical Order of the Proper Names occurring in the principal Greek Authors, by HENRY DRISLER, M.A. Royal 8vo, Sheep, $5 00.

The Recent Progress of Astronomy,

Especially in the United States. By ELIAS LOOMIS, M.A. New Edition. 12mo, Muslin, $1 00.

Cosmos:

A Sketch of a Physical Description of the Universe. By ALEXANDER VON HUMBOLDT. Translated from the German, by E. C. OTTE. Complete in 3 vols. 12mo, Muslin, $2 55.

Bickersteth's Memoirs.

A Memoir of the late Rev. EDWARD BICKERSTETH, Rector of Watton. By Rev. T. R. BIRKS, M.A. With a Preface, &c., by Rev. STEPHEN H. TYNG, D.D., of New York. 2 vols. 12mo, Muslin, $1 75.

Foster's Christian Purity.

The Nature and Blessedness of Christian Purity. By Rev. R. S. FOSTER. With an Introduction by Bishop JANES. 12mo, Muslin, 75 cents.

Elements of Natural Philosophy.

Designed as a Text-book for Academies, High-Schools, and Colleges. By ALONZO GRAY, A.M. Illustrated by 360 Woodcuts. 12mo, Muslin, 70 cents; Sheep, 75 cents.

Lord Holland's Foreign Reminiscences.

Edited by his Son, HENRY EDWARD LORD HOLLAND. 12mo, Paper, 60 cents; Muslin, 75 cents.

Curran and his Contemporaries.

By CHARLES PHILLIPS, A.B. 12mo, Paper, 75 cents; Muslin, 87½ cents.

The Irish Confederates,

And the Rebellion of 1798. By HENRY M. FIELD. Portraits and a Map. 12mo, Paper, 75 cents; Muslin, 90 cents.

The Harmony of Prophecy;

Or, Scriptural Illustrations of the Apocalypse. By Rev. ALEXANDER KEITH, D.D. 12mo, Muslin, $1 00.

The Bards of the Bible.

By GEORGE GILFILLAN. 12mo, Muslin, 35 cents.

Abbott's Illustrated Histories:

The following Works of the Series are now ready: Josephine, Cleopatra, Madame Roland, Xerxes the Great, Cyrus the Great, Darius the Great, Charles I., Charles II., Hannibal, Julius Cæsar, Alfred the Great, Maria Antoinette, Queen Elizabeth, Alexander the Great, William the Conqueror, Mary Queen of Scots. 16mo, Muslin, with Illuminated Title-pages and numerous Engravings, 60 cents per Volume.

Abbott's Franconia Stories:

Comprising Malleville, Beechnut, Mary Bell, Wallace, Mary Erskine. 16mo, beautifully bound in Muslin, Engraved Title-pages and numerous Illustrations, 50 cents per Volume.

Kings and Queens;

Or, Life in the Palace: consisting of Historical Sketches of Josephine and Maria Louisa, Louis Philippe, Ferdinand of Austria, Nicholas, Isabella II., Leopold, and Victoria. By J. S. C. Abbott. With numerous Illustrations. 12mo, Muslin, $1 00; Muslin, gilt edges, $1 25.

A Summer in Scotland.

By Jacob Abbott. With Engravings. 12mo, Muslin, $1 00

Five Years of a Hunter's Life

In the Far Interior of South Africa. With Notices of the Native Tribes, and Anecdotes of the Chase of the Lion, Elephant, Hippopotamus, Giraffe, Rhinoceros, &c. By R. Gordon Cumming. With Engravings. 2 vols. 12mo, Muslin, $1 75.

Sydney Smith's Moral Philosophy.

An Elementary Treatise on Moral Philosophy, delivered at the Royal Institution in the Years 1804, 1805, and 1806. By the late Rev. Sydney Smith. 12mo, Muslin, $1 00.

Travels in the United States, etc.

During 1849 and 1850. By Lady Emmeline Stuart Wortley. 12mo, Paper, 60 cents; Muslin, 75 cents.

Dealings with the Inquisition;

Or, Papal Rome, her Priests, and her Jesuits. With Important Disclosures. By the Rev. Giacinto Achilli, D.D., late Prior and Visitor of the Dominican Order, &c. 12mo, Muslin, 75 cts.

Leigh Hunt's Autobiography,

With Reminiscences of his Friends and Contemporaries. In 2 vols. 12mo, Muslin, $1 50.

Campbell's Life and Letters.

Life and Letters of Thomas Campbell. Edited by WILLIAM BEATTIE, M.D. With an Introductory Letter, by WASHINGTON IRVING. 2 vols. 12mo, Muslin, $2 00.

Doctor Johnson:

His Religious Life and Death. 12mo, Muslin, $1 00.

Southey's Life and Correspondence.

Edited by his Son, Rev. C. C. SOUTHEY, M.A. Portrait. 8vo, Muslin, $1 75.

Southey's Common-place Book.

Edited by his Son-in-Law, JOHN WOOD WARTER, B.D. 3 vols. 8vo, Paper, $1 00 per Vol.; Muslin, $1 25 per Vol.

History of Greece,

From the Earliest Times to the Destruction of Corinth, B.C. 146; mainly based upon that of Bishop THIRLWALL. By Dr. L. SCHMITZ, F.R.S.E. 12mo, Muslin, $1 00.

History of Rome,

From the Earliest Times to the Death of Commodus, A.D. 192. By Dr. L. SCHMITZ, F.R.S.E. With Questions, by J. ROBSON, B.A. 18mo, Muslin, 75 cents.

A Treatise on Popular Education:

For the Use of Parents and Teachers, and for Young People of both Sexes. Printed and Published in accordance with a Resolution of the Senate and House of Representatives of the State of Michigan. By IRA MAYHEW, late Superintendent of Public Instruction. 12mo, Muslin, $1 00.

The Conquest of Canada.

By the Author of "Hochelaga." 2 vols. 12mo, Muslin, $1 70.

Health, Disease, and Remedy,

Familiarly and practically considered in a few of their Relations to the Blood. By G. MOORE, M.D. 18mo, Muslin, 60 cents.

Hume's History of England,

From the Invasion of Julius Cæsar to the Abdication of James II., 1688. By DAVID HUME. A new Edition, with the Author's last Corrections and Improvements. To which is prefixed a Short Account of his Life, written by Himself. With a Portrait of the Author. 6 vols. 12mo, Cloth, \$2 40; Sheep, \$3 00.

Macaulay's History of England

From the Accession of James II. By THOMAS B. MACAULAY. With an Original Portrait of the Author. Vols. I. and II. Library Edition, 8vo, Muslin, 75 cents per Vol.; Sheep extra, 87½ cents per Vol.; Calf backs and corners, \$1 00 per Vol.—Cheap Editions, 8vo, Paper, 25 cents per Vol: 12mo (uniform with Hume), Cloth, 40 cents per Vol.; Sheep, 50 cents per Vol.

Gibbon's History of Rome.

History of the Decline and Fall of the Roman Empire. By EDWARD GIBBON. With Notes, by Rev. H. H. MILMAN and M. GUIZOT. Maps and Engravings. 4 vols. 8vo, Sheep extra, \$5 00.—A new Cheap Edition, with Notes, by Rev. H. H. MILMAN. To which is added a complete Index of the whole Work, and a Portrait of the Author. 6 vols. 12mo (uniform with Hume), Cloth, \$2 40; Sheep, \$3 00.

History of Spanish Literature.

With Criticisms on the particular Works and Biographical Notices of prominent Writers. By GEORGE TICKNOR. 3 vols. 8vo, Muslin, \$6 00; Sheep, \$6 75; half Calf, \$7 50.

Pictorial History of England.

Being a History of the People as well as a History of the Kingdom, down to the Reign of George III. Profusely Illustrated with many Hundred Engravings on Wood of Monumental Records; Coins; Civil and Military Costume; Domestic Buildings, Furniture, and Ornaments; Cathedrals and other great Works of Architecture; Sports, and other Illustrations of Manners; Mechanical Inventions; Portraits of Eminent Persons; and remarkable Historical Scenes. 4 vols. imperial 8vo, Sheep, \$12 00; half Calf, \$13 50.

The War with Mexico.

By R. S. RIPLEY, U.S.A. With Maps, Plans of Battles, &c. 2 vols. 8vo, Muslin, \$4 00; Sheep, \$4 50.

Ancient and Mediæval Geography.

For the Use of Schools and Colleges. By CHARLES ANTHON, LL.D. 8vo, Muslin, $1 50; Sheep extra, $1 75.

Findlay's Classical Atlas

To Illustrate Ancient Geography. Comprised in 25 Maps, showing the various Divisions of the World as known to the Ancients. By ALEX. FINDLAY, F.R.S. With an Index of the Ancient and Modern Names. 8vo, half Bound, $3 25.

A First Book in Latin.

Containing Grammar, Exercises, and Vocabularies, on the Method of constant Imitation and Repetition. By Prof. M'CLINTOCK, of Dickinson College. 12mo, Sheep, 75 cents.

A First Book in Greek.

Containing full Vocabularies, Lessons on the Forms of Words, and Exercises for Imitation and Repetition, with a Summary of Etymology and Syntax. By Professor M'CLINTOCK. 12mo, Sheep, 75 cents.

A Second Book in Greek.

Containing Syntax, with Reading Lessons in Prose; Prosody, and the Dialects, with Reading Lessons in Verse; forming a sufficient Greek Grammar. By Prof. M'CLINTOCK. 12mo, Sheep, 75 cents.

The Pillars of Hercules;

Or, a Narrative of Travels in Spain and Morocco in 1848. By DAVID URQUHART, M.P. 2 vols. 12mo, Paper, $1 40; Muslin, $1 70.

The Valley of the Mississippi.

History of the Discovery and Settlement of the Valley of the Mississippi, by the three great European Powers, Spain, France, and Great Britain; and the Subsequent Occupation, Settlement, and Extension of Civil Government by the United States, until the Year 1846. By JOHN W. MONETTE. Maps. 2 vols. 8vo, Muslin $5 00; Sheep, $5 50.

Moral and Political Philosophy.

With Questions for the Examination of Students. By WILLIAM PALEY, D.D. 12mo, Muslin, 60 cents.

History of the Confessional.

By JOHN HENRY HOPKINS, D.D., Bishop of Vermont. 12mo, Muslin, $1 00.

History of the American Bible Society,

From its Organization in 1816 to the Present Time. By Rev. W. P. STRICKLAND. With an Introduction by Rev. N. L. RICE, and a Portrait of Hon. E. BOUDINOT, LL.D., first President of the Society. 8vo, Cloth, $1 50; Sheep, $1 75.

Gieseler's Ecclesiastical History.

From the Fourth Edition, Revised and Amended. Translated from the German, by SAMUEL DAVIDSON, LL.D. Vols. I. and II., 8vo, Muslin, $3 00; Sheep, $3 50.

History of the Girondists;

Or, Personal Memoirs of the Patriots of the French Revolution. By A. DE LAMARTINE. From Unpublished Sources. 3 vols. 12mo, Muslin, $2 10.

History of the French Revolution.

By THOMAS CARLYLE. Newly Revised by the Author, with Index, &c. 2 vols. 12mo, Muslin, $2 00.

Letters and Speeches of Oliver Cromwell.

With Elucidations and connecting Narrative. By THOMAS CARLYLE. 2 vols 12mo, Muslin, $2 00.

Past and Present, Chartism,

And Sartor Resartus. By THOMAS CARLYLE. A new Edition, complete in One Volume. 12mo, Muslin, $1 00.

Latter-Day Pamphlets.

Comprising, 1. The Present Time; 2. Model Prisons; 3. Downing Street; 4. The New Downing Street; 5. Stump Orator; 6. Parliaments; 7. Hudson's Statue; 8. Jesuitism. By THOMAS CARLYLE. 12mo, Muslin, 50 cents.

Not so Bad as we Seem;

Or, Many Sides to a Character. A Comedy in Five Acts. By Sir E. BULWER LYTTON. As first performed at Devonshire House, in the Presence of her Majesty and Prince Albert. 16mo, Paper, 30 cents; Muslin, 37½ cents.

Sketches of Minnesota,

The New England of the West. With Incidents of Travel in that Territory during the Summer of 1848. By E. S. SEYMOUR. 12mo, Paper, 50 cents; Muslin, 75 cents.

History of the Conquest of Peru;

With a Preliminary View of the Civilization of the Incas. By WILLIAM H. PRESCOTT. 2 vols. 8vo, Muslin, $4 00; Sheep, $4 50; half Calf, $5 00.

History of the Conquest of Mexico,

With the Life of the Conqueror, Hernando Cortes, and a View of the Ancient Mexican Civilization. By WILLIAM H. PRESCOTT. With Portraits and Maps. 3 vols. 8vo, Muslin, $6 00; Sheep, $6 75; half Calf, $7 50.

History of Ferdinand and Isabella,

The Catholic. By WILLIAM H. PRESCOTT. With Portraits, Maps, &c. 3 vols. 8vo, Muslin, $6 00; Sheep, $6 75; half Calf, $7 50.

Harper's Illustrated Shakespeare.

The complete Dramatic Works of William Shakespeare, arranged according to recent approved Collations of the Text; with Notes and other Illustrations, by Hon. GULIAN C. VERPLANCK. Superbly Embellished by over 1400 exquisite Engravings by Hewet, after Designs by Meadows, Weir, and other eminent Artists. 3 vols. royal 8vo, Muslin, $18 00; half Calf extra, $20 00; Morocco, gilt edges, $25 00.

Herman Melville's Works.

TYPEE; 12mo, Paper, 75 cents, Muslin, 87½ cents.——OMOO; 12mo, Paper, $1 00, Muslin, $1 25.——MARDI; 2 vols. 12mo, Paper, $1 50, Muslin, $1 75.——REDBURN; 12mo, Paper, 75 cents, Muslin, $1 00.——WHITE-JACKET; 12mo, Paper, $1 00, Muslin, $1 25.——MOBY-DICK; 12mo, Muslin, $1 50.

The Country Year-Book;

Or, the Field, the Forest, and the Fireside By WILLIAM HOWITT. 12mo, Muslin, 87½ cents.

Dark Scenes of History,

By G. P. R. JAMES. 12mo, Paper, 75 cents; Muslin, $1 00.

Upham's Life of Faith:

Embracing some of the Scriptural Principles or Doctrines ol Faith, the Power or Effect of Faith in the Regulation of Man's Inward Nature, and the Relation of Faith to the Divine Guidance. 12mo, Muslin, $1 00.

Upham's Life of Madame Adorna;

Including some leading Facts and Traits in her Religious Experience. Together with Explanations and Remarks, tending to illustrate the Doctrine of Holiness. 12mo, Muslin, 50 cents; Muslin, gilt edges, 60 cents.

Upham's Life of Madame Guyon.

The Life and Religious Opinions and Experience of Madame Guyon: together with some Account of the Personal History and Religious Opinions of Archbishop Fenelon. 2 vols. 12mo, Muslin, $2 00.

Upham's Principles of the Interior or Hidden

Life. Designed particularly for the Consideration of those who are seeking Assurance of Faith and Perfect Love. 12mo, Muslin, $1 00.

Sacred Meditations.

By P. L. U. 48mo, Muslin, gilt edges, 31¼ cents.

Thankfulness.

A Narrative. Comprising Passages from the Diary of the Rev. Allan Temple. By the Rev. C. B. Tayler. 12mo, Paper, 37½ cents; Muslin, 50 cents.

Book of Common Prayer:

Elegantly printed, according to the revised Standard adopted by the General Convention, in the following varieties of binding and size:

Standard 4to. A splendid volume, suitable for the desk. Turkey Morocco, gilt edges, $10 00.

Standard 8vo. From the same stereotype plates as the preceding. Sheep extra, $2 00; Calf extra, $2 50; Turkey Morocco, gilt edges, $5 00.

Royal 8vo. Hewet's Illustrated Edition. Turkey Morocco, gilt edges, $6 00.

Medium 8vo. Double Columns. Sheep extra, $1 25; Turkey Morocco, gilt edges, $4 00.

12mo, Sheep extra, 62½ cents; Roan extra, 75 cents; Turkey Morocco, gilt edges, $1 75.

18mo, Roan or Sheep extra, 75 cents; Calf or Turkey Morocco, gilt edges, $1 75.

24mo, Sheep extra, 35 cents; Roan extra, 40 cents; Calf or Turkey Morocco, gilt edges, $1 25.

32mo, Roan or Sheep extra, 40 cents; Calf or Turkey Morocco, gilt edges, $1 25.

Pearl, Roan or Sheep extra, 40 cents; Pocket-book form, gilt edges, $1 00; Calf or Turkey Morocco, gilt edges, $1 25.

Saurin's Sermons.

Translated by Rev. R. ROBINSON, Rev. H. HUNTER, and Rev. J SUTCLIFFE. New Edition, with additional Sermons. Revised and corrected by Rev. S. BURDER. With Preface, by Rev. J. P. K. HENSHAW. Portrait. 2 vols. 8vo, Sheep extra, $3 75.

Hall's complete Works:

With a brief Memoir of his Life, by Dr. GREGORY, and Observa tions on his Character as a Preacher, by Rev. J. FOSTER. Ed ited by O. GREGORY, LL.D., and Rev. J. BELCHER. Portrait 4 vols. 8vo, Sheep extra, $6 00.

Barnes's Notes on the Gospels,

Explanatory and Practical. Designed for Bible Classes and Sunday Schools. With an Index, a Chronological Table, Tables of Weights, &c. Map. 2 vols. 12mo, Muslin, $1 50.

Barnes's Notes on the Acts of the Apostles,

Explanatory and Practical. Designed for Bible Classes and Sunday Schools. With a Map. 12mo, Muslin, 75 cents.

Barnes's Notes on the Epistle to the Romans,

Explanatory and Practical. Designed for Bible Classes and Sunday Schools. 12mo, Muslin, 75 cents.

Barnes's Notes on the First Epistle to the Corinthians,

Explanatory and Practical. Designed for Bible Classes and Sunday Schools. 12mo, Muslin, 75 cents.

Barnes's Notes on the Second Epistle to the Corinthians,

and the Epistle to the Galatians, Explanatory and Practical. Designed for Bible Classes and Sunday Schools. 12mo, Muslin, 75 cents.

Barnes's Notes on the Epistles to the Ephesians,

the Philippians, and the Colossians, Explanatory and Practical. Designed for Bible Classes and Sunday Schools. 12mo, Muslin, 75 cents.

Barnes's Notes on the Epistles to the Thessalonians,

Timothy, Titus, and Philemon, Explanatory and Practical. Designed for Bible Classes and Sunday Schools. 12mo, Muslin, 75 cents.

Barnes's Notes on the Epistle to the Hebrews,

Explanatory and Practical. Designed for Bible Classes and Sunday Schools. 12mo, Muslin, 75 cents.

Barnes's Notes on the General Epistles of

James, Peter, John, and Jude, Explanatory and Practical. Designed for Bible Classes and Sunday Schools. 12mo, Muslin, 75 cents.

Barnes's Questions on Matthew.

Designed for Bible Classes and Sunday Schools. 18mo, Muslin, 15 cents.

Barnes's Questions on Mark and Luke.

Designed for Bible Classes and Sunday Schools. 18mo, Muslin, 15 cents.

Barnes's Questions on John.

Designed for Bible Classes and Sunday Schools. 18mo, Muslin, 15 cents.

Barnes's Questions on the Acts of the Apostles.

Designed for Bible Classes and Sunday Schools. 18mo, Muslin, 15 cents.

Barnes's Questions on the Epistle to the Romans.

Designed for Bible Classes and Sunday Schools. 18mo, Muslin, 15 cents.

Barnes's Questions on the First Epistle to the Corinthians.

Designed for Bible Classes and Sunday Schools. 18mo, Muslin, 15 cents.

Barnes's Questions on the Epistle to the Hebrews.

Designed for Bible Classes and Sunday Schools. 18mo, Muslin, 15 cents.

Neal's History of the Puritans;

Or, Protestant Non-conformists; from the Reformation in 1517 to the Revolution in 1688; comprising an Account of their Principles, their Attempts for a further Reformation in the Church, their Sufferings, and the Lives and Characters of their most considerable Divines. Reprinted from the Text of Dr. Toulmin's Edition: with his Life of the Author, and Account of his Writings. Revised, corrected, and enlarged, with additional Notes, by J. O. Choules, D.D. With Nine Portraits on Steel. 2 vols. 8vo, Muslin, $3 50; Sheep extra, $4 00.

Noel's Essay on the Union of Church and State.

12mo, Muslin, $1 25.

Abercrombie's Miscellaneous Essays.

Consisting of the Harmony of Christian Faith and Christian Character; the Culture and Discipline of the Mind; Think on these Things; the Contest and the Armor; the Messiah as an Example. 18mo, Muslin, 37½ cents.

Jarvis's Chronological Introduction to Church History:

being a new Inquiry into the true Dates of the Birth and Death of our Lord and Savior Jesus Christ; and containing an original Harmony of the four Gospels, now first arranged in the Order of Time. 8vo, Muslin, $3 00.

Butler's Analogy of Religion,

Natural and Revealed, to the Constitution and Course of Nature. To which are added two brief Dissertations: of Personal Identity—of the Nature of Virtue. With a Preface by Bishop Halifax. 18mo, half Bound, 37½ cents.

www.ingramcontent.com/pod-product-compliance
Lightning Source LLC
LaVergne TN
LVHW010220110826
845151LV00004B/1154

* 9 7 8 1 4 2 5 5 2 6 2 7 6 *